Dave Scott

Bulk discounts available. For details visit:
www.amacombooks.org/go/specialsales
Or contact special sales:
Phone: 800-250-5308 / E-mail: specialsls@amanet.org
View all the AMACOM titles at: www.amacombooks.org
American Management Association: www.amanet.org

This publication is designed to provide accurate and authoritative information in regard to the subject matter covered. It is sold with the understanding that the publisher is not engaged in rendering legal, accounting, or other professional service. If legal advice or other expert assistance is required, the services of a competent professional person should be sought.

Various names used by companies to distinguish their software and other products can be claimed as trademarks. AMACOM uses such names throughout this book for editorial purposes only, with no intention of trademark violation. A list of trademarked terms in this book can be found on pages iii–iv. Individual companies should be contacted for complete information regarding trademarks and registration.

Library of Congress Cataloging-in-Publication Data

Scott, David T.
The new rules of lead generation : proven strategies to maximize marketing ROI / David T. Scott.
    pages cm
Includes bibliographical references and index.
ISBN 978-0-8144-3261-7 (hbk.) — ISBN 0-8144-3261-1 (hbk.) 1. Marketing—Management.
2. Strategic planning. I. Title.
HF5415.13.S3896 2013
658.8'02—dc23

                                                                                    2012045472

About AMA
American Management Association (www.amanet.org) is a world leader in talent development, advancing the skills of individuals to drive business success. Our mission is to support the goals of individuals and organizations through a complete range of products and services, including classroom and virtual seminars, webcasts, webinars, podcasts, conferences, corporate and government solutions, business books, and research. AMA's approach to improving performance combines experiential learning—learning through doing—with opportunities for ongoing professional growth at every step of one's career journey.

Printing number
10 9 8 7 6 5 4 3 2 1

Trademarked Terms

The following trademarked terms appear in this book.

AdCenter
AdWords
Aetna Insurance
Android
Ask
Atlas Advertiser Suite
Atlas Solutions
Axciom
Bank of America
Barron's Online
Best Buy
Bing
Bing Content Network
Blackberries
BMW
Body Bugg
BodyMedia
Cadillac
Caterpillar
Clearwire
ClickBank
Coca-Cola
Coke
Comcast
CommissionJunction
Consumer Electronics
 Show
Culligan

CursorMania
Dahaner Corporation
DART
DART for Advertisers
Dell
Delta Airlines
Dictionary.com
Direct Marketing
 Association
Discover
DoubleClick
Dow Jones
Eloqua
E-Mail Experience
 Council
ESPN.com
ExactTarget
Excite
Expedia
Facebook
FINS.com
Flash
Flowers.com
Fluke Corporation
Geico Insurance
General Electric
General Motors
Gifts.com

Gist
Godfrey Group
Google
Google Display Network
Google Network
Google Search Network
HBO
Hoover's
Ifficient Interactive
InfoUSA
Intel
InterActiveCorp
Internet Advertising
 Bureau
iPad
iPhone
IWON!
JCPenney
Kimberly-Clark
LeadFEED
LinkedIn
LinkShare
L.L.Bean
LoveandSeek.com
Lucky Strike
Marketo
MarketWatch.com
Marriott

Match.com

McKinsey

Merkle

Microsoft

Microsoft Media
  Network

MSNBC

MyPoints

National Retail
  Federation

Nike

OKCupid.com

Oldsmobiles

Open AdStream

OutletBuy.com

Pandora

Pepsi

Point.com

Progressive Insurance

RealMedia

Redfin

RedState.com

Retro Gamer

ShareASale

Sheraton Hotels

ShoeBuy.com

Showtime

SmartMoney.com

Smash Hit Displays

SmileyCentral

Sobe

Swagbucks

Thesaurus.com

Twitter

United Way

U.S. Postal Service

Via Luna Group

Visa

Wall Street Journal

Walmart

WebFetti

Xobni

Zillow

ZoomInfo

Contents

Introduction:
Who Should Read
This Book?

THINK OF *The New Rules of Lead Generation* as a Lead-Generation Marketing 101 course for companies with a growth agenda. This book is designed for companies that have resources and staff, as well as a budget for growth.

If you're reading this book, chances are you already know something about lead-generation marketing. Maybe you're a marketing manager at a company that is using lead-generation tactics (such as e-mail marketing, search engine marketing, attending trade shows, etc.). Maybe your lead-generation campaigns are not doing as well as you'd like. Maybe they *are* doing well, but you'd like to achieve better lead-generation results as your company grows.

Or maybe you're a marketing novice just entering the field of lead-generation marketing. In that case, you'll want to study this book very carefully. You can use the tools and techniques provided here in the real world of marketing. Your knowledge of lead-generation marketing will make you a valuable, in-demand asset for employers.

Lead-generation marketing is often the unseen power behind a company's marketing success. If brand marketing is the face that a company shows to the world (through TV commercials, billboard ads, etc.), then lead-generation marketing is the backbone of the company's marketing efforts. Brand marketing makes the customers aware that the company and its products or services exist. Lead-generation marketing helps to bring in prospective customers as leads and convert them into actual sales.

Yet lead-generation marketing is one of the least understood forms of marketing! Most graduate and undergraduate business and marketing programs focus almost exclusively on the brand-oriented fundamental principles of marketing (as taught by my mentor, Philip Kotler). Also, future MBAs and marketing grads often see brand marketing as the creative, sexy side of marketing, whereas lead-generation marketing is seen as a "necessary evil"—something that most companies must do, but which doesn't get as much attention. Most business and marketing programs place little emphasis or study on lead-generation tactics. This is surprising, considering how many large to midsized companies depend on these tactics to produce quality leads and drive sales.

Lead-generation marketing is often the real world of corporate marketing. Yet so many business and marketing graduates enter the workforce knowing nothing about it! Many marketers will tell you they had to learn lead-generation tactics on the job.

If you're like many marketing managers, your knowledge of lead-generation marketing may be limited to the tactics you regularly use. Few marketing managers and executives really understand all the lead-generation tactics or the theories behind them. They don't know which tactics will provide them with the best, most actionable leads, or how to use these tactics to find and target the best customers for their products or services. Some lead-generation tactics may generate more leads and be more cost-effective for your company than other tactics. For example, depending on your type of product, e-mail marketing may generate more leads and be more cost-effective than attending trade shows. But you may not have the tools you need to measure and compare tactical results to determine which tactic is more effective.

Some companies use only one lead-generation tactic at a time—simply because "that's the way we've always done it"—when they could use five or six lead-generation tactics to their advantage. Others are still using a lead-generation tactic that served them well in the past, but may not be the most effective tactic for their present needs. Just as your company's products and target audience may change over time, lead-generation tactics evolve and change. If your company is stuck using the same lead-generation tactic in exactly the same way year after year, eventually the tactic will prove less effective in providing you with leads. Even if your company wants to adopt new lead-generation tactics, you may not know how to budget the new tactics outside of your existing resources. Or you may not know how to compare the results of the new tactics against your current ones to find out which give you the best return on investment.

This book helps marketers to better understand how to use lead-generation marketing to its maximum effect. The goal is to help you develop a strategic action plan for using the seven most successful lead-generation tactics to your best advantage. I'll show you how to set targeted goals, execute smart campaigns, and use testing and measurement to find out which lead-generation tactics work best for you. I'll also show you how to combine strategies and tactics in an integrated lead-generation campaign to help you get the maximum number of leads for your company at the best cost-per-lead.

What's in This Book?

The New Rules of Lead Generation gives you the following:

- *An in-depth look at lead-generation marketing itself:* I'll explore what lead-generation marketing is, how different types of companies use it, and how it can work to support your organization. I'll look at the strategic elements of lead generation, and show you how to develop effective strategies for managing, planning, and executing your lead-generation campaigns.

- *An in-depth look at the seven most successful lead-generation tactics that companies are using today:* I'll discuss how each tactic works, when to use each tactic, and why these tactics are effective. I'll give you strategies and tips for getting the best results from each tactic. I'll also look at how each tactic has evolved over the years, and how they will continue to evolve in the future.

- *Testing methods that will help you to measure the results and cost-effectiveness of each lead-generation tactic:* This will help you determine which of the seven lead-generation tactics are most effective for your company. And I'll show you how to adopt new tactics without breaking the bank or disrupting your existing marketing program.

- *A plan for developing a successful, integrated lead-generation campaign:* I'll explore how to use different lead-generation tactics in coordination with each other (and with your brand marketing) to provide maximum benefits for your sales organization and your company.

Until now, no book has provided a comprehensive look at lead-generation marketing from a *strategic* point of view. Most lead-generation marketing books are written for small-business owners or self-employed consultants (writers, photographers, graphic designers, etc.). These books focus on things that small-business owners worry about (designing websites, attending networking events, etc.), but which most marketing managers for large to midsized growth companies have well in hand. These books provide basic step-by-step procedures for small-scale lead-generation tactics (effective cold-calling techniques, writing a direct mail piece, etc.). But they don't examine the strategies behind the techniques, or talk about how to use them in a corporate-level campaign to generate the maximum number of leads you can get from them.

Today's corporate marketers need a book about enterprise-level lead-generation marketing, a book that provides them with *principles and strategies* of lead generation that can be applied on a large scale in a variety of industries.

Who Are You?

If you're a small business owner, you can certainly benefit from understanding and using the lead-generation strategies and tactics in this book. But this book is not written specifically for small businesses. Small businesses and self-employed consultants have different priorities and concerns in regards to lead-generation marketing. This book focuses on how growth corporations can use lead-generation strategies to their best advantage in order to generate thousands, if not millions, of actionable leads.

So I'll assume a number of things about you, as a reader of this book, and about your company.

- First, you're a marketing manager or executive for a *midsized to large company*, maybe even a Fortune 1000 company. (Or, if you're a marketing novice, someday you hope to be a marketing manager for a midsized to large company.)

- Your company is in a *state of growth*, not interested in just maintaining the status quo. You have a *lead-generation mission*, a consistent need for leads and lead-generation strategies (as most companies do).

- I'll assume that, as a marketing manager or executive, you have a *lead-generation budget* that's at least 3% of your company's annual revenues. This percentage might vary based on your type of business, but, as a general guideline, you need an appropriate marketing budget. In other words, you're not operating on a shoestring.

- You have marketing staff and/or the resources—either through your staff or a marketing agency—to carry out a lead-generation campaign. You can produce the "creatives" that will help you to bring in warm leads and scale up your lead-generation efforts as you learn how to use new tactics to your advantage.

- When it comes to how your company handles sales, I'll assume one of two possibilities: Either your company's marketing efforts support a *global or national sales organization,* or you are a strict e-commerce company, and all sales are made through your online catalog. In fact (for reasons I'll explain later), e-commerce marketers may benefit more than companies with traditional sales organizations from using the lead-generation strategies in this book.

- Maybe your company is in the initial stages of developing a lead-generation strategy, and you want to know how to do it right. Or maybe your company is already using lead-generation tactics, but they aren't giving you the quality leads you need to support your sales organization. Maybe you need to obtain a higher, more consistent level of quality leads to support your company's continued growth. If any of these situations apply, this book is for you.

- Finally, you are *serious* about lead-generation marketing and want to *learn how to do it right.* You are an executive who *has the authority* to make changes in how your organization handles lead-generation marketing. If you're reading this book, you're ready to engage in lead-generation marketing as a *discipline;* you're not just looking for a few extra tips and tricks to add to your current lead-generation efforts. You are genuinely interested in developing a lead-generation plan that will provide your company with quality leads over the long run.

Who Am I?

By now you might be wondering, "Who is David T. Scott? And how does he know so much about lead-generation marketing?"

Let me tell you a little bit about myself. . . .

I got into lead-generation marketing by accident. I attended the Wharton School of Business at the University of Pennsylvania. Although I received a great education there, my MBA was in strategic management, so I didn't concentrate much on marketing. But the few courses I took were about brand marketing. I don't remember a single class being offered on lead-generation marketing at Wharton.

I was serving as vice president of corporate strategy for a $3.5 billion, publicly traded software company with a worldwide sales organization. Then the vice president of marketing got fired, and his job duties were passed on to me! In my new position, I was one of several marketing executives in charge of generating a weekly quota of quality leads for the president of my division, who was a former vice president of sales.

Like most lead-generation marketers, I had to educate myself on the job. My team was using multiple competing lead-generation tactics, on a limited budget, and I had to decide which tactics to concentrate on and which to use less. My background included corporate strategy and computer programming, two fields that emphasize mathematics and analysis. Lead generation requires a great deal of analytical thinking, so I was comfortable working with the lead-generation processes. But in the beginning, my efforts were mostly trial and error.

In my next job, as chief marketing officer for a billion-dollar mobile devices company, I had a bit more authority. I started to create testing and measuring tools to find out which lead-generation tactics were providing us with the most effective, actionable leads and to measure the cost-effectiveness of each tactic. Through trial and error, I learned how to coordinate different tactics, as part of an effective, integrated lead-generation strategy.

As I moved on to other marketing executive positions, I found I could easily transfer these strategies and measurement tools to lead-generation efforts at other companies. Originally, I'd thought that when I moved on to new companies, I'd focus more on brand marketing. Instead, I found that the more I understood lead-generation marketing, the more in demand I was to new employers.

Today, I'm the CEO and founder of a company that specializes in automation technology for lead-generation marketing. But in my conversations with other marketers, I'm often surprised to learn how many of them don't really understand the lead-generation process or how to make the best use of it for their company's needs and goals.

The science and analysis of lead generation have become very important for me to examine as a marketer. This book is about the tools I've created to test and measure lead generation. By using these tools, you can make your lead-generation efforts as effective as possible, and you'll know which tactics are the best and most cost-effective for your company and your goals.

Changing with the Times

Lead-generation marketing is in a constant state of evolution. One challenge of writing a book like this is making sure the tools I provide don't go out-of-date in a few years. Many lead-generation marketing books have a short shelf life because they focus on current trends and tactics, instead of looking at how tactics evolve over time. Some books published in the past decade don't cover emerging trends like social media advertising on Facebook. Instead, they cover subjects like newspaper classified ads and telemarketing, a lead-generation tactic that has now been legislated out of existence.

This book provides strategies and tactics that will still be of use to marketers one year, five years, or even ten years from now. I focus on three tried-and-true lead-generation tactics (direct mail, trade shows, and cold calling) and four emerging digital lead-generation tactics (e-mail marketing, search engine marketing, display advertising, and social media advertising). Lead-generation marketers will be using all seven of these tactics for the foreseeable future.

But even if one of these seven tactics is eventually replaced by a future lead-generation tactic, *you can still apply the strategic approaches and the testing and measuring tools provided in this book.* You'll be able to test and measure the effectiveness of any new lead-generation tactics and to compare their effectiveness with your current ones.

No doubt, the seven lead-generation tactics in this book will evolve over the next decade. Companies and industries will develop new ways to use them. And marketers will apply future technology innovations to these seven tactics to bring leads in more easily. Who knows? In 10 years or so, hypertargeted marketing offers may be sent directly to our 3-D television sets. We may see the development of new forms of social advertising, such as text message advertising. As you'll see in this book, Twitter has released its own advertising platform, which can be used for lead-generation marketing.

The movie *Minority Report*, starring Tom Cruise, gives us an interesting and insightful look at what advertising might be like in the future. In the year 2054, advertising has evolved to the point where every ad experience is extremely personalized. Video billboards in shopping malls instantly identify shoppers by scanning their eye retinas when they walk into a store and determine their clothing sizes by scanning their bodies. The video billboards then give the shoppers customized suggestions on what to buy, based on their style preferences and other recorded information about them.

Even today, marketers are using new technologies to apply these same principles to lead-generation tactics. For example, in online display advertising, ad networks like DoubleClick are using ad-serving technologies, such as Internet cookies and IP-tracking programs, to follow a Web user's click trail and see what sites he visits. The ad network can then target the user by serving display ads that are appropriate to that user's needs and interests. If, for example, your click trail indicates that you are looking for a new car, the ad network can serve you online ads about the latest car models. (I'll talk more about these technologies when I discuss display advertising in Chapter 10.)

The goal of this book is to give you the fundamental tools that allow you to *evolve your own lead-generation strategies* over time. I place great emphasis in this book on mathematics and analytics. I focus on *how to test and measure your lead-generation efforts* to find out how well they provide you with leads and, most importantly, how cost-effective they are.

As lead-generation tactics evolve and change, you'll be able to continuously evaluate their effectiveness in supplying your company with cost-effective leads. You'll be able to determine which new tools and technologies you should embrace and which you should discard in your ever-changing lead-generation efforts.

Before We Begin: How to Read This Book

BEFORE WE explore the complex subject of lead-generation marketing, let me suggest—no, let me *urge* you—to read this book from start to finish. If you're a lead-generation marketer, you may be tempted to skip ahead to the later chapters that explore individual tactics (e.g., direct mail, e-mail marketing) that you are currently using. But you will get *much, much more* out of this book if you read it from Chapter 1 to the end—even the chapters about tactics you are not currently using.

This book is divided into two parts. In *Part One: The Basic Tools of Lead-Generation Marketing*, I'll show you how to lay the foundation for successful lead-generation marketing campaigns.

Chapter 1: What Is Lead-Generation Marketing?—This is a basic overview of lead-generation marketing. What is it? Who uses it? And how does it fit into the marketing mix?

Chapter 2: Defining Your Leads—How do you define the types of leads you are seeking in terms of who your customers are and what kind of action you want them to take as a result of your lead-generation marketing?

Chapter 3: Developing Your Lead-Generation Strategy—How do you develop strategy and set goals for your lead-generation campaigns? And how do you test and measure your lead-generation results to determine the success of your efforts?

Chapter 4: Using Lead-Generation Tactics—You can apply this basic five-step process to each of the seven most successful lead-generation tactics.

Chapter 5: Calculating the Costs—This chapter shows how qualified leads get turned into sales, and how this process can affect your return on marketing investment (ROMI). Only by understanding and measuring the overall costs of your lead-generation efforts can you determine how successful and cost-effective they are.

These first five chapters are heavy with lead-generation marketing theory. But it's *essential* that you read these chapters, and read them carefully. These chapters provide you with a set of valuable tools that will be the basis of your lead-generation marketing campaigns.

You can't build a strong house without a strong foundation. The tools I provide in these first five chapters will help you to lay a strong foundation for your lead-generation marketing efforts. By learning these tools, you will give your lead-generation campaigns the best chance of success.

In *Part Two: Lead-Generation Marketing Tactics*, each chapter covers one of the seven most successful lead-generation marketing tactics:

1. Search engine marketing

2. Social media advertising (Facebook, LinkedIn, and Twitter)

3. Display advertising (also known as banner ads)

4. E-mail marketing

5. Direct mail marketing

6. Cold calling

7. Trade shows

In each chapter, I'll explore how each tactic works and give you strategies for using it effectively. (Actually, there are two chapters on social media advertising, one for advertising on Facebook and LinkedIn and another for advertising on Twitter. The reason is that Twitter's advertising program is a bit unusual and requires a closer look.)

The tactics chapters in Part Two deal with the new lead-generation tactics first, before moving on to the older tactics. Chapters 7 to 10 and Chapter 12 are about online lead-generation tactics: search engine marketing, social media advertising, display advertising, and e-mail marketing. Chapters 13 to 15 are about traditional lead-generation tactics: direct mail, cold calling, and trade shows.

The tactics chapters are in this order for several reasons. I've decided to explore the online lead-generation tactics first, because I think those are of greatest interest to marketers. Then, I'll return to the traditional "tried and true" tactics, and show you some new ways to use those tactics to your advantage.

Also, it makes more sense to explore the online lead-generation tactics at the beginning of Part Two, while the principles and strategies introduced in Part One are still fresh in your mind. In Part One, I explore the basic principles of lead-generation marketing and give you a five-step tactical strategy that you can apply to each lead-generation tactic. So it's important for you to see that these principles and strategies work with the new tactics as well as the old.

Finally, some chapters in Part Two cover additional strategies and elements that apply to more than one lead-generation tactic and that can be used with both online lead-generation tactics and traditional tactics. For example, Chapter 6, "Introduction to Online Lead-Generation Advertising," presents an overview of online lead-generation advertising tactics (e.g., social media advertising, search engine marketing, display advertising). I'll explore some common elements (e.g., online bidding, testing tactics) that you can apply to each of these tactics. I'll also talk about how to create and use landing pages, an online conversion tool that you can also use with e-mail marketing, cold-calling, and direct mail campaigns. And Chapter 11, "Selecting and Targeting a Mailing or Contact List," shows you how to rent or buy targeted lists of potential customers for your e-mail marketing, direct mail, and cold-calling campaigns.

These additional strategies and elements apply to more than one lead-generation tactic, and in some cases to both online and traditional tactics. So it's better for me to introduce and talk about them in separate chapters. That way, I don't repeat myself too much in the tactic chapters when I talk about using these additional strategies and elements with each lead-generation tactic.

Chapter 16, "Integrated Lead-Generation Marketing" (the last chapter in the book), shows you how to use several marketing tactics at the same time, as part of an integrated lead-generation marketing campaign. You'll learn how using several lead-generation tactics in combination with one another will help you to achieve a much more effective marketing campaign.

Now let's get to it. . . .

PART ONE

The Basic Tools of Lead-Generation Marketing

1

What Is Lead-Generation Marketing?

TO BEGIN, we need to answer two basic questions: What exactly is lead-generation marketing? And what exactly is a lead?

Lead-generation marketing is getting people to "raise their hands" and say they are interested in buying, or learning more about, your product or service. By "raise their hands," I mean they show interest in a very palpable way.

Leads are people who have identified themselves as candidates who can potentially be turned into sales. Depending on where they are in the buying cycle, they may be "thinking about buying" or "shopping around" or "considering alternatives" or "ready to buy." Whatever their stage, they have a genuine interest in your products or services, and are considering you as a viable option to meet their needs.

Lead-generation marketing is a way to generate what I call *marketing-qualified leads* (MQLs). An MQL is a lead that is legitimate, honest, and actionable. *Legitimate* and *honest* mean your prospective customers have a true intent to buy. They have the money and the authority to buy, and are serious about evaluating your product or service for possible purchase. *Actionable* means your sales engine can act on the lead.

A *sales engine* is whatever mechanism you use to engage the sale of your goods and services. It used to be that "sales engine" referred almost exclusively to a company's sales department, but a shift in practices is taking place. In the 21st century, lead-generation marketing is changing not only how companies handle marketing but, in some cases, how they handle sales as well.

A Paradigm Shift

We live in an interesting time for lead-generation marketing. It is (and always will be) a sales support function. Its traditional goal in corporate marketing is to provide warm, actionable leads to the company's sales force, enabling salespeople to close more deals and generate more revenue. A sales force used to be an essential requirement for any business, and lead-generation marketing provided support for the sales. Previously, only a few specialty companies, such as L.L.Bean, were able to get by without a sales force, relying exclusively on print catalogs to drive sales.

But the role of lead-generation marketing is evolving, as more companies adopt e-commerce and mobile technologies as sales vehicles. With the evolution of online catalog marketing and self-service sales, some e-commerce companies don't even need a sales force. They just need highly effective lead-generation marketing.

This is one of the most exciting transformations that has occurred in the world of business over the last decade. With the development of e-commerce, some organizations have been able to take the sales force entirely out of the equation. This development puts greater influence on the marketing discipline, to the point where, in some organizations, lead-generation marketing could effectively serve as both sales and marketing for the company. It's a very powerful paradigm shift.

This shift first played out in the travel industry. Companies like Expedia introduced self-service travel concepts that essentially put travel agencies out of business. You no longer have to hire a travel agent to purchase an airline ticket or to book hotel or rental car reservations. Now you can make your own reservations online.

This paradigm shift is extending to the real estate field. Companies like Redfin and Zillow now provide real estate search engines and databases that allow Web users to offer or search for homes for sale online. As a home buyer, you can check the location, property values, and other information about the house, get a home price estimate, compare mortgage options with different lenders, and ask advice from a community of real estate experts. As a home seller, you can offer your home for sale and post information about it. You may not even need a real estate agent to buy or sell a home.

The car buyer's market is also being affected by this paradigm shift. Auto industry marketers are now providing car buyers with information that was formerly provided by salespeople in the dealer's showroom. These days, 80% of the car-buying experience is done online. People research car models, read consumer reports and reviews, check out the 360°-view on the car maker's website, download a list of the car's features, and get an estimate of the price. When the buyer walks into the dealership, marketing has already done most of the work for the sales force. You may never be able to buy a car without a salesperson to sell it to you, but it's a definite power shift.

What's driving this shift in business practices that gives lead-generation marketing more influence and importance in e-commerce businesses? Consumers want more control over the buying experience. They want to do their own research on products and understand their options before making a purchase. The Internet provides a means for consumers to find product information quickly and easily and, in many cases, to make purchases more conveniently.

As companies seek to fulfill the consumer's need for more buying information and control, they are relying more on lead-generation marketing. This reflects a dramatic shift in the importance of marketing in relation to sales.

To further understand this shift, let's look at where lead-generation marketing falls in the world of marketing, and how it relates to its "brother"—brand awareness marketing.

Brand Awareness vs. Lead Generation

In general, the world of marketing is dominated by two disciplines: brand awareness marketing and lead-generation marketing. These two disciplines are the "big brothers of marketing," and they have a kind of yin/yang relationship with each other. (There are other equally important forms of marketing, of course, such as product marketing. But these other forms have only a casual relationship to lead-generation marketing, so I won't focus on them in this book.)

Brand awareness marketing (commonly known as brand marketing) is all about making people aware of your product and/or your company. It's about creating an impression of what your brand stands for in people's minds, and repeating that impression until they have an explicit or implicit awareness of your brand. Coca-Cola spends billions of dollars a year for just this purpose. They plaster their brand and pictures of their soft drink across billboards, posters, print ads, TV commercials, online ads, and many other places so that, when you're thirsty and looking for something to drink, you automatically think of Coke. Or if a Coca-Cola bottle is sitting next to a Pepsi bottle, you've already formed your opinion of Coca-Cola's product in your mind, and you can make your choice.

For decades, brand awareness marketing has been considered the sexy part of marketing. The hit TV show *Mad Men* is built around the lives of advertisers in a top New York ad agency in the 1960s. During this time, ad marketers were perfecting the concepts of art and copywriting, and the concepts of advertising aimed at building awareness of a brand (Chevrolet Oldsmobiles, Lucky Strike cigarettes, etc.) in the public mind, and then invoking an implicit desire to buy the product.

Lead-generation marketing has long been considered the underbelly of marketing. Lead-generation marketers ask this question: Once you have established an awareness of your brand and/or product in the marketplace, how do you get the customer to move from considering your product to actually *buying* it? It's one thing to make your customers aware that you offer the newest, most innovative smartphone; it's another thing to convince them to spend $479.99 to buy it. That is the art of lead-generation marketing.

Who Uses Lead-Generation Marketing?

It's difficult to measure the exact percentage of companies that use lead-generation marketing. But here's an interesting statistic: A McKinsey Global Survey found that 83% of companies worldwide use some kind of online lead-generation tactic (e-mail marketing, search engine ads, etc.).[1] If we include the few companies that use only traditional lead-generation tactics (trade shows, direct mail, and cold calling) without using *online* tactics, we might estimate that roughly 85 to 90% of all companies worldwide use some form of lead-generation marketing.

The companies that have the most use for lead-generation marketing are those that acquire sales through a website or sales staff. Any company that has a direct sales process and/or a direct sales force—either an internal sales force or a field sales force—will receive significant benefits from using lead-generation marketing tactics.

The ways that companies employ the two major marketing disciplines—brand awareness and lead generation—fall across a range of three categories. Figure 1.1 shows the breakdown of how companies fall into each category.

Lead generation–dependent companies rely exclusively, or almost exclusively, on lead-generation marketing. Usually, these companies are manufacturers or service providers (e.g., Intel or Caterpillar) who may sell directly to a targeted set of customers who have a specific need for their products or services. (For example, Caterpillar usually sells its equipment products and vehicles to construction companies, mining companies, warehouse companies, or whoever has a specific need for it.)

Or these companies may be original equipment manufacturers (OEMs) that sell directly to client companies, who then install the OEM's components in their own products and sell them under their own brand name. (For example, Intel manufactures microprocessor chips and sells them to manufacturers of computers, mobile devices, entertainment systems, etc.)

For these companies, brand doesn't matter nearly as much as lead generation because the company relies more on the sales team, the catalog, or the website to push their wares. Yes, their brand helps in terms of recognition.

FIGURE 1.1. Marketing Mix

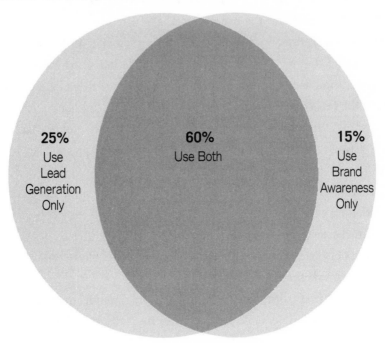

(Among businesses that use their products, Intel and Caterpillar are very recognizable brand names.) But the company's direct efforts in marketing and sales really drive the business. Their audience is so targeted that branding to a larger audience would be a waste of money. The challenge for these companies is to make contact with the customers who have a need for their products and to build a personal or business relationship with them.

An excellent example of this type of company is the Fluke Corporation, headquartered in Everett, Washington. Owned by the Dahaner Corporation, Fluke is a billion-dollar company that manufactures electronic testing devices such as calibrators and waveform generators. Fluke uses lead-generation marketing to market their products exclusively to electricians and companies that have a need for them. Because their target market is so specific, they don't need to spend much money on brand advertising. Among electricians, Fluke enjoys 95% name recognition, but very few people outside their customer base have ever heard of the company.

Brand awareness–dependent companies rely exclusively, or almost exclusively, on brand awareness marketing. Companies like Coca-Cola and Delta Airlines need brand marketing because their target audience includes "everyone." So these companies pay millions of dollars for advertising to make sure their brand is top-of-mind for anyone with a reason to buy their types of products or services.

In many cases, these companies don't need to rely on lead-generation marketing because they have channels (e.g., supermarkets or retail stores) to do their selling for them. For example, a consumer electronics manufacturing company like Panasonic might sell its flat-screen TVs, DVD players, and other products through retail stores like Target, Walmart, and Best Buy, as well as online through Amazon.com.

Many consumer electronics companies don't focus on direct sales of their products. They care only about whether their brand has enough value and awareness to command the high premiums that the company demands, and whether the stores will carry the brand. A consumer electronics company has no reason to generate leads for their products because retail stores that offer or specialize in consumer electronics do it for them, through their own brand awareness marketing.

Brand awareness/lead generation–dependent companies use a combination of brand awareness and lead-generation marketing. Usually, these companies have numerous competitors, along with numerous potential customers in their target markets. In these situations, their target audience must take some kind of action. Whether that action is simply to become aware of the product, to show interest, or to actually purchase the product depends on where the potential customers are in the buying cycle. (I'll talk more about this in Chapter 2.)

An example of a company that uses a balance of brand awareness and lead-generation marketing is Progressive Insurance or any other large insurance company. Progressive Insurance has hundreds of agents throughout America, whom they must fuel with leads every month. So Progressive does a tremendous amount of lead-generation marketing through direct mail, e-mail marketing, and display ads. But Progressive also uses national TV advertising to make customers aware of their brand. They want to make sure that anyone who is thinking about buying insurance thinks about them.

As shown in Figure 1.1, the companies that use only brand awareness marketing or only lead-generation marketing are fewer in number than those that use both. Most companies fall at the center of the graph, using some combination of brand awareness and lead-generation marketing. The more successful companies are the ones that have learned not only how to use lead-generation marketing to maximum effect, but also how to coordinate lead-generation and brand awareness marketing.

When lead-generation and brand awareness marketing work in tandem, it produces a *halo effect*, in which the positive effect of one marketing tactic benefits other marketing tactics. For example, when people see a commercial for your company on TV, they come away with a positive impression of your product. While surfing the Web, they see a display ad for your product that reinforces the message. A few days later, they get an e-mail from you, inviting them to learn more about your product, and they click on the link to your website. They may not have clicked on the e-mail invitation without the positive impressions they received from previous ads. (I'll talk more about the halo effect in Chapter 16, when I discuss integrated marketing campaigns.)

What sets lead-generation marketing apart from brand awareness marketing is that brand marketing is more intuitive and creative, whereas lead-generation marketing is more mathematical and analytical.

Analytical vs. Emotional

Brand awareness marketing is a "bright idea," "thinking-outside-the-box" kind of discipline. Brand awareness marketers focus on creating impressions in the prospect's or customer's mind and on displaying or broadcasting those impressions in ways calculated to reach as many consumers as possible. For example, in marketing a soft drink, they work on creating ads and TV commercials to convey the impression that the soft drink is "cold," "tasty," and "thirst-quenching."

Brand awareness is a battle of creative ideas, whose goal is to connect emotionally with the customer. Once a brand awareness campaign is sent out into the world, there's no way to correct it. You can only determine the effectiveness of the ad or commercial after it is released, not before.

Lead-generation marketing focuses more on mathematics and scientific methods. You must constantly perform testing and analysis as part of your lead-generation efforts. This testing and analysis process occurs on multiple levels. On a tactical level, you need to continuously test the results of your lead-generation tactics to find out how well they provide quality leads and how cost-effective they are. On a lead-generation management level, you need to compare the results of different tactics (e.g., direct mail versus trade shows) to find out which tactics are the most efficient and cost-effective.

Within each tactic, you test variables against a constant to determine which combination of variables works best in attracting leads from your customers. For example, in an e-mail marketing campaign, you may have two e-mail creatives with the same offer. You send each creative out with a different subject header, and compare the results to see which subject header gets the better response from your potential customers.

In lead-generation marketing, there is no "correct answer," or right tactic or variable. One tactic (e.g., direct mail) may be your best performing tactic this year, but five years from now, another tactic (e.g., search engine marketing) may be more efficient and cost-effective in meeting your goals. One type of customer may respond well to one type of offer from you, while another customer in another demographic may respond better to another type of offer. The point is, you are *constantly testing and analyzing your results* to see which lead-generation tactics and variables work best for you. Your success in lead generation depends on what you learn from testing and analysis and on how you use the results to improve your efforts.

Analytical vs. Creative Mindset

Most of the lead-generation marketers I know come from a mathematical or business background, not a creative one. I started as a computer programmer before earning my MBA in strategic management. Other lead-generation marketers I know were formerly accountants, electrical engineers, or economists. You don't need a degree in computer science or economics to do lead-generation marketing, but you do need an analytical mindset. You must be able to think structurally, in terms of the different levels of the planning, organization, testing, and analysis used in a lead-generation campaign.

Lead-generation marketing is all about the science of the approach. Very little creativity is involved. In fact, I could argue that too much creativity actually inhibits the effectiveness of lead-generation marketing. Many lead-generation campaigns didn't work because the marketers tried to be too creative.

For example, you might have a gorgeous creative e-mail with beautiful graphics, and a plain-text e-mail that simply states your value proposition and offer, along with a call-to-action. The plain-text e-mail will often outperform the beautiful creative e-mail, because a plain-text e-mail (1) has a better chance of getting past the recipient's spam filters and (2) looks less like an advertisement. The creative e-mail may look great, but the benefits of your offer may get lost in the graphics. Or the imagery may distract customers from the call-to-action that tells them how to respond to the ad. It's a matter of substance over style.

Successful lead-generation marketing involves making a series of calculated decisions about how you will approach your potential customers and what information you will provide to them about your products and services. In a way, these decisions are like the choices a general or other military leader has to make on the battlefield.

Going into Battle

Think of lead-generation marketing as being like a medieval army going into battle. Historically, armies have always organized themselves into tactical divisions. Each combat division had a specialized tactic—infantry, cavalry, artillery, archery, pikemen, spearmen, etc. The great military generals of history knew how to use each tactic to their advantage in battle, as well as how to use different tactics in combination with each other for maximum effect against the enemy.

For example, in attacking an armed fortress, a general might use artillery to soften up the walls and outer defenses. (In ancient times, artillery usually took the form of catapults firing large stones at a fort to break through the walls. As warfare moved into the modern age, artillery usually meant cannons and mortars.) If the fort had manned trenches, bastions, and other defenses, the general might use archers or spearmen to try to take them out or a cavalry charge to overrun them. Finally, when the fort's defenses had been softened to the point that it could be taken, the general would mount a full infantry charge to break through the gates and enter the fortress.

At the same time, many great military leaders have understood the importance of brand awareness marketing (although they didn't call it that). Historians tell us that Genghis Khan had to fight only 30% of his battles. His Mongol hordes sacked and pillaged so many cities that Khan's reputation preceded him wherever he went.

When Khan appeared on the battlefield, he rode on horseback, dressed in shining gold armor topped with a horned headdress. He would make a magnificent appearance, surrounded by his generals and flanked by heralds carrying flags, banners, and other regalia. With his Mongol divisions marching in formation behind him, his army was an impressive sight. Many of his enemies who chose to face him in battle simply lost the will to fight. Often, towns and villages would surrender to him rather than be destroyed.

However, Khan knew that brand awareness can carry you only so far. Occasionally, he faced an enemy (such as the Shah of Khwarezmia, in the region of modern Iran) who was not intimidated by his reputation or the size of his army. When that happened, Khan would have to assemble his forces, march out to meet his enemy, and rely on his tactical teams.

The same principles apply to using lead-generation tactics (although I wouldn't recommend the sacking and pillaging approach). For most businesses, brand awareness is not enough to help you achieve success in all the potential markets for your products or services. You must use lead-generation marketing when you want to take over and achieve market dominance in certain strategic market areas.

Just as generals had their combat divisions of infantry, cavalry, and artillery, lead-generation marketers have their tactics, such as direct mail, trade shows, cold calling, etc. Like combat units, each lead-generation tactic has its own specific role, its own strengths and weaknesses. If you use only one tactic, it may be fairly effective, provided you choose the *right* tactic to reach your target customer. But if you use several lead-generation tactics in combination, you could increase the range of potential customers you reach with your message, thus achieving much better results.

But like the great generals of old, you must understand how each tactic works and how to use it effectively. You must understand how to determine which tactics will be the most effective and how to coordinate different tactics in a lead-generation plan to achieve the best results. Only a combination of tactics, based on the situation at hand, will create the optimum battle plan.

Calculating the Cost

We can learn another lesson from military history. The great generals knew that sometimes you have to take risks to achieve results. They knew how to use combat tactics to their strategic advantage so that a minimum number of their troops would be lost in securing a military objective.

For example, a general might look at a heavily armed enemy fortress and determine that a full frontal assault on the fortress gates would require 100,000 troops with the potential for 20,000 casualties. However, the general notices a nearby ridge overlooking the fort. The ridge is also occupied by enemy troops, but its defenses are weak. The general foresees that his artillery could soften up the enemy's defenses on the ridge with a two-day barrage of shelling. He could send a cavalry charge up the ridge, followed by an infantry assault, to capture this strategic advantage point. Afterward, the general's artillerymen could drag their cannons up to the ridge to fire down on the fort and force it to surrender. If the plan works, the general can capture the objective, and the casualties to his army from the ridge assault would be fewer than 1,000.

Thankfully, a lead-generation marketer doesn't need to make such life-or-death decisions regarding combat troops. But you do need to determine which lead-generation tactics will be the most cost-effective for your marketing goals. Like the general in command of troops, you don't want to waste your entire lead-generation budget on one tactic that may not provide you with the results you need. You may get better results with a combination of tactics, but you must first determine which of the seven tactics are more cost-effective for you and which are less cost-effective. You must then develop a strategy to use the most cost-effective tactics to your advantage.

In this book, I'll show you how to plan your lead-generation strategy using your most cost-effective tactics. For now, remember this: The overall goal of your lead-generation efforts should be to achieve the *highest-quality, most cost-effective leads for your company.*

> > > **What You Should Know** < < <

To review, here is what you should remember about lead-generation marketing:

- Lead-generation marketing is getting people to "raise their hands" and say they are interested in buying your product or service. It is a way to generate marketing-qualified leads—that is, leads that are legitimate, honest, and actionable.

- The two most widely used disciplines of marketing are brand awareness marketing and lead-generation marketing. The majority of companies use some form of lead-generation marketing, usually in some combination with brand awareness marketing.

- Lead-generation marketing is based more on mathematics and scientific methods than on creative thinking. It is more analytical and less emotional. Successful lead-generation strategy requires continuous testing and measurement on several levels to achieve the best results.

- A successful lead-generation strategy is one that employs several tactics in coordination. The secret lies in knowing which tactics will be the most effective for you and how to combine those tactics to achieve the best results.

- A major part of lead-generation strategy is determining which tactics are the most cost-effective for your marketing goals and budget. The overall goal of your lead-generation efforts should be to achieve the highest-quality, most cost-effective leads for your company.

2

Defining Your Leads

THE NEXT FOUR chapters focus on the terminology and qualifying processes of leads themselves, the fundamentals of lead-generation strategy, and the principles and methods for using lead-generation tactics. In reading these four chapters, you might think I'm overexplaining the principles and theories of lead-generation marketing.

Be patient with me. It's very important that you understand these terms and concepts, because *they provide a common framework for all lead-generation campaigns.*

As I said in the "Before We Begin" chapter, the goal for Part One is to lay a strong foundation for your lead-generation campaigns. Using the terms and concepts I provide in these next four chapters will help you to define your campaign objectives and strategies. You'll be able to plan and execute your campaigns more effectively, no matter which lead-generation tactics you use. And you'll be able to test and measure your results to find out how well your campaigns and tactics worked.

Before we explore lead-generation strategies and tactics, we need to examine the nature and context of leads themselves. In this chapter, I'll examine the different kinds of leads, and also look at how to define "leads" or other "actions" that you may be seeking from your potential customers.

What Is a Lead?

One of the first questions you should ask in planning your lead-generation efforts is, "What is a lead to me? How do I define a lead in terms of the goals and needs of my organization?"

The common term for the subject of this book is lead-generation marketing, so I tend to use the word *lead* as a generic term for customer actions. However, technically, the subject of this book might be called *action*-generation marketing. An *action*, in this case, is any distinct action that a potential customer takes as a result of a lead-generation marketing tactic. A *lead*—or rather, the act of signing up as a lead—is one type of customer action.

But there are *other* types of customer actions. The objective of *your* lead-generation marketing efforts (in whichever tactic you use) may not be to obtain an actual lead. Depending on your company's goals and your marketing efforts, you may be seeking some other type of action from your customer.

For example, if you're an e-commerce company (or have e-commerce tools on your website), the action you are seeking from your customer may be an actual purchase. If, for example, you are an online shoe retailer, and you send out an e-mail with a "Buy one pair of shoes, 20% off" special offer, the action you seek is to have customers take advantage of the discount and purchase a pair of shoes from you.

Or, if you're a software company, and you send out an e-mail announcement about version 2.0 of your latest software package, available to version 1.0 users at the reduced price of $24.95, the action you seek is to have customers purchase the upgrade.

Depending on your goals, you may be seeking more than one type of action from your potential customer. Often, you want customers to take an action that compels them to become a lead. For example, if your goal is to educate your customers about a new type of product or service they haven't seen before, you may ask them to download a white paper about your product or service. That's one action you want them to take. But to download the white paper, they need to enter their e-mail addresses on your landing page and sign up for your e-mail newsletter. In doing so, the customers become leads.

It's important to determine the goals for your lead-generation efforts, in terms of the action you want to elicit from customers. Your goal may be an actual lead, or it may be some other customer action. But the number of leads or actions that you acquire, measured against the cost to acquire them, is the crucial measure of success for your lead-generation efforts.

Very often, the type of lead you are seeking depends on where your target customers are in the buying cycle.

The AIDA Curve

In defining the type of lead or other customer action you want to obtain, the most crucial question is, "Where do my target customers stand in the buying cycle? In what stage of buying are they in relation to my type of product or service?" To answer this question, you need to compare your potential customers against the AIDA curve.

The AIDA curve is a well-known principle of contextual marketing. *Contextual marketing* is the concept of organizing your marketing campaigns in context with the mindset of the buyer at the time. It is one of the simplest and most effective tools a marketer can use.

Without knowing where your potential customers are in the buying cycle and how close they are to making a buying decision, you may send them the wrong offer or the wrong message at the wrong time. If this happens, you will end up wasting your lead-generation budget on an unsuccessful campaign.

In Figure 2.1, you can see how the AIDA concept covers the four stages of the buying cycle. AIDA is an acronym for Attention, Interest, Decision, Action.

The AIDA curve examines the mentality of your potential customers when you grab them as a lead. According to AIDA curve theory, not every

FIGURE 2.1. The AIDA Curve

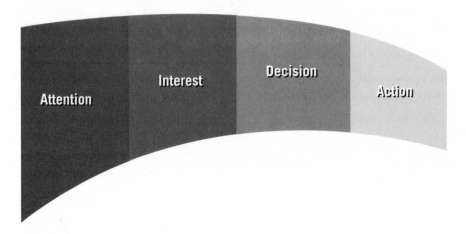

customer is in the same frame of mind or at the same decision point in con-sidering your offer. Therefore, you need to learn which stage of the buying cycle each customer is in, and then cater your lead-generation tactics to reach the customer in that stage.

You may already be familiar with the AIDA curve. In the movie *Glengarry Glen Ross,* based on the play by David Mamet, Alec Baldwin plays Mr. Blake, a ruthless sales executive at the corrupt Chicago real estate firm of Mitch & Murray. He gives an iconic "chalk talk" speech to the salespeople at his firm, trying to motivate them to sell shoddy real estate packages. In his speech, Baldwin explains the AIDA curve (and even writes it on a black-board), and orders the sales force to concentrate on pushing the customer through the Attention-Interest-Decision-Action buying cycle in order to make sales.

In recent years, the AIDA curve has fallen out of fashion in the business world. Maybe because of Alec Baldwin's famous speech, it's now consid-ered a cliché. But examining your potential customers through the prism of the AIDA curve is an absolutely essential part of planning your lead-generation strategy.

Throughout the AIDA curve process, the potential customer is asking a series of questions about your product or service or your type of product or service. It's up to you to provide him or her with answers.

THE ATTENTION PHASE

Potential customers in the Attention phase have just become aware of your type of product. It's not that they've just learned of your particular brand of product or service; *it's that they've just learned about the product or service itself!*

If your product or service is brand new, then customers never knew it existed until you came along. Or, if it's a new variation on an existing product or service (e.g., a hybrid electric car that uses less gas and gives off less carbon emissions), it solves a problem in a way that they've never heard of before.

At this stage, the customer is asking the following questions:

- *Why does this class of products/services exist?*

- *What is its purpose?*

- *What makes this class of products or services interesting?*

An example from my own experience helps to illustrate the AIDA curve. A few months ago, I became aware of a weight-loss device called a Body Bugg, a small electronic calorie counter that you attach to your arm with an arm band. The Body Bugg measures how many calories your body is burning at any given time. Every day, you download the measurements to your laptop or mobile device. A Body Bugg application lets you compare your daily caloric burn against how much you are eating to determine whether you're doing enough daily physical activity to meet your weight-loss goals.

A few months ago, I didn't know the Body Bugg existed. Once I became aware of it, I was intrigued enough to do some research. At this point, I was asking myself, "What exactly is this computer-aided weight device? How can it help me to lose more weight?"

In the Attention phase, you're selling potential customers on the whole purpose of the product class *in general,* not necessarily on your version of the product. You're informing them that the product exists and what it can do for them.

Tread carefully when educating customers in the Attention phase. One of the classic mistakes of lead-generation marketing is to try to close a sale, or do a hard-sell, in this phase. Customers contact you, wanting to know more about your product in general—and you send them an offer to buy your product at a 30% discount.

The problem is, these customers are not ready to buy. They are still learning about the product, and don't know whether they really need it or not. When you send Attention-phase customers a discount offer, it's often a turnoff for them. They may decide that you are being too pushy with your product. They may lose interest in it, or at least lose interest in your brand. They won't move on to the Decision or Action phases with your company, and you've thrown away the opportunity.

Instead, try to educate your Attention-phase customers using case studies, webinars, your website, and other vehicles. Give them basic product information, and explain its benefits. Help them to figure out whether this product is of interest to them.

THE INTEREST PHASE

Once potential customers become aware of the type of product you sell, they may have some interest in it. But they are still unsure about buying it. At this stage, the customer is asking the following questions:

- *Why should I use these classes of products?*

- *Why should I consider buying one over some other type of device that provides a similar solution, or to replace the solution I have now?*

Or if you're offering a service, the customer is asking:

- *How will this service help me?*

- *Do other types of services accomplish the same goal?*

- *If so, why should I use this service instead of the others?*

Once I became aware of the Body Bugg, I was in the Interest phase. I started to do research to find out if it was the right product for my needs. I compared it to other weight-loss products, and decided that the concept and features of the Body Bugg could help me. At that point, I decided I was in the market for a product like this.

With Attention-phase customers, you are selling the general benefits of your type of product. With Interest-phase customers, you are trying to interest them in your type of product versus other products on the market with similar solutions.

This is where a webinar or a well-written website can be very effective for you, by providing information that will inspire the reader's interest in the product. You should also use white papers, case studies, and customer testimonials. You need to sell the benefits of your type of product, not the features of your particular brand.

If you send out an e-mail to Interest-phase customers, you should ask them to download a white paper or product sheet. You want to educate them so they quickly recognize (1) their need for a product like yours, and (2) that your product provides the solution they are looking for.

THE DECISION PHASE

Customers in the Decision phase have decided that they like the product or service enough to buy it. You need to prompt them to act now, and most importantly, to act in your favor.

At this stage, the customer is asking:

- *Why should I buy your brand of this type of product over someone else's?*

- *What makes your brand of product better than the others?*

- *Where can I get the best deal on the product?*

If you're offering a service, the customer is asking:

- *Why should I purchase your service instead of someone else's?*

• *What makes your service better than the others?*

Here, you should focus on the quality or uniqueness of your product. You also need to make sure that your version of the product is in the customer's "consideration set." If competitors manufacture other versions of your product under their own brand, they will likely be in the potential client's consideration set as well.

In my research, I discovered that there was more than one Body Bugg brand on the market. Each calorie-counting device had the same function, but vendors were charging different prices and bundling different services with each model. I had to decide which version of the Body Bugg was the best bargain, which one fit my budget, and which store I should visit to purchase my Body Bugg.

The vendor I went with (www.bodymedia.com) did a very good job of giving me reasons to buy their version of the Body Bugg. Their website allowed me to compare the advantages of the Body Bugg over other weight-loss devices.

For Decision-phase customers, you should use white papers, sell sheets, and product comparisons to explain to the customer why your version of the product is the best on the market. You should also use customer testimonials: "Don't take *our* word for it. Let our customers tell you how good our product is."

Also, with Decision-phase customers, you should start to focus on where they can buy the product, how easy it is to buy, what kind of support they get for it, and other helpful information. You might not ask them to *buy* the product at this point, but you may, for example, offer them a free 30-day trial to convince them that it is worth buying.

THE ACTION PHASE

In the Action phase, your potential customers buy a product or service. They have made a decision on one particular vendor or service provider, so they contact the vendor or service company, go to a store, or go to an e-commerce site and make the transaction for the purchase.

The Action-phase customer is asking one question: *"Why should I buy this product or service right now?"*

When I decided to buy the Body Bugg, I chose the vendor (BodyMedia) with the best overall product and the best support package. BodyMedia's website provided a list of local fitness stores where I could buy the device, rather than having to order it online.

You need to offer Action-phase customers reasons to buy *now*. This is where you should make special offers, such as sales, 30% discounts, and timed coupons (e.g., "Buy within the next two weeks, and get 50% off").

You must be timely and strategic in making your offer to customers who are ready to buy. Again, you don't send a discount offer to customers in the Attention or Interest phase; these customers are still seeking information about the product and haven't made up their minds whether they really want it.

Likewise, potential customers who have visited your website 26 times are most likely in the Decision and Action phases. This is the time to send them a special offer, since these customers are probably interested in buying something from you. They just need a little prompting from you to take action. Don't send them white papers or product data sheets (unless they request them), since these customers already have all the information they need.

The AIDA Curve Table

Table 2.1 summarizes the questions that your customer is asking about your product or service and that you need to answer for them in each stage of the AIDA curve. By understanding the decision-making process of your customer and by deciding how to answer these questions for them, you can better define what kind of lead, or customer action, you are seeking from them.

Table 2.1 uses two product examples to demonstrate the kinds of questions a customer might ask about those products. The first example is a series of questions that a potential customer might ask about the Body Bugg calorie counter. The second is a series of questions that a potential customer might ask about a brand of sales management software.

TABLE 2.1. Questions to Ask in Each Stage of the AIDA Curve

Stage	Questions Your Customer Is Asking	Body Bugg Example	Sales Management Software Example	Sales Tools to Use in This Stage
ATTENTION	• Why does this class of products exist? • What is its purpose? • Why is this class of products interesting?	• What is the Body Bugg? What is its purpose? • What is the function of the Body Bugg? What will it do for me?	• What is sales management software? What is its purpose and function? • How does sales management software differ from other business software?	• Webinars • Website content • Case studies
INTEREST	• Why should I use these classes of products? • Why should I consider buying this product over some other type of device that provides a similar solution or replaces the solution I have now?	• How will the Body Bugg help me to lose weight and/or exercise more effectively? • What are the advantages of the Body Bugg over other types of weight-loss or exercise devices?	• How will sales management software help my sales force to manage its sales activities more effectively? • How is sales management software better than our current sales management system?	• Interest • Webinars • Website content and features
DECISION	• Why should I buy your brand of this type of product over someone else's? • What makes your brand of product better than the others'? • Where can I get the best deal on the product?	• Which brand of the Body Bugg should I buy? • Which brand of Body Bugg has the best special features and support? • Where can I get the best bargain for the product?	• What brand of sales management software should I buy? • Which brand is the best for my business needs? • Which brand has the best features and customer support? • Which brand offers the best quality and ROI for me?	• White papers • Sell sheets • Product comparisons • Customer testimonials
ACTION	• Why should I buy this product now?	• Is there a sale on the Body Bugg? Is a special offer available for it if I buy it today?	• Is a special offer available for the sales management software I want to buy?	• Special offers • Timed coupons

Tracking the AIDA Curve

How do you determine which phase of the AIDA curve your customers are in? This question is one of the hardest aspects of marketing. You need a big-picture understanding of your customers and what they know about your product or service.

First, look at where your company is in terms of development. Where does your product or service fit into the market? How familiar, in general, are your target customers with your type of product or service? How much information do you need to give them about it?

For example, if your company is selling a high-tech product that has never existed before, most of your potential customers will be in the Attention and Interest phases. So your lead-generation efforts will concentrate on educating the market about what your product does (or what this genre of products does), along with the advantages of using it.

If your product is an improvement on a well-known product, the Attention and Interest phases are quicker. For example, almost everyone in the world knows what a laptop computer is. Those who have never owned a laptop will usually check online or at a local electronics store to make sure that laptops offer the same features as their regular desktop computers. But, in general, most of these people are already computer literate, so you don't need to educate them on the advantages of using computers.

If your potential customers are familiar with your type of product and its advantages, they will be looking for reasons to buy from you. In this case, most of your potential customers will jump straight to the Decision and Action phases. For example, people who have previously owned laptops will be looking at the benefits and features of your laptop brand to see if it is worth buying over other brands. Your lead-generation efforts should focus on giving them quick information about the special features of your laptop brand, easy ways to buy the product, and a good value and price for the product. This is when you should offer your customers a "50% off" coupon.

When using lead-generation tactics, you should develop creative assets (marketing e-mails, social media ads, etc.) with different offers targeted at customers in different AIDA stages, and test those offers to see which ones get the best response. For example, you might send out two types of e-mails: one targeted at Interest-phase customers, and another targeted at Decision- and Action-phase customers.

I once worked for a company that specialized in sales automation tools. We did a lot of testing to determine our customer's place in the AIDA curve. Our customers had the same basic target profile, but we needed to pinpoint where they were in the buying process. Our offers ran the gamut from webinar invitations for Interest-phase customers to discount offers for Action- phase customers. And we tried to identify which campaign within each lead-generation tactic had the greatest pull.

Through much testing, we found that about 50% of our potential clients were in the Interest phase, and the other 50% were in the Action phase. We realized we had two different types of customers: those who were familiar with our product and those who were not. So we decided we needed two different messages and two different offerings, one for each type of customer. And we needed a way to let customers self-segment themselves into either the Interest or the Action phase.

We were using e-mail marketing, so we created two different e-mails, each with a different call-to-action. For Interest-phase customers, we sent out an e-mail with the subject line and message, "Learn more about sales automation software." If customers clicked on this e-mail, it took them to a landing page on our website where they could download a white paper about our software. For Action-phase customers, we sent out an e-mail with the subject line and message, "7-day free trial." If customers clicked on this e-mail, it took them to a different landing page where they could try our software for free. (See Chapter 6 for information about landing pages and Chapter 12 regarding marketing e-mails.)

We sent both e-mails to the same customers. We hoped the customers would click on the appropriate e-mails based on their AIDA curve position. In other words, we were counting on our customers to "engage" with the right e-mail (e.g., "learn more" versus "free trial"), based on whether they were in the Interest or Action phase.

Of course, there was always the chance that Interest-phase customers would read the "free trial" e-mail or that Action-phase customers would read the "learn more" e-mail. If so, we'd lose those customers because they read the "wrong e-mail"—that is, the e-mail not intended for them. But the two–e-mail strategy was the best idea we could find to reach out to customers and determine their stage in the buying cycle. Once they responded to our offer and we knew whether they were in the Interest or Action phase, we could hone our message to them, through landing pages, white papers, and other marketing materials.

Marketing-Generated Leads vs. Sales-Generated Leads

Before we close this chapter on leads, you need to understand the difference between a marketing-generated lead and a sales-generated lead. This book focuses exclusively on marketing-generated leads.

A *marketing-generated lead* is a warm, inbound lead generated by marketers. To obtain marketing-generated leads, you send out an offer using lead-generation tactics, and any interested customers approach you through that process. The customer usually comes to your company with an interest in your products or services, with an intent to buy, or with questions in hand.

A *sales-generated lead* is usually generated by people in the sales department. This type of lead is primarily used for cold calling, and usually consists of the name, phone number, or e-mail address of somebody in your company's target demographic. For example, if you are a beverage company marketing a new energy drink, you may purchase a list of all convenience stores in a metropolitan area. The leads on this list are unqualified, so the customer may be completely unaware of your product. It's up to your sales reps to work these leads into warm leads and convert them into sales.

There's a distinction between sales-qualified leads and sales-generated leads. A sales-*qualified* lead starts out as a warm, inbound marketing lead, which is then handed over to the sales department and qualified as a legitimate sales lead for possible conversion into a sale. (In Chapter 5, I'll talk briefly about sales-qualified leads and how the process of qualifying leads fits into lead-generation marketing.)

In this book, I won't talk about sales-*generated* leads or how to acquire them. Salespeople use a different strategy to acquire sales-generated leads, and a lot of great books already discuss these strategies. Instead, I'll talk about how lead-generation marketing can provide warm leads that your company's sales engine (either your sales department or your automated e-commerce website) can act on to turn them into sales.

> > > *What You Should Know* < < <

To review, here's what you should know about defining your leads:

- A *lead* (in the context of this book) is a generic term for the type of action you want your customer to take as a result of a lead-generation tactic. Based on your company's goals, a lead can be an actual lead, or some other customer action, such as a purchase of your product. But you must define the type of lead or action you are seeking from your customer as a basic means of measuring the success of your lead-generation efforts.

- Often, the type of action you are seeking depends on where your customer is in the buying cycle. The AIDA curve (Attention-Interest-Decision-Action) is a well-known marketing principle that defines the four stages of a customer's mindset when they purchase a product or service.

- In the Attention phase, customers become aware of the *type* of product or service. They become aware of its function and its purpose. In the Interest phase, customers compare the benefits of a product or service with similar products or services on the market to find which type of product or service will meet their goals.

- In the Decision phase, customers consider different brands of the same product or different providers of the same service, to find out which one will best meet their needs. In the Action phase, customers take action to buy the product or service.

- You need to find out which phase of the AIDA curve your customers are in and market to them according to those phases. Customers in the Attention or Interest phases are learning about your type of product or service. You need to provide them with information such as case studies, white papers, and Web content that answers their questions. Don't try to hard-sell them on the product or service while they are still learning about it.

- Customers in the Decision or Action phase are making a decision about whether to buy your brand or another brand of the same product or service. Send them special offers or other incentives to buy your brand.

Developing Your Lead-Generation Strategy

THIS CHAPTER contains an overview of how to plan and execute a lead-generation marketing strategy. It introduces the themes of strategy that I talk about throughout the book. In this chapter, I'll assume that at least one of the three following scenarios applies to your company. (Ideally, all three should apply.)

1. You are currently using one or more lead-generation tactics (e.g., direct mail, e-mail marketing) but would like to learn how to use them more effectively to increase the number of qualified leads you get from each tactic.

2. You would like to adopt new lead-generation tactics (e.g., social advertising, search engine marketing) that your company has not used before.

3. You would like to *integrate* your lead-generation marketing tactics so that they will work in conjunction with each other (and with your brand) to achieve a higher level of success.

To achieve these goals, you first need to understand the three levels of strategy that apply to lead-generation marketing:

1. *Tactical Strategy:* You use this strategy to plan and execute campaigns using *individual* tactics. For example, you would use a tactical strategy to plan and execute an e-mail marketing campaign. I'll talk extensively about tactical strategy in Chapter 4, and in each chapter on a specific lead-generation tactic.

2. *Integration Strategy:* This is the strategy of using two or more lead-generation tactics in conjunction with each other (and with your brand), as part of an integrated lead-generation marketing campaign. For example, you might use direct mail, e-mail marketing, and search engine marketing as part of an integrated campaign. I'll talk about how to develop an integrated campaign strategy in Chapter 16.

3. *Lead-Generation Management Strategy:* Use this strategy to manage your *overall* lead-generation marketing efforts.

These three levels of strategy are interconnected. To achieve success in lead-generation marketing, you need to apply all three levels simultaneously.

The Importance of Lead-Generation Management Strategy

This chapter focuses primarily on lead-generation management strategy. This is high-level strategy, but learning how to use lead-generation marketing to your advantage requires planning and forethought. You need to think through your management strategy *before* you begin your efforts to improve lead generation in your company.

Many people in your organization depend on your lead-generation efforts, so any changes you make to your current lead-generation strategy will have effects, positive or negative, on those people. A well-planned management strategy will help you to maximize the positive effects and minimize the negative ones. A poorly planned management strategy has the opposite effect; it can disrupt your lead-generation efforts and cause chaos in your organization.

A well-planned management strategy allows you to work with your executives, sales department, and fellow marketers to increase your lead-generation results as quickly and painlessly as possible. You can make positive changes to your lead-generation efforts and achieve positive results that will be noticeable and long lasting. (If you have a good management strategy, any negative effects should be minimal and short-lived.)

A well-planned lead-generation management strategy allows you to:

- Make gradual and steady improvements to your existing lead-generation tactics

- Adopt and learn new lead-generation tactics with minimal trouble and without breaking your budget

- Test and measure your results for each tactic

- Test lead-generation tactics against each other, so you know which tactics provide the best results and are the most cost-effective for your company

- Justify your efforts and your budget to your executives

- Show a positive ROMI (see page 56 for a definition), which in turn may help you to justify an increase in your marketing budget

Developing a Management Strategy and Setting Goals

Developing a good lead-generation management strategy begins with setting goals for your organization. Your goals tell you what you (and your organization) hope to achieve. Your goals should define how much you wish to increase your lead-generation efforts, by when, and at what cost. By measuring your lead-generation results against these goals, you can tell how well you've succeeded and where you need to improve.

It's amazing to me how many marketing organizations don't set goals for their lead-generation efforts. They plunge into lead-generation marketing campaigns with no idea of what they're shooting for, how many leads they're trying to bring in, or what level of cost-effectiveness they need to observe. When their campaign is over, they have no idea how well their lead-generation efforts have worked or how well specific tactics are working to provide them with the leads they need. They have no idea if they've really provided a positive ROMI to their company. Often, they've gone over budget or executed a campaign that has provided them with a minimal number of actionable leads.

Overall, your goal for lead-generation marketing should be to use as many tactics as possible to your advantage. In defining your lead-generation management strategy, you should focus your goals on three areas:

1. Meeting or exceeding your *lead quotas*

2. Using the best-quality lead-generation tactics for your organization—that is, focusing your marketing efforts on the tactics that will give you the *largest number of high-quality leads*—to help you meet your lead quotas

3. Using the most cost-effective tactics for your organization

Now let's take a very quick look at each of these types of goals.

MEETING OR EXCEEDING YOUR LEAD QUOTAS

When it comes to the numbers of leads you wish to obtain, your goals should be very general. It's impossible to predict the exact number of leads that you will get from using any given lead-generation tactic or any combination of tactics. You can't say, "My goal is to get 1,000 leads per month from e-mail marketing and 2,000 leads per month from search engine marketing." That's like saying, "I'll plant 1,000 corn seeds and get exactly 10,000 ears of corn this summer."

However, if you're working in an organization that has a sales team, chances are that your marketing department is required to deliver a certain quota of leads to them each month. You might want to set goals according to that quota. For example, if the quota is 2,000 leads per month, and your marketing team is producing only about 1,500 leads per month, you're perceived as underperforming. You might set a goal to get the monthly number of leads your department delivers up to 2,000 per month within three months, and to keep it at 2,000 per month for the rest of the year.

If your marketing team is performing at quota (e.g., 2,000 leads per month) but you think you can do better, you might set your goal to exceed the quota. For example, you might set a goal for your department to deliver 3,000 leads per month, and to meet this new goal within three months. Exceeding your monthly quota will provide recognition for you and your marketing team and will also help your organization to move into a state of growth.

How do you accomplish the goal of increasing the number of leads you deliver? You do it by adopting new lead-generation tactics and/or using your current tactics more effectively. The strategies and tools I provide in this book will show you how to do this.

USING THE BEST-QUALITY TACTICS

To help you meet your lead quotas, you should concentrate your marketing efforts on using lead-generation tactics that provide your organization with the largest number of high-quality leads.

How do you identify the best-quality tactics for your organization? You test tactics against each other, and compare their results. I'll show you how to do this a little later in this chapter.

USING THE MOST COST-EFFECTIVE TACTICS

In addition to using tactics to obtain the most actionable leads, your goal should be to use tactics that are the most cost-effective for your organization. In Chapter 5, I'll talk about how to determine your cost-per-lead (CPL) and other measurements you should use to test and measure the cost-effectiveness of your lead-generation tactics.

Again, you will need to test tactics against one another to find out which are the most cost-effective for you. I'll talk about comparing and testing tactics against each other shortly. First, let's take a look at how you go about adopting new lead-generation tactics that your organization may not have used before.

Adopting New Tactics

If you wish to adopt new lead-generation tactics, you need to have a management plan in place for introducing those new tactics into your organization. You cannot simply switch to the new tactics and expect to achieve instant success. You first need to learn how to use the new tactics effectively. (I'll talk about this in Chapter 4, and in each chapter on a specific tactic.) Then, you need to test your results to find out how well the new tactics work for your business, and how well they work against your current lead-generation tactics.

It may be that your current tactics work very well, but the new tactics you adopt can supplement them in lead generation. Or maybe the new tactics will eventually be more efficient at providing quality leads and/or more cost-effective than your current ones. But be aware: It will take you a few tries with the new tactics to learn how to make them work to your best, most cost-effective advantage.

Adopting new lead-generation tactics can be expensive, so you need to do it carefully and systematically. You need to maintain your current lead-generation efforts while you test new sources or tactics. Obviously, you don't want to suddenly switch to new, untested tactics or divert essential marketing budget resources from existing successful tactics. This could cause a sudden drop-off in your incoming leads, which would make you very unpopular with your sales team. (There's an old saying: "Leads are to sales what catnip is to the cat.")

When you adopt a new lead-generation tactic, you need to make a plan for what your organization wants to achieve from it. You should determine a *test budget*—the budget you need to effectively employ and test the tactic. You should also estimate your target CPL—the amount you want to spend to acquire each lead—and use your test budget to try to achieve that target CPL. (Again, I'll discuss this concept in detail in Chapter 5.)

Also, you need to have a plan in place for how you will qualify and use the leads you acquire. Don't take this step for granted, especially with new tactics. Even if you have a well-established lead-qualifying system in place, make sure your organization knows how to capitalize on the additional leads, so that you get maximum benefit from them. You don't want to spend a lot of money acquiring leads with a new tactic and then have those leads slip through the cracks because your marketers or sales teams aren't sure what to do with them.

In presenting your plan for new lead-generation tactics to your chief financial officer (CFO) or executive board, make sure they understand several things. First, they need to understand that the new lead-generation tactics will require (if possible) a test budget that is separate from your current lead-generation budget. If your CFO can't (or isn't willing to) provide more money for testing new lead-generation tactics, consider diverting money from some of the current less-effective lead-generation efforts.

For example, if your marketing department is doing 10 trade shows per year, and not all of those shows are providing a high number of actionable leads, you might consider dropping the worst-performing trade shows. Then divert your budget for those shows into testing new lead-generation tactics. Or suppose you're purchasing seven e-mail address lists per month for your marketing campaigns. You might cancel one or two underperforming lists—those that aren't getting a good response rate for your offers—and use the extra money to finance the testing of a new tactic.

Your CFO and executives also need to understand that adopting new lead-generation tactics is a trial-and-error process. Your marketing team will probably need several tries with a new lead-generation tactic before you learn how to use it to your company's best advantage. Above all, your executives should understand that the overall goal of your new lead-generation tactics is to *increase* the number of inbound leads and thus increase sales and revenue for the company over the long run.

The Power of Testing

Once you determine your goals for lead-generation marketing, you need to plan and execute your campaigns with your chosen tactics. Again, I will explore tactical strategies in the chapters to come. Right now, I want to talk about one of the most important aspects of managing your lead-generation marketing, an element that applies to all the lead-generation tactics you will use: testing.

It's extremely important to continuously test and measure the results of your lead-generation efforts. The art of successful lead-generation marketing lies in understanding which tactics will acquire the most profitable leads for your company, and then using those tactics on a regular basis.

Without testing and measurement, you have no idea which lead-generation tactics work best for your company. You have no idea which tactics give you the highest number of quality leads at the most effective cost-per-lead. Nor do you know how to use those tactics in combination to obtain the maximum number of leads you can get. Furthermore, you have no way to measure your ROMI for your lead-generation campaign.

I can't overemphasize the importance of testing and measuring your lead-generation efforts. (Notice I'm using italics for emphasis here!) Time and again, I've seen companies pour large amounts of money into lead-generation tactics without having any way to measure their success or failure. After a few months of using these tactics, they have no way of knowing if the $10,000 they've spent on the campaign has made a difference. When they want to justify the next $10,000 they need to spend to their executives, they have no way to do it.

I always tell people you *must* have a testing budget and a testing mentality. If you have a lead-generation marketing budget of, say, $1 million per year (or even per month), you should put 10% of it into testing your efforts. With lead-generation marketing, you are never, ever out of the testing mode, even when your tactics are successful.

Testing One Tactic vs. Another

Testing the results of your individual lead-generation tactics is just the first step. You also need to test and measure lead-generation tactics against each other until you know which tactics give you the best results. You should then spend more of your marketing budget on tactics that provide the most high-quality leads and are the most cost-effective for your company.

To test tactics against each other, you should establish a baseline tactic (often called a control) and a test tactic. A baseline tactic is a lead-generation tactic that you are currently using. A test tactic is a tactic you want to test against the baseline. (It doesn't have to be a new tactic. It can be one that you have used for some time.) After developing and employing a lead-generation campaign for the test tactic, you should measure your results against the baseline to find out which tactic provides more leads and is more cost-effective.

However, you may have to compare the test tactic against the baseline more than once. It may take you several tries to learn how to use a test tactic effectively, especially if it is a new one for your company. On your first campaign, the test tactic may not perform as well as your baseline tactic, but that doesn't mean you should abandon the test tactic. After three or four campaigns, the test tactic may start to produce better lead results and be more cost-effective. After you've tested the test tactic against the baseline several times, you will start to get a clearer idea of how well the test tactic is performing for your company.

Once you've tested a tactic against a baseline, you can start to determine which are your primary and secondary tactics. Your *primary tactics* are the most efficient and cost-effective tactics in providing leads for your company. Again, once you've determined your primary tactics, you should devote more of your marketing budget and resources to them. You may have more than one primary tactic. For example, after several rounds of testing tactics, you may discover that two or even three of the tactics you use (e.g., direct mail, e-mail, social advertising) produce a similar number of high-quality leads (e.g., approximately 5,000 per month for each tactic)

Bowl ad), but they had no way to qualify how spending that money would provide an ROMI and benefits for the company.

But in the past 10 years, even before the 2008 economic downturn, shareholders have asked businesses to become more accountable. With the IT revolution, budgets and ROIs have become more measurable. As a result, good managers and executives have learned how to tell their ROI story. They can justify their department budget and describe how time and money investments will provide a payback for the company. They can predict results by explaining their plans and the potential benefits. Unfortunately, many marketers have yet to learn how to explain their ROMI.

As a marketer, you may find it easier to articulate and justify your marketing projections (e.g., "Give me a $10 million budget for this campaign, and I'll return $100 million") if you use a set of tools to test and measure your marketing efforts over the long term. You can often make more accurate predictions of the results for your next campaign if you use these tools to defend the results of your previous campaigns. Using these results will help you to win your budgets; you may even see them increased. If you have no way to predict the results of your marketing campaigns, you may find your budget decreased. Even worse, if you can't deliver a significant and measurable ROMI through your efforts, you may find yourself out of a job.

> > > **What You Should Know** < < <

To review, here's what you should remember about the strategy of lead-generation marketing:

- There are several levels of strategy in lead-generation marketing. At the highest level, you must develop a lead-generation management strategy and set goals for your efforts in order to implement a successful lead-generation campaign.

- Your overall goal should be to use as many lead-generation tactics as possible in your organization. In terms of lead-generation management strategy, you want to center your goals around (1) meeting or exceeding your lead quota, (2) focusing your marketing efforts on best-quality lead-generation tactics that deliver the largest number of high-quality leads for your company, and (3) using the most cost-effective lead-generation tactics.

- When adopting new lead-generation tactics, you should do it carefully and systematically. It may take you a few tries to learn how to use the new tactics effectively. Continuously measure the results of the new tactics against the results of your current tactics. Also, make sure your CFO and other executives know what to expect when you are testing new lead-generation tactics.

- You must continuously test and measure your lead-generation efforts to find out which tactics are the most successful in acquiring leads, and which tactics you should focus your efforts and marketing budget on.

- In testing tactics against one another, you must establish a baseline tactic and a test tactic to test it against. Compare the results of the test tactic against the results of the baseline in order to find out which tactic is more or less successful in acquiring leads and which is more or less cost-effective.

- Once you have tested your tactics against each other, you should establish primary tactics (tactics that are more successful and cost-effective) and secondary tactics (tactics that may be less effective than primary tactics, but may still be cost-effective and a good source of leads). You should devote more of your marketing budget and resources to primary tactics, and use secondary tactics to supplement your primary tactics.

- Testing and measuring lead-generation tactics against each other is an ongoing, continuous process. This is necessary to ensure that the tactics you use are successful and cost-effective for your company over the long run.

- Testing and measuring your lead-generation results will help you to justify your ROMI to your executives. The more you can demonstrate the results of your lead-generation efforts, the more your marketing budget will be protected and even increased.

Using Lead-Generation Tactics

THIS BOOK focuses on the seven most successful lead-generation tactics:

1. Search engine marketing

2. Social media advertising

3. Display advertising

4. E-mail marketing

5. Direct mail marketing

6. Cold calling

7. Trade shows

This chapter deals with tactical strategy—that is, how to use and test individual lead-generation tactics. Each of the seven most successful lead-generation tactics has its own characteristics, advantages, and disadvantages, but you can apply certain fundamental strategies and principles to all seven tactics. You should use these strategies and principles as a foundation for planning and executing each lead-generation campaign, no matter which tactic you use.

As I've said, your overall goal should be to test and deploy as many of these tactics as possible. Depending on the types of products or services you sell, your company may not need to use all seven tactics, but you should at least be aware of them, and understand how each tactic works. If possible, you should test *all seven tactics* to find out which ones are the most efficient and cost-effective for your business.

If only five of the seven tactics work for your company, use those five to maximum effect. If you find that certain tactics work better for you, scale up your efforts on those tactics to help meet the goals of your enterprise. The more actionable leads you can drive using these tactics in combination, the happier your sales department (and ultimately your shareholders) will be.

I will devote one chapter to each of these seven lead-generation tactics (except social media advertising, which requires two chapters). I'll examine each tactic in depth, explore the theory behind it and how it works, and provide strategies for how to use each tactic to your best advantage. Most important of all, I'll show you how to set goals and test and measure your results when using each of these lead-generation tactics. *Only by continuously testing and measuring your results can you know how well each lead-generation tactic works for you.*

Before we get into the details of tactical strategy, let's take a quick look at how lead-generation tactics have evolved over the years.

The Evolution of Lead-Generation Tactics

Of the seven most successful tactics, direct mail, trade shows, and cold calling have proven themselves to be enduring, tried-and-true tactics. Some may argue that these traditional tactics are out of fashion, because they require more effort and are more expensive than the new, digital tactics.

But smart marketers keep using them, because traditional tactics continue to produce large numbers of actionable leads for many companies. These tactics can be just as successful and cost-effective as online tactics, provided you know when and how to use them effectively.

The other four tactics—e-mail marketing, search engine marketing, display advertising, and social media advertising—are digital tactics that have emerged within the last decade or so. These tactics have great potential. As marketers become more adept at using them, I have little doubt that these emerging tactics will become staples of their lead-generation marketing efforts.

What's interesting about the four digital tactics is that each one represents the next step in the evolution of a traditional form of marketing.

- E-mail marketing has evolved from direct mail marketing.

- Display advertising and social media advertising have both evolved from print ads and outdoor advertising (such as billboard advertising).

- Search engine marketing has evolved from advertising in the Yellow Pages.

You could also say that webinars have evolved from trade shows, because webinars provide an online medium for companies to explain the advantages of their products or services to an audience of potential customers. Trade shows accomplish the same goal for a live audience of potential customers.

But this illustrates what I explained in Chapter 1: Lead-generation marketing is in a constant state of evolution. And it will continue to evolve as new tactics and new mediums of marketing come along. That's why you need a set of strategic tools that you can adapt to all lead-generation marketing tactics. Even as these tactics continue to evolve, the tools I provide in this book will enable you to effectively plan, execute, and test the results of the tactics you use.

The Other Tactics

Here are some marketing tactics that are not officially lead-generation tactics, and which I won't talk about in this book:

- Basic word-of-mouth marketing or business networking

- Traditional advertising channels (print/TV/outdoor/radio)

- Public relations/analyst relations

- Social media (e.g., creating a Facebook or LinkedIn page for your company), which is different from social media advertising that involves posting pay-per-click ads on social media sites

- Search engine optimization

Not every marketing tactic is a lead-generation tactic. The tactics in the preceding list are traditionally used for brand awareness marketing. They are also occasionally (and sometimes quite successfully) used for lead generation, but they are not specifically *designed* to acquire large numbers of qualified leads for a company. If you use these tactics specifically to acquire leads, they will prove to be very costly. Also, it's very hard to measure your rate of success in acquiring leads with these tactics.

Using brand awareness tactics for lead generation is like using a grenade to hit a bull's-eye target, when what you really need is a sniper rifle. You will hit your targeted customer, but you will also hit a lot of other non-customers as well (I call this "collateral damage"). You may end up spending large amounts of money trying to convert thousands of people who don't want your product, in the hopes of finding the few people who do.

Lead-generation marketing is the sniper rifle. It allows you to hit exactly the type of customer who meets your criteria. In lead-generation marketing, you use targeting and scientific methods to identify the prospects most likely to buy your product.

Active vs. Passive Marketing

The seven lead-generation tactics provide a mix of active and passive marketing. Each tactic falls into one category or the other, as illustrated in Table 4.1.

TABLE 4.1. Active vs. Passive Marketing Tactics

Active Marketing Tactics	Passive Marketing Tactics
• Direct mail	• Trade shows
• E-mail marketing	• Search engine marketing
• Cold calling	• Social media advertising
• Display advertising (in some cases)	

Active marketing is when you are actively reaching out to customers who may or may not be aware of your product. Direct mail and e-mail marketing are forms of active marketing. Using lead-generation marketing tactics provides an extremely effective way to gain your customer's interest, and to transact with them.

Passive marketing is when your customer is actively seeking out your types of products or services. You want to be in the places where you know they are looking (e.g., trade shows, search engines), so you can be a part of their consideration set, and so they can transact with your product.

It's important to use a mix of active and passive lead-generation tactics. You want to reach out to customers who know your products well and who are ready to buy (passive marketing). However, you also want to use lead-generation tactics to actively reach out to customers who may not be so familiar with your products.

Perhaps your potential customer doesn't *realize* yet that they have a need for your product. Or maybe their current solution isn't working as well as they'd like, but they prefer to stick with it because they don't know of a better solution. If you can get your value proposition for an *improved* product or solution in front of them at the moment when they are fed up with their current solution, they may click on the e-mail link, or call the 800 number, or take a phone call to hear what your salesperson has to say.

A great example: Until recently, my own company had a bottled water dispenser in our Seattle offices, the kind with the enormous blue bottle that sits in the break room and gurgles a lot. But we had a problem. Even though we had scheduled regular monthly bottle replacements, our water supply company kept forgetting to deliver a refill bottle on the first Monday of each month. Every month, I had to call the water supply company to remind them to come back and replace the bottle.

Then I received an e-mail from a different water company, Culligan, advertising a "bottleless water system"—a water-dispensing machine that takes water from your existing office water system. The bottleless water machine has a built-in device that filters the water and dispenses it as clean drinking water. It also has a water heater to provide hot water for tea and coffee.

The e-mail I received included a link to Culligan's webpage, inviting me to learn more about the bottleless water system. I clicked on the link and filled out a form on the website. A day later, a salesperson from Culligan called me to provide more details about this system. I was sold on it, and, a week later, a Culligan representative installed a new bottleless water system in our offices. Our new water system provides exactly the same type of filtered water that we received from our old bottled water dispenser, at the same price, but we no longer need weekly bottle refills.

Until I received the e-mail about Culligan's bottleless water system, I wasn't aware the product existed. If I hadn't received that e-mail, I would have kept going through the cycle of calling our previous water supply company every month when they forgot to bring refill bottles. Who knows how long that would have gone on? But thanks to Culligan's use of active marketing, I was introduced to a new solution. Culligan proved the value of the proposition to me, and now we have a bottleless water system that works beautifully.

Five Steps of a Lead-Generation Campaign

You need to follow a five-step tactical strategy for any lead-generation campaign. No matter which lead-generation tactic you are using, you should use all five steps to get the best results for your efforts:

1. Determine and plan your approach.

2. Research and discover your target customer.

3. Build your assets.

4. Execute your test campaign.

5. Measure, measure, measure!

To this five-step process, we might add a sixth step:

6. Repeat.

To ensure maximum results for your lead-generation efforts, you should repeat this five-step process with each campaign and with each tactic you use.

In this chapter, I will examine each of these steps in depth, and show you how to apply each step to your lead-generation campaign, no matter which tactic you are using. In the chapter for each tactic, I'll show you how the steps apply in executing each tactic.

As I explained in Chapter 3, a successful lead-generation strategy depends on finding out which tactics work best for your business and which ones are the most cost-effective. But to truly measure the effectiveness of a lead-generation tactic, you must make sure that you are "doing it right." If you are regularly using a certain lead-generation tactic (e.g., direct mail, e-mail marketing) but the tactic is not giving you the desired results, it may be time to reassess your strategy for using the tactic.

Also, remember that when you adopt a new lead-generation tactic, it will usually take you several tries to find out how well that tactic works for your company and how cost-effective it is. But if you use these five steps to plan and execute your campaign, you'll increase your chances of success and shorten the time it takes to measure the effectiveness of any new tactic.

Step 1: Determine and Plan Your Approach

It's essential that you think through your approach and develop a plan for how you will use a certain tactic. You should do this with *each* tactic you use, whether it is a direct mail campaign, attending a trade show, etc. Determining and planning your approach lays the foundation for a successful lead-generation campaign.

It's amazing to me how many marketers jump into their lead-generation process without identifying their target audience or the objective for their campaign. This is one of the most common reasons why these campaigns fail. Without a strategic plan, marketers have no idea how to reach the people most likely to buy their products or services, and no way to measure their success or failure when the campaign is over. Often, they spend a big budget on the campaign, but end up reaching only a minimum number of potential customers.

Even worse, the marketers get frustrated and abandon a tactic too quickly. They assume "it just doesn't work for us," when that tactic might have served them well if they had stuck with it and learned how to use it properly. They also have to report bad results to their bosses, which, in turn, puts pressure on their jobs and may even cause them to doubt their own ability to generate leads. This turns into a vicious cycle: The marketers keep failing to produce the leads they need due to a lack of planning in their tactics.

The more planning and strategic evaluation you do before employing a tactic, the more you can define success, and the more you will increase your chances of achieving it. You need to think through three areas of planning:

1. Who is your *target customer*? What are their demographics and psychographics? What is their buying behavior?

2. What are your *goals and/or projected outcomes* in using this lead-generation tactic? What action do you want your target customer to take? And what do you plan to do when they take that action?

3. How do you *measure success* (both quantitatively and qualitatively)?

Each of these questions requires some discussion. In the next few pages, I'll go deeper into each question and talk about how to determine your own answers.

WHO IS YOUR TARGET CUSTOMER?

The first questions to ask in planning your tactical approach are: "What is my target market? Who is my target customer?"

Surprisingly, many companies don't take the time to—or don't even know *how to*—(1) identify and pinpoint their target market and (2) research their customer to understand their lifestyles, their wants, and their needs. You'd think this would be an obvious first step for any marketing effort, but many companies plunge headlong into lead-generation campaigns with only a vague idea of what kinds of people might be interested in buying their product or service. As a result, they waste their lead-generation efforts and budget trying to market their products or services to the wrong people.

The more successful lead-generation marketers understand how crucial it is to know your target customer. Everything you know about how they think, and how they behave as consumers, serves as a guide to your lead-generation efforts.

With some lead-generation tactics, your ability to target your customer is limited. For example, trade shows offer demographic information (usually available on the show's website) about the people who normally attend their annual show. You can choose to attend trade shows where the majority of attendees match your target audience. But once you get to the show, you are marketing to everyone who attends it, whether they fit your target profile or not.

Other tactics, such as e-mail marketing, allow you to do very specific targeting to potential customers in very well-defined demographics. Either way, your goal should be to learn as much as you can about your target customer, and to find the best, most effective tactics for reaching out to those customers and turning them into leads or sales.

RESEARCHING YOUR TARGET CUSTOMER

In general, you should try to define your target customer according to three measurements:

1. *Demographic Attributes:* This basic information about your target customer may include your customer's median age (e.g., 25–35 years old), sex, ethnicity, marital and family status, household income, level of education, etc. If you are marketing to a business, it may include your target customer's industry, job title, typical role in the business, and that sort of information.

2. *Psychographic Attributes:* What is your target customer's mindset? Are they professionals? Working class? Do they have a propensity to travel? Do they use credit cards? How much credit are they personally willing to bear? Do they prefer to buy brand labels? Do they give to charities?

3. *Buying Behavior:* Historically, what other types of things do your target customers like to buy? Are they into luxury goods? Or are they satisfied with midprice, quality-brand items? Do they keep up with current trends and fads? Or do they simply prefer to buy only what they need when they need it? What are their spending habits? Do they generally buy in cash or credit?

> **Note:** *Buying behavior can be very specific and current information. For example, has your target customer purchased an airline ticket or other travel product in the last six months?*

You can gather this information in several ways. First, if you already have an established base of customers, spend a little time gathering data about them. Customer surveys and interactive follow-up phone calls are the most reliable way to do this. Also, marketing research companies, such as Axciom and Merkle, can help you gather data about potential customers.

I think it's mission critical that every company should do this kind of research and introspection. Understanding your current customers—who they are and why they buy from you—can give you valuable insight about your prospective customers. Again, it amazes me how many companies *don't* do this. They have an established customer base, and yet they have no information about the people who buy their products or services.

E-commerce companies have a special need to know their customers, because their transactions are always done at arm's length. Traditional brick-and-mortar companies with a sales force have an advantage over e-commerce companies, in that their salespeople often interact with target customers and get to know their wants and needs.

E-commerce companies can only gather a limited amount of information about their customers from online sales. They get some information about buying behavior based on the products their customers purchase from them. Also, e-commerce companies do occasional online customer surveys. But these surveys often get a minimal response, and usually provide very limited information about their customers. So e-commerce companies must find other ways to establish their customer profile.

If you are an e-commerce company or if you feel uncomfortable asking your customers for personal information about their lives and spending habits, marketing research companies will do the job for you. If you give them a postal or e-mail address list for your customers, these companies will research customer information and share that data with you. (Usually, they match your customer contact information against profiles they've already established in their consumer databases.)

EARLY ADOPTERS VS. MAINSTREAM BUYERS

Understanding who buys your product can be difficult if you don't have a large enough customer base. If you are a brand new company, you know that millions of potential customers are out there, waiting for your product. The trick is to not fall into the trap of thinking that you know your potential customer, based on the handful of customers you have now. The first hundred or so customers who have already bought your product are not necessarily representative of all your prospective customers.

In his books *Crossing the Chasm* and *Inside the Tornado*, author Geoffrey Moore explores the marketing strategies invented by Silicon Valley's high-tech companies to introduce and market their products. Moore recalls that in the early days of the high-tech revolution the products themselves were so new that mainstream consumers were reluctant to try them. So high-tech companies in Silicon Valley marketed their products to "early adopters"— mostly techies and visionary business owners who believed that having the latest technology (whatever it was) would give them a competitive edge. But high-tech companies soon discovered they were targeting too narrow an audience. Their marketing messages, according to Moore, were criticized for being "too long, too complicated, and, well, too nerdy."[1]

Eventually, high-tech companies realized that the best target audience for their innovations were pragmatic and conservative business owners, who would buy a technology only when it had a proven track record for serving other businesses. It took some time and effort for high-tech marketers to "cross the chasm," as Moore put it. They had to make the transition from marketing to techies and visionaries to marketing to mainstream business owners who really had a need for their products and solutions—and, from there, to marketing to everyday consumers.

WHAT ARE YOUR GOALS?

The second question you need to ask in planning your tactical approach is, "What are my goals or objectives in using this particular lead-generation tactic?" The answer goes back to how you define a lead. Is a lead, for you, a person who is ready to buy? Or is it a person who's interested but just wants more information? What kind of action do you hope the customer will take in response to your tactic?

As I explained in Chapter 2, the type of lead or other action you are seeking often depends on where your potential customers are in the buying cycle, according to the AIDA curve. If your customers are in the Attention or Interest phases, they are still learning about your products. You may be seeking actual leads or actions (such as downloading your online catalog, or accepting an invitation to a webinar) that will cause your customers to become leads. If your customers are in the Decision or Action phases, they are making a decision to buy. You may be seeking a transaction or sale from them.

To further define your goals, you need to answer other questions:

- How many potential customers do you plan to reach out to using this lead-generation tactic?

- How do you plan to qualify and use the leads once you've obtained them?

- What is your overall budget for using this lead-generation tactic?

- And, of course, what is your target "cost-per-lead"? How much money do you plan to spend to acquire each lead, or other customer action?

I'll explore the concept of cost-per-lead in full detail in Chapter 5.

HOW DO YOU MEASURE SUCCESS?

The third question to ask in planning your tactical approach—and the question that too many marketers forget to ask—is: "How do I measure the success of my lead-generation campaign?"

What does success mean for you, in terms of leads (or other customer actions)? Is your campaign a success when you get the leads to raise their hands? Do you measure success by the number of people who say they are seriously considering buying your product? Or is it enough for them to say they would like more information? Do you measure success by the number of people who simply respond to your lead-generation tactic, whatever the response is?

Or is your campaign a success only when a lead is converted to an actual sale? Is it a success when your customers transact and have a pleasant experience? Is it successful when your customers refer someone to you?

Every company will have a different set of priorities for what they want their lead-generation efforts to achieve. And different lead-generation campaigns will have different goals in terms of how to measure success. But you must *define the measurements for your success* before you begin your efforts to connect with your customers. Without measurements, you will have no way of knowing whether your lead-generation campaign has succeeded.

Step 2: Research Your Target Customer

Step two of deploying your lead-generation tactic is researching your target customers to find out what makes them tick.

One important advantage of each lead-generation tactic is the ability to reach out to your specific target customers. The golden rule of thumb is that the more targeted, the better. For trade shows, this means picking the right trade show, where your target customers are most likely to show up. For e-mail marketing, this means sending your e-mail offer only to the people who are most likely to click through on the offer.

But targeting your customers means doing research so that you know who your target customers are and where to find them. You have to be very specific in defining them. As mentioned, you want to avoid as much as possible what I call collateral damage, that is, wasting your lead-generation efforts to reach out to people who have no intention of buying your products.

For example, if you are conducting an e-mail marketing campaign to sell products for cats (toys, vitamins, etc.), you want to send your e-mail creative to a very specific list of cat owners. You don't want a list of pet owners because many of the people on that list will own dogs, parakeets, fish, etc.

Doing research gives you the opportunity to determine the right target audience for your product, and how best to go after them. Each of the seven lead-generation tactics involves some component of research to help you find your target audience. I'll get into the specifics of how to research and discover your target audience in each chapter on individual tactics.

Step 3: Build Your Assets

Step three in your lead-generation campaign is building your assets. And here, I need to define a few terms:

- *Assets* are the creative materials that you send out or employ to try to connect with your potential customers. (You might refer to them as creatives.) If you're doing a direct mail campaign, the asset is the direct mail piece you send out. If you are attending a trade show, your assets are the trade booth, the displays, the one-sheet information flyers, and the giveaways you have for prospective customers.

- *Asset building* is the task of designing and producing marketing materials for the purposes of lead generation. Building your assets involves completing a series of tasks in order to create each asset.

- *Tasks* are the individual components of each asset. For a direct mail package, the tasks include designing the package, determining the unique selling proposition, writing the headlines and sales letters, etc. For a trade show, you need to design the trade booth, displays, giveaways, and other assets.

Each lead-generation tactic has a series of assets that you need to create in order to effectively build your tools for that tactic. I will examine asset building in each of the chapters devoted to the individual tactics.

Before I leave the subject of asset building, I want to introduce three more terms. You may already be familiar with these terms, because they are standard concepts of marketing. But I want to introduce them here because *they should be included in every creative asset you produce.*

- A *value proposition* is a promise of value to be delivered to customers if they accept your offer. For example, if you are using e-mail marketing to advertise car insurance, the value proposition in your creative may read, "Save up to 20% on car insurance today." Or, if you are sending out an e-mail invitation to a webinar, your value proposition might read, "Join this webinar, and hear our CEO explain the six ways our new accounting software can help your company save time and money."

- A *call-to-action (CTA)* is a statement that tells the customer what to do right now to accept your offer. For example, in an e-mail creative, your call-to-action might say, "Click here to sign up for our service." Or, "Click here to sign up for this webinar."

- Include an *offer* in the creative to entice the customer to buy your product or service, sign up with you as a lead, or take some action. Usually, the offer is a combination of the value proposition and the CTA: "Act today, and get 25% off your next purchase." Or, "Act today, and get free shipping on purchases over $25." Or the ever-popular "Buy one, get one free." Including a special offer is a very effective way to prompt your potential customers to take the action you are seeking from them.

Step 4: Execute Your Test Campaign

How you execute and deploy a lead-generation campaign is just as important as how well you design and create your assets. You can have a terrific value proposition and great creative assets to offer your potential customers, but your entire campaign can fall flat if you don't know how to execute it properly. That's why it's important to do a test campaign before you commit yourself to a full deployment.

If you've never used a lead-generation tactic before, a test campaign will give you some indication of how well the tactic works for you. But even when using one of your regular tactics, a tactic you have used for years, testing is essential! A test campaign provides valuable insight into how well the various elements of your creative assets work, and how receptive your audience is to your offer. This insight allows you to make improvements to your assets and your tactical plan, which, in turn, helps you to get a better response rate for the campaign.

For example, say you are conducting an e-mail campaign, but you have no idea how well your creative assets will work for you. Maybe you have two separate lists of two types of prospective customers (e.g., women ages 25 to 40 and women ages 40 to 60), but you don't know which list will respond better to your e-mail offer. Or maybe you have two different versions of the subject header for your e-mail offer (e.g., "Get 25% off" vs. "Buy one, get one free"), but you don't know which one will get the better response (or open rate) from your customer.

You can do certain types of testing—such as A/B split testing or champion-versus-challenger testing—to determine how well different versions of your assets work, how well your value proposition appeals to different target audiences, and how well the tactic itself works for you. These testing techniques can help you to execute your campaign without wasting a lot of money before you know whether the tactic or the assets are good.

A test campaign also gives you insight into how to spend your budget wisely. Some marketers decide they want to go out big, and will spend a lot of money up front before they know whether the tactic works. I strongly suggest you do small tests to establish whether the economics of the lead-generation tactic will work for you. Once you've established how well the tactic works, you can then begin to execute the tactic on a larger scale.

For instance, say you are a new consumer electronics company with a brand-new suite of products that has never been seen before at the annual International Consumer Electronics Show (CES). Does it make sense for you to buy a large booth and put on an expensive showing for your first appearance at the show? Or would it be better to buy a smaller booth and keep expenditures low for the first year, to see how well the trade show tactic works for you and how well trade show visitors respond to your products?

I will talk more about testing and executing each type of tactic in each chapter on individual tactics.

Step 5: Measure, Measure, Measure!

Once you have the performance data from your lead-generation campaign, you need to consistently measure your results to find out how well the tactic worked for you, and how well your marketing message and other components worked in bringing in leads. It's important to remember that measurement requires a great deal of setup, and you must do this setup *before* you execute the campaign.

I will talk about how to test and measure each tactic in the chapters on individual tactics. For now, here is a quick example: Say you are doing an e-mail campaign, and you want to know which of two CTAs works better for you. You should create two e-mail creatives with two different offers: one that offers a coupon for $10 off, and another that offers your product at a 25% discount. You should then set up two different landing pages, one for each e-mail. The landing page that receives the larger response from its e-mail will tell you which CTA works better.

> > > *What You Should Know* < < <

- The seven most successful lead-generation tactics are search engine marketing, social media advertising, display advertising, e-mail marketing, cold calling, direct mail, and trade shows.

- You should test as many of these tactics as your company can use. If possible, use all seven. If not, use a healthy mix of whatever tactics will work and are cost-effective for your company.

- In using any lead-generation tactic, tactical strategy involves five steps: (1) determining and planning your approach, (2) researching your target audience, (3) building your assets, (4) executing a test campaign, and (5) measurement.

- In step 1, you determine and plan your approach for using a lead-generation tactic. In planning your approach, you must answer three questions: (1) Who is your target customer? (2) What are your goals for using this tactic? (3) How will you measure your success in using this tactic?

- In step 2, you research your target customers to find out about their wants and needs.

- In step 3, you build your creative assets. You must perform a series of tasks in order to build each asset you will use.

- In step 4, you execute a test campaign. Before unleashing the full campaign, test your assets to see how well customers respond to them and what types of customers respond best to each asset.

- In step 5, you measure the results of your lead-generation efforts to find out how well the target customers responded to your assets, your product, and your offer. To measure your success, you should set up specific testing tools prior to sending out your creative assets or making contact with target customers.

5

Calculating the Costs

IN THIS CHAPTER, I'll look at how to define the costs of obtaining leads or customer actions. I'll look at how leads work in the overall process of selling your products to customers, as well as the effect that qualifying your marketing or sales leads can have on the cost-effectiveness of your lead-generation campaigns. I'll also look at different ways to assess the lifetime value of your customer in terms of the number of sales you receive from a lead, and how this can affect how you calculate the ROMI for your lead-generation efforts.

Making an Impression

When buying marketing services, marketers usually measure the cost in cost-per-milia (CPM), or the cost per 1,000 customer impressions. Most marketers refer to cost-per-milia as either *CPM* or *cost-per-impression*. For example, if you are doing an e-mail marketing campaign, you may buy a list of 5,000 e-mail addresses for $500. Your CPM, in this case, is $100 (5,000 addresses = 5 × 1,000 impressions = 5 × $100 = $500).

An *impression* is simply any exposure, positive or negative, to your brand or message that helps to form an awareness of it in the consumer's mind. When customers see an e-mail from you in their inbox, that's an impression (even if they delete it without clicking on it). If they receive a direct mail piece from you, see an online ad from your company, or receive a phone call from one of your salespeople, those are impressions too.

The concept of CPM originated with print and outdoor ads. Advertisers would charge clients by the estimated number of people who would see a print ad (based on the circulation of the magazine in which it appeared) or an outdoor billboard (based on how many people drove by the billboard every day).

I won't talk much about impressions in this book because creating impressions is more the goal of brand awareness marketing. But I need to mention impressions as one of the basic hypothetical units used to negotiate payment for marketing services.

Lead-generation tactics often provide a more accurate estimate of the number of impressions that we pay for in purchasing services. For example, if you send out an e-mail offer to everyone on the list of 5,000 e-mail addresses, you know that nearly all those people, at the very least, will read the subject line. Even if they didn't actually open the e-mail, they knew what it was about and whom it was from, and thus they received some kind of impression about your product or company.

One more concept I need to mention is pay-per-click (PPC), which, like CPM, has become a standard measurement for how companies pay for marketing services using online ads. PPC is usually done either on a flat rate or a bid basis. (I'll talk more about the PPC process in the chapters about online lead-generation advertising tactics, such as display advertising and search engine marketing.)

Measuring Your Cost-Per-Action

The success and cost-effectiveness of your lead-generation campaigns are based on another form of measurement. The *cost-per-action (CPA)* is the average cost of each customer action, based on the number of people who actually respond to an ad or marketing technique.

With CPA, it's not enough for potential customers to see an online ad, such as a search engine ad or display ad, from your company. They also have to take some sort of specific action, such as (1) clicking on the ad, (2) visiting the landing page on your website, and (3) purchasing the product, or filling out the online form to take advantage of the special offer in the ad.

In the example of the 5,000-name e-mail list, purchased for $500, your CPM—the fee you pay per 1,000 names—is $100. But of the 5,000 people who receive your e-mail promotion, only 10% (500 recipients) may actually open it and click on the link to the landing page on your website. And then only 10% of those recipients (50 out of 500 recipients) may purchase the product offered in the e-mail, sign up for the webinar, or fill out the form to download your product white paper (thus becoming leads for you)—or perform whatever action you're seeking from them. Your CPA, in this case, is $10 per action ($500 to purchase the list ÷ 50 customer actions = $10 CPA).

The CPA is a major factor in determining your ROMI, which, in turn, determines the success of your lead-generation efforts. For example, if you are selling a $100 product, and you are seeking an actual sale from your customer, a $10 CPA is very good. It gives you a return rate of 1,000%.

CPA has become an especially popular form of measurement in the digital world. With digital measuring tools, we can actually measure the number of actions that result from using an online lead-generation tactic, such as search engine marketing or display advertising. Previously, with, say, billboard advertising, it was almost impossible to count the exact number of people who saw the billboard ad every day, or to measure the effect that the ad might have on any given potential customer.

CPA encompasses a few concepts that I will talk about in the chapters to come, such as:

- *Cost-Per-Open (CPO):* If you're using e-mail marketing, how much does it cost you to get customers to open an e-mail that you've sent them?

- *Cost-Per-Click (CPC):* Once they've opened the e-mail, how many potential customers will click the "Click here" button that takes them to a landing page on your website? How much does it cost you to get the customer to click on the e-mail? Or if you're using online lead-generation ads (such as display ads, search engine ads, or social media ads), how much does it cost you to get a potential customer to click on the ad?

> **Note:** *CPC is often used interchangeably with PPC. PPC is a negotiated rate (e.g., $1 per click) that you agree to pay each time someone clicks on your online lead-generation ad. For display ads, search engine ads, or social media ads, the CPC—the amount you* actually *pay each time someone clicks on the ad—is equal to the negotiated PPC rate. (In this case, your CPC is $1.)*
>
> *But you can also use CPC as a measurement for e-mail campaigns, where the cost of buying an e-mail contact list is measured in CPM (that is, cost-per-1,000 names). In this case, the CPC is the amount you spend for each potential customer who actually clicks on your e-mail and goes to the landing page on your website. If you buy an e-mail list with 1,000 addresses for a $100 CPM rate, and exactly 100 people click on the e-mail to visit the landing page, your CPC is $1 per click.*

- *Cost-Per-Lead (CPL):* This is a synonym for CPA. Use cost-per-lead when your objective is to obtain an actual lead (as opposed to a sale of the product). CPL is the cost of obtaining an actionable lead that may be turned into a sale.

  In the case of e-mail marketing, how much does it cost you to get the potential customer to open the e-mail, click the link to the website, and fill out the form to show interest in buying or learning more about your product? If you buy an e-mail list with 1,000 addresses for a $100 CPM rate, and only 50 people fill out the form to become a lead, your CPL is $100 ÷ 50 = $2 per lead.

- *Cost-Per-Sale (CPS):* This is the total cost of making an actual product or service sale.

Determining your CPA will provide an important basic measurement for the effectiveness of your lead-generation marketing campaigns, whether the action you are seeking is a warm lead, a purchase, or a webinar reservation from a potential client.

Questions You Should Ask

In planning your lead-generation efforts, you should ask certain questions:

- How much should it cost you to obtain each customer action using lead-generation tactics? Will the CPA be cost-effective and eventually lead to a sale?

- Will the money you spend to obtain a customer action using a lead-generation tactic be more or less than the amount you will eventually make on a sale?

- After performing that action, will customers make a one-time purchase from you? Or will they be a long-term customer, continuously buying additional products from you over many years?

Target CPA vs. Actual CPA

One more thing you should know. When you use each of the seven most successful tactics in lead-generation marketing, you will deal with two types of CPA: your target CPA and your actual CPA.

- Your *target* CPA is the ideal CPA. It is the goal for the average amount you *plan* or *hope* to spend to acquire each customer action (whether that's an actual sale, signing up for a webinar, etc.). You should try to determine your target CPA before launching your lead-generation campaign, based on how much you want to spend to acquire that lead and on the questions listed in the previous section.

- Your *actual* CPA is the CPA you *actually* get each time you use a lead-generation tactic. You determine the actual CPA *after* the campaign is over. You should then compare the actual CPA with your target CPA to see how close you came.

Your goal, of course, is to have the actual CPA be equal to or less than your target CPA. For example, if you set a target CPA of $20 per customer action on an e-mail marketing campaign, and your actual CPA in the campaign is $18, you've met your goal. If, however, your actual CPA turns out to be $30 per customer action, you might need to rethink how you use a certain tactic in order to make it more cost-effective.

Keep in mind that it will probably take you several tries with a tactic before you can get your results to the point where it is cost-effective for you, especially if the tactic is one you haven't used before. If your target CPA for your first e-mail marketing campaign is $20 per customer action, and the actual CPA is, say, $40, it doesn't necessarily mean you shouldn't use e-mail marketing. The results may simply mean that you need to make some adjustments so you get a better, more cost-effective response on your next campaign.

If the actual CPA for your second e-mail marketing campaign is $35, and your actual CPA for your third campaign is $27, you are moving closer to your $20 target CPA. In this case, you should probably keep experimenting with e-mail marketing, until you can make it a cost-effective tactic. If, however, your actual CPA remains consistent at $40 over multiple campaigns, you might want to consider whether e-mail marketing is the best tactic for your company, or if other tactics will be more cost-effective.

When you use multiple lead-generation tactics, you will need to establish common goals and use the same target CPA for all the tactics you employ. For example, if you have a $50 target CPA, you will need to apply it across all your tactics. And you will need to measure your success in each tactic according to that $50 target CPA.

Also, when you use multiple lead-generation tactics, you will need to compare the actual CPAs for different tactics against each other to find out which tactics are the most cost-effective for your company in the long run.

How much does it cost you, for example, to obtain an action from your potential customer using direct mail vs. using trade shows vs. using social media marketing? (I'll talk more about comparing actual CPAs across multiple tactics later in this chapter and again in Chapter 16.)

Determining Your Target CPA

If you've been doing lead-generation marketing for some time, you probably have an idea of what your target CPA is for the tactics you use. However, it can be tricky to determine your average cost for a tactic you've never used before. In some cases, it may help to know the average return for that tactic.

For example, in the chapters about online lead-generation marketing tactics (e-mail marketing, search engine marketing, etc.), I talk about the concepts of the click-through rate and the conversion rate. The *click-through rate (CTR)* is the number of clicks an online ad or marketing e-mail gets from your potential customers. If you send out 100,000 marketing e-mails, and 1,000 people click on the e-mail to go to the landing page on your website describing the offer, you have a 1% CTR.

The *conversion rate* is the number of people who actually buy your product, sign up as a lead, etc., after clicking on the marketing e-mail. Your conversion rate is calculated *from your CTR*. If 1,000 people click on your e-mail, but only 150 people follow through and buy the product advertised in the e-mail, your conversion rate is 15%.

A 1% CTR and a 15% conversion rate are good rates for an e-mail marketing campaign. When calculating your target CPA, it may help to use these average numbers as placeholder numbers in order to figure out the CPM you can afford. For example, in calculating your target CPA, you might assume a 1% CTR and a 15% conversion rate. If you plan to spend $10,000 at $100 CPM to purchase 100,000 e-mail addresses, you can calculate that a 1% CTR will give you 1,000 clicks. From this, a 15% conversion rate will give you 150 conversions. In this case, you can estimate a target CPA ($10,000 ÷ 150) of about $66 per action.

But you really won't know your actual CTR, conversion rate, or actual CPA until you send out the e-mails and measure the results. At the end of your campaign, you may find that your initial CTR is 2% (2,000 clicks), but your conversion rate, calculated from that CTR, is only 5% (100 conversions). This gives you an actual CPA of $100 ($10,000 ÷ 100 conversions).

Comparing these results to what you originally assumed is very useful. For your next e-mail marketing campaign, you can either adjust your marketing tactics or message to get a better CTR and conversion rate, and/or adjust your budget for the campaign to better fit your target CPA. (I'll talk more about measuring your returns for e-mail marketing in Chapter 12.)

The Big Picture: Qualifying Leads

Most companies have a process of qualifying leads. This process enables them to separate the good leads from the bad and to focus attention on *actionable* leads—that is, on courting potential customers who might actually buy the product or service. As a lead-generation marketer, you need to understand the "big picture" of how the lead-qualifying process works and how this process can have a positive or negative effect on your business's bottom line.

There are several levels of leads that lead up to an actual sale of your product. A *marketing lead (ML)* is any lead that comes in to your organization. It may be a lead that will lead to a sale. Or it may be from a person who has no interest in the product, and just filled out the form because they liked the look of it, or to get whatever free giveaway you are offering on your website, at a trade show, etc.

Some of the initial MLs you collect will be useless to you (which is fine). There will usually be some bad leads from people with no interest in your products. There may be duplicate leads where the potential customer accidentally sent you the same online form twice, or leads where the customer provided bad data (i.e., the wrong phone number or an incomplete e-mail address).

Also, some leads may be from prospective customers who are not ready to buy, but who are still interested in the product. Most companies save these leads and continue to send appropriate marketing materials to the prospective customers until they are ready to make a buying decision.

Usually, these leads go into a "drip bucket" so that the company can "drip" marketing communications to these potential customers in the hopes that they will eventually become active buyers.

Your responsibility as a marketer is to qualify leads before handing them off to your sales organization. Unless you are a strict e-commerce company, you need to have a process or measures in place to weed out the bad or duplicate leads. For example, you might have a member of your marketing staff give a phone call to marketing leads to see how interested they are in your products. Or you might have questions in your fill-out form to help you gauge the potential customer's interest. (Example: "How often do you buy our type of product? ( ) Once a month. ( ) Once a year. ( ) Once every 10 years.")

Once you qualify certain leads as being good ones that might result in a sale, those leads become *marketing-qualified leads (MQLs)*. You then pass your MQLs on to your sales organization, where they become *sales leads (SLs)*.

Often, sales departments have their own procedures to further qualify SLs, turning them into *sales-qualified leads (SQLs)*. For example, a salesperson may place a follow-up call to ask customers whether they currently have a budget to buy the product. In some cases, the sales department may narrow the list even further by separating SQLs from *sales-qualified opportunities (SQOs)*. An SQO may be a potential customer who is not yet ready to buy but who is definitely planning to buy within the next year. (*Note:* SQOs may also be defined as potentials, prospects, etc., depending on the kind of sales management software you use.)

The final stage in the process is getting the customer to buy. This is where the SQL turns into an actual sale.

Here's the important thing to keep in mind: Each time you go through a qualification step, *the number of leads that can potentially be turned into sales will probably be reduced.* You may start with 100 MLs, but, once you qualify those leads, you reduce the number to 50 MQLs. Those 50 MQLs become 50 SLs, but your sales staff then reduces them to 20 SQLs.

In general, the overall cost of turning a lead into a sale increases each time you qualify leads. For example, it may cost you $1,000 to obtain every

100 MLs. At that point, your cost-per-ML is $1,000 ÷ 100 = $10 per ML. But let's say that out of 100 MLs you obtain, only 10 of those MLs become MQLs. Your cost-per-MQL is $1,000 ÷ 10 = $100 per MQL. Your sales organization will take those MLs, turn them into SLs, and further qualify them. If only 5 SLs become SQLs, your cost-per-SQL is $1,000 ÷ 5 = $200 per SQL. If only one of those five SQLs results in a sale, your CPS is $1,000 ÷ 1 = $1,000 per sale.

This $1,000 CPS may provide either a positive or negative ROMI to your company. It depends on your product and the price at which you sell it. If you are selling pleasure yachts at a price of $700,000 each, a $1,000 CPS may be quite attractive. But if you are selling a $50 gift certificate to a restaurant, a $1,000 CPS is *way* too much.

Determining Customer Value

Once you've figured out the overall cost of turning a lead into a sale, you need to figure out the ROMI (if any) to your company from acquiring that customer and making the sale. You can do this in two ways. First, you can assess the overall CPA against the purchase value of that single purchase. Second, you can assess the overall CPA against the *lifetime value (LTV)* of that customer.

It's a common notion among marketers that the cheapest actionable leads you can obtain are the most cost-effective. If you are selling a product for $100, it seems logical to use a tactic that generates actionable leads at an overall CPA of less than $100. A tactic with a CPA of $5 per acquired action-able lead might be ideal.

Some lead-generation tactics, of course, will never be that inexpensive, but in some cases, they don't need to be. If you use the concept of the life-time value of your customers, you can apply the CPA not just to a one-time sale but to every purchase the customer makes from then on. By using the LTV assessment, you can sometimes get higher-quality leads by paying a bit more money. If you think in terms of LTV, you may decide to use a lead-generation tactic that will cost a bit more but that still provides you with a good ROMI.

For example, say you own a company that creates and produces DVD video training courses for other companies. You have a five-DVD sales training package that you sell for $200, and your margin on the DVD is $100. You might argue that your CPA therefore needs to be less than $100.

But what if the buyer is a company that has a regular, ongoing need for the kinds of training videos you provide? Over the long run, they could be a very loyal customer and might conceivably buy a $200 DVD package from you every month. That customer is now worth $2,400 per year to you. And your CPA could be more like $1,200 because the value of that customer goes far beyond a single sale.

Companies like BMW have embraced this concept of LTV and have incorporated it into their marketing efforts. When you buy a BMW, the company looks at you as a customer whom they have acquired for life, hoping you will buy every car you will ever own from them. They spend money to keep you engaged as a valued customer through customer events, touch points such as letters and gifts, and other means.

When I leased my BMW, I received a hat, a shirt, and a coffee mug with the BMW logo on it. Over the term of the lease, I received branded BMW magazines with reports on new car models, customer testimonials, and travel articles (e.g., "Driving the Swiss Alps in your BMW"). BMW also entered me into various drawings for road trip excursions in Europe. Also, a friend of mine who had just bought a BMW roadster received a set of branded luggage that fit perfectly in the trunk of her new car.

All of these efforts were designed to keep me and my friend as lifetime customers. By keeping you engaged and by continuously measuring your satisfaction with their product and their company, BMW lets you know that they appreciate your value as a customer. They want to increase the likelihood that you will continue to buy BMWs for the rest of your life.

Return on Marketing Investment

Your overall CPA, the cost of making the one-time sale, and the possible LTV of a customer are all factors that you need to consider in determining the ROI of your lead-generation efforts. Concerning ROI, the question is,

"Did the money I spent in acquiring this lead generate positive net value to my business?" In marketing, we talk about ROMI. In this case, the question is, "Am I spending less money to acquire the customer than I am making on the customer?"

A Case Example: Display Ads vs. Trade Shows

Let's look at a hypothetical example of how the overall costs of lead-generation tactics can affect your ROMI, for better or worse. In this example, we'll compare the costs and results of using online display ads rather than trade shows.

At first, this might seem like an odd comparison, since these tactics are so diverse. If you use these two tactics, your efforts will look very different in terms of how you invest in either one. But if you use the terms I've introduced in this chapter, it's easier to compare their results and cost-effectiveness. You can find out which tactic provides better results in generating leads and/or is driving the better ROMI value.

Let's begin with a couple of assumptions. First, let's assume that your product can be sold using either display ads or trade shows. Also, let's assume that you know how to use both tactics to effectively reach your target customer. (For example, you know which trade shows your target customers are most likely to attend.)

You have a choice between spending $5,000 for PPC online display ads or spending $25,000 to attend a trade show. You want to determine which tactic will give your company the most actionable leads and the best ROMI.

> **Note:** *I use* choice *here in terms of comparison. As I said before, you should use as many of the seven lead-generation tactics as possible. If you find that using* both *display ads and trade shows will provide a good ROMI for your company, there's no reason not to use both.*

At first glance, the choice between using display ads rather than trade shows might seem like a no-brainer. It might seem more sensible and cost-effective to use the display ads because this tactic will be far less expensive than the trade show. But if you look closely at each type of campaign and at the ROMI that each tactic gives you, you might be surprised at how the results compare.

For the display ads, you might negotiate a PPC rate of 10¢ per click. A budget of $5,000 gives you 50,000 clicks. But of the 50,000 clicks on your online display ad, only a few will turn into actual leads. Most Web surfers who see the ad will click on it out of curiosity. Some will click on the ad more than once. Many of them will take a quick look through your website, but only a few will actually fill out the online form to say they are interested in buying your product. Of the 50,000 clicks your display ad receives, only 1% may convert to an actual lead. This gives you 500 MLs.

When you start to qualify those leads, separating the good leads from the bad, that number will probably be reduced even further. Only 33% of the MLs may convert to MQLs. This gives you about 166 MQLs. At this point, your CPA is around $30 ($5,000 ÷ 166 MQLs = $30.12 per MQL). But the process doesn't end there.

Once you hand the leads over to sales, perhaps only one-third (i.e., 33%) of the 166 MQLs may be converted into SQLs, for about 55 SQLs. And only one-third of the SQLs may result in an actual sale. From 55 SQLs come about 17 sales. Therefore, your CPS is about $294 per sale ($5,000 ÷ 17 sales = $294.12).

Whether display ads in this case give you a positive or negative ROMI depends on what type of product you are selling, the cost of it, and how many sales you hope to make from one potential customer.

If you are selling a product for $300 and it is a one-time sale, your display ad campaign was not very cost-effective. With a $294 CPS, you've made a profit of only $6. If your product sells for less than $294, you're in trouble. In this case, you've just lost money using this tactic.

However, the display ad tactic might still be cost-effective if your new customer has an LTV. If you think this customer might buy 10 products from you over the next year at $300 apiece, you stand to gain revenue of $3,000. If so, your $294 CPS (and the $20 CPA) will be very cost-effective in the long run because you may get more than one sale. In time, you may get a larger profit and a better ROMI.

Now let's take a look at the trade show tactic. You may determine that it will cost you $25,000 to attend an appropriate industry trade show. This cost includes the expenses of renting space at the show, designing and building a display booth, creating additional creatives (marketing materials, giveaways, tchotchkes, etc.), airline fares, hotel rooms, car rental, and other expenses for sending three company reps there.

Use of display ads would, of course, be less expensive. But trade shows have several advantages. First, trade shows give you better access to your target audience than online display ads. In today's economy, attending a trade show is a serious investment. People and companies must spend money to register for a trade show and to travel to it. So if they attend a show, they are usually in the market for your type of product. In other words, they may be looking to buy.

If 250 trade show attendees sign up as leads for you (assuming, again, that you attend the right show), those leads will usually be more qualified than the 500 or so leads you would receive from display ads. Of your 250 MLs, maybe 80%, or 200, will convert to MQLs. This gives you a CPA of about $125 ($25,000 ÷ 200 MQLs = $125). That is a more expensive CPA than the $30 CPA that you pay for using display ads. But because the leads from the trade show are more qualified, they will eventually pay for themselves.

The second advantage of the trade show is, because the leads are more qualified, your marketing staff can spend less time and effort weeding out the good leads from the bad. It may take your staff less time to qualify 200 MQLs from the 250 trade show MLs than it would take them to qualify 166 MQLs from the 500 MLs from the display ads.

Also, since the leads from the trade show are usually looking to buy, your salespeople can focus on leads that have a better chance of turning into sales. Of the 200 MQLs that you get from the trade show, maybe 100 will convert into sales. This is more than the 17 sales received from the display ads. Your CPS for the trade show is $250 per sale ($25,000 ÷ 100 sales = $250). This is less than the $294 CPS for the display ads. Plus, you made more sales (100) and earned more income.

Again, whether the trade show provides a positive or negative ROMI—and whether it is actually more or less effective than using the display ads—depends on your product, its cost, and the customer's LTV. If you sell a $300 product and the trade show results in 100 sales at a $250 CPS, you make a $50 profit per sale. This is slightly more (at least initially) than the $6 profit per sale on the sales of the same $300 product to 17 customers at a $294 CPS using the online display ad. But the $50 profit you make on each trade show sale is still a rather small profit.

However, if your customers have LTV, the trade show sales may lead to additional sales. If, for example, you're promoting a business-to-business product at industry trade shows, your customers are more likely to make additional purchases. If 70 companies out of the 100 trade show sales are impressed with your product, they may decide to buy 5 or 10 more units, perhaps for use in all their business locations.

On the other hand, maybe your product sells better online. Maybe you have an innovative website that people will want to return to many times after they've made their first purchase. You may see additional sales from them. If so, using display ads to bring new potential customers to your website and turn them into longtime customers might be a better option. In that case, you would limit your use of trade shows for lead generation.

Again, there's no right tactic to use in all cases. The point is not to prove that one tactic is better than another but rather to determine which tactics will be cost-effective and provide a positive ROMI for *your* business and *your* products. If using both display ads and trade shows will provide your company with actionable leads and a positive ROMI, then by all means, you should use both. But you should know *which* tactics provide you with the best ROMI.

Once you know which tactics result in the best ROMI, you can concentrate on making those tactics your primary ones. You can also use them as baseline tactics and test other tactics against them. It may turn out that your test tactics will eventually produce a better ROMI and become your new baseline tactics.

> > > *What You Should Know* < < <

To review, here's what you should know about calculating the costs of your lead-generation campaigns:

- Payment for marketing services often uses the cost-per-milia (CPM), or cost-per-1,000 impressions unit of measurement. An impression is any exposure, positive or negative, that a consumer has to your brand or message. [Pay-per-click (PPC) is another common measurement used in online marketing.]

- You should base the success and cost-effectiveness of your lead-generation campaign on your cost-per-action (CPA). A CPA may be a cost-per-lead (CPL), cost-per-click (CPC), cost-per-open (CPO), etc., depending on the action you hope customers will take when they receive your creatives.

- In planning your lead-generation efforts, you must determine your target cost-per-action. This is your ideal CPA that you hope to achieve in using a certain lead-generation tactic, based on how much of your marketing budget you wish to assign to the campaign.

- When comparing results of lead-generation tactics, you should, for each tactic, compare your target CPA against the actual CPA. This helps you to determine how cost-effective each tactic is.

- In qualifying leads, you must separate actionable leads that might result in a sale from unqualified leads. As you go through the qualifying process, the number of qualified leads will probably be reduced. For example, 200 marketing leads (MLs) might become 100 marketing-qualified leads (MQLs), which then become 50 sales-qualified leads (SQLs). By the time you make an actual sale, your cost-per-sale (CPS) may provide a positive or negative ROMI for your company, depending on your product, its price, and the potential long-term value of the customer.

- Customers who have a lifetime value (LTV) may buy more than one product from you over the long run. In some cases, you can get higher-quality leads by using a more expensive lead-generation tactic (like a trade show). Customers who have a regular, ongoing need for your type of product may provide a ROMI that goes beyond a single sale.

- In determining your ROMI, you must determine whether the money you spend to acquire the customer is less than what you make from that customer.

PART TWO

Lead-Generation
Marketing Tactics

6

Introduction to Online Lead-Generation Advertising

THERE ARE THREE lead-generation tactics—search engine marketing, social media advertising, and display advertising—that might be grouped under the heading of *online lead-generation advertising*. Each of these three tactics uses online ads as a basis for reaching out to target customers.

This chapter gives you a short overview of some common principles and secondary elements associated with online lead-generation advertising. Since these common principles and elements apply (in one form or another) to all three tactics, I think it's best to take a quick look at them. In Chapters 7–10, I'll look at specific ways you can apply these principles and elements to each online advertising tactic.

It's very important that you should understand the difference between creating an online ad for lead generation and creating one for brand awareness. Brand awareness ads are based on creativity, and your hook for the ad usually tries to spark an emotional response from the person who sees it.

When you create an online ad for lead generation, your approach is based more on the medium of expression. Search engine ads on Google and Bing, as well as social media ads on Facebook, are text-based ads. These ads are very functional and don't give you a lot of room for branding.

Search engine and social media ads only offer a limited number of characters for each ad you post (e.g., 25 characters for the headline, and 70 characters for the message on search engine ads). Your ad must include a title, value proposition, CTA, and offer using that limited number of characters. In creating your ad, you will concentrate more on creating compelling copy that will prompt your target audience to click on the ad.

The many types of display ads (image ads, video ads, Flash animation ads, etc.) give you more room for branding. But the *function* of these ads is still to bring in leads. As we'll see in Chapter 10, display ads have evolved beyond the simple brand advertising tools that they once were, and have become a very useful lead-generation tool.

Understanding the Online Bid Process

A second important element of online lead-generation advertising is the online bid process. Online lead-generation advertising works like an auction. When you post online ads, you make a PPC (or CPM) bid for how much you are willing to pay each time someone clicks on your ad. Your bid is used to determine how often (or how highly placed) your ad will be served. Advertisers compete with each other by offering different PPC (or CPM) bids for each ad they post. The ads with the highest bids get the best placement or highest positioning.

The bid process is used with:

- *Search Engine Ads:* On Google and Bing, advertisers bid a PPC rate for certain keywords and keyword phrases (e.g., "office Realtors in Atlanta"). Search engine ads with the highest PPC bids get placed in the "ad spaces" at the top of the natural search results list, or in the margins on the side of the page, when someone searches for those keyword terms.

- *Social Media Sites:* On Facebook, LinkedIn, and Twitter, advertisers bid a PPC rate to have their ads displayed to certain target demographics (e.g., Facebook users ages 20–25 who are married or engaged). You bid a rate for each ad you post, according to the target demographics you choose. In general, the highest-bidding ads appear first on the Facebook pages of users in the selected target demographic. (LinkedIn also gives you the option to bid and pay by CPM rate.)

- *Some Display Advertising:* Some websites that offer display advertising use the bid process, allowing advertisers to bid PPC or CPM rates. Ads with the highest-bidding rates get the most coverage, or get placed in premium ad spaces on the website.

Note: *Not every website that sells display ad space uses the bid process. Many sites or content networks simply sell you available space.*

When you set up your ad campaign, the search engine, social media site, or website will ask you to give a PPC (or CPM) bid for each ad you post. Again, with a PPC bid, you pay a certain amount (e.g., $2.50) to the search engine or site each time someone clicks on your ad. (With a CPM bid, you pay a certain amount for every 1,000 times a webpage or social media page presents your ad, regardless of whether someone clicks on it or not.)

You can bid any PPC or CPM rate to have your ad placed on these search engines or sites. But the higher you bid, the better positioned your ad will be. In general, *only the ads that represent the highest bids* will be served, or given top space, on search engines, social media sites, or websites.

For example, on a search engine, ads with the top five to seven bids will be placed in the premium ad spaces at the top or in the side margins of the first page of natural search results for the keywords (e.g., "office Realtors in Atlanta") for those ads. Ads with lower bids may be placed in the ad spaces on the second or third page of search results, where they are less likely to be seen.

On social media sites, only the ads with the top five bids are served on the page of a user within the target demographic (e.g., Facebook users ages 20–25 who are married or engaged) when the user logs onto their page on the site. Ads that bid a lower rate may not be served at all.

Fortunately, there are ways to use the bid process to maximize the effectiveness of your online ad campaigns. I'll provide more information on how the bid process works for each of the online lead-generation advertising tactics in Chapters 7–10.

Testing Your Online Lead-Generation Ad Campaign

You will need to do testing of multiple elements at the beginning of an online lead-generation campaign. An *initial test campaign* is essential because it tells you what works and what doesn't. You can test different ads against each other to see which ads, and which offers, get the highest response. You can also use testing to tailor the elements of your campaign, so that you give your ads the best chances of success.

Each of the three online lead-generation advertising tactics provides you with different opportunities to test your ad campaign once it is deployed. However, some basic principles and common elements apply to testing all three tactics.

YOUR TEST TIME PERIOD

When you do a test of an online ad campaign, you should allow yourself adequate time and budget to test the effectiveness of your ads. I recommend a time period of one week for a test campaign. On search engine marketing, social media advertising, or display advertising, running one or more online ads for a week gives you an adequate time period to monitor the response to each ad, and to measure and understand the data you collect from the response.

TESTING YOUR BUDGET

Search engines, social media sites, and some ad-serving software tools used in display advertising allow you to set a daily or weekly budget for how much you want to spend on each ad you post, based on your PPC or CPM bid. Your ad will continue to run on a website, social media site, or search engine until it gets the maximum number of clicks to equal your set budget.

For example, if you post an ad on a search engine or social media site with a maximum budget of $1,000 at a PPC rate of $2 per click, the ad will continue to run on that site until it gets 500 clicks. Depending on how popular your ad is, it may get 500 clicks in one day, one week, or one month.

Online lead-generation advertising gives you opportunities to test your daily budget, to find out how much money you need to allow for each ad. I recommend setting a high daily budget for the first week of your campaign. If you can afford it, I recommend an initial daily budget of $1,000 for each ad you post. This is expensive, but your goal is to test the true effectiveness of your ads. You want to get an idea of the maximum number of leads you can obtain each day with your ad.

If you set a daily budget of $1,000 at a bid of $2 per click, your ad will run every day on the search engine, social media site, or website until it gets 500 clicks. If you're lucky, on some days, you may get the maximum number of clicks. On other days, you may get less. For example, say you run an ad on Facebook for a product that appeals more to weekend users. On Friday through Sunday, you may get 500 clicks per day, but on Monday through Thursday, you may get an average of only 200 clicks per day. This is fine, because now you know the average number of clicks you can get per day with your ad. You can then adjust your daily budget rate down to around $400–$500 for those days when you know you will get only about 200 clicks.

But if you set a low daily budget for the ad, you may be throwing leads away. For example, if you set a daily budget of $50 with a $2 per click bid, your ad will run only until you get 25 clicks. You will get 25 leads when you could have gotten 200 or more. So it's better to set a high daily budget for the first week of your campaign in order to get a sense of the highest number of leads you can obtain with that ad.

If you need to start out with a smaller test budget, you can still test your daily budget. For example, you could set a $200 daily budget for each ad, at a PPC rate of $2 per click. If your ad reaches its click limit (e.g., 100 clicks per day) on three separate days, you might increase the ad's daily budget to $300. If the ad continues to reach its click limit (e.g., 150 clicks per day), you can keep increasing the ad's daily budget in $100 increments every few days, until you know the maximum number of clicks (e.g., 500) you can expect from the ad on a given day. This testing strategy may take a bit longer to determine your maximum daily budget for each ad. But it may also save you money if you can't afford a higher test budget.

OTHER TESTING AREAS

For each online ad campaign, you should test three other areas:

1. *Testing Ads Against One Other:* Test different ads, and different versions of the same ad, against one another to see which gets the best response. For example, you might test an ad with a "Buy one, get one free" offer against an ad with a "Buy now, get 20% off" offer.

2. *Testing Your Target Demographics:* If you're not sure which target audience will be most interested in your ads, you can run variations on your ads for each group of target customers. For example, you might test one ad aimed at recent college graduates against another aimed at recent retirees, to see which demographic group gives you a better response.

3. *Testing Your Ad Schedule:* Search engines allow you to run your ads on days and times when people in your target audience are likely to see them. For example, you may choose to run a search engine ad aimed at college students Monday through Friday from 6 p.m. to 3 a.m.

In the next four chapters, I'll talk about how to test each of these areas for the individual online lead-generation advertising tactics.

Now let's take an in-depth look at a creative element that is an essential part of any online lead-generation campaign: the landing page.

A Look at Landing Pages

A *landing page* is the page on your website that potential customers see when they click on the link provided by your online ad or e-mail promotion. Landing pages are not, by themselves, a primary marketing tactic, but they are an essential companion piece to online lead-generation tactics.

Landing pages are used with all three forms of online lead-generation advertising—search engine ads, display ads, and social media ads. They are also used with e-mail advertising. In addition, landing pages can be used as a marketing tool with direct mail packages, and sometimes with cold calling.

The purpose of a landing page is to reinforce the ideas or offer you present to potential customers in your online ad, marketing e-mail, or direct mail package. In lead generation, the creative is the "swing" that connects you with your customer. The landing page is the "follow-through," by which the customer takes an action either to become a lead (e.g., by downloading a white paper, accepting a webinar invitation, etc.) or to make a purchase from you.

Whether you create it for e-mail marketing, online advertising, or direct mail, a good landing page is mission critical to the success of your campaign. You therefore need to follow a few guidelines in creating your landing page.

MAKE IT A SOFT LANDING

First, your landing page should be a soft landing for prospective customers. You shouldn't try to hard-sell the product. Instead, you should reinforce the message of your e-mail, direct mail piece, or online ad. For example, if you send out a marketing e-mail with the theme, "Five reasons to buy now," your landing page should list and reinforce those "five reasons," and allow the potential customer who clicked on the e-mail to buy now.

Make sure the landing page your customer opens is consistent with the call-to-action in the lead-generation creative. If your marketing e-mail invites potential customers to sign up for a webinar, the e-mail link should send them directly to a webinar signup page. If your online ad asks the customer to buy the product (e.g., "Buy now, get 20% off"), the destination link in the ad should send them to a landing page with a "buy" message. It should not send them to a landing page that invites them to download a white paper about the product.

Also, make sure the landing page reflects the "look and feel" of the lead-generation creative. The brand, colors, and graphics on your landing page should be consistent with those in the online ad, marketing e-mail, or direct mail piece that you show or send to the potential customer.

KEEP IT FOCUSED

Your landing page needs to be very focused. Make sure the link in your e-mail, online ad, or direct mail piece sends or points the customer *directly* to the landing page, and nowhere else. For example, if you use a marketing e-mail to advertise a product, the e-mail link should *not* send your potential customers to a page about a different product. Nothing frustrates a potential customer more than clicking on an e-mail link or online ad and being sent to a page that has nothing to do with the e-mail or ad.

Also, you should never use your home page as a landing page. If potential customers click on a marketing e-mail or online ad that takes them to your home page, they may get lost searching for the offer featured in the e-mail or ad. They may even give up searching for it and leave the page without taking the offer.

I recently received an e-mail that invited me to download a white paper about a product. When I clicked on the e-mail link, it took me to the company's home page, which featured information on *all* the company's products. I had to search around on the home page for the white paper that the e-mail had invited me to download. I finally found it hidden about two-thirds of the way down the page.

Although you don't want to use your home page as a landing page, the landing page itself should at least have a relationship with the home page. You want to make sure that potential customers know they've come to the right place when they reach your landing page. You don't want them to think they've been directed to the wrong webpage or site, or worse, make them suspect that the e-mail you sent is a phishing scam.

For example, the destination URL should make it obvious that the landing page is a genuine page on your website (e.g., www.acmecompany.com/special-software-offer). It should not be an unrelated URL (e.g., www.software-offer.com). Also, your landing page should have the same look and feel as your home page and as the other pages on your site (i.e., the same colors, border graphics, branding, text style, etc.).

Limit the options for things the potential customer can do on your landing page. Whatever action you want them to take (e.g., signing up for a webinar, downloading a white paper) should be front and center on the landing page. Visitors should be able to take that action right away. They shouldn't have to hunt around the page for the signup form or download link.

The landing page should be free of distractions. If you want customers to sign up for a webinar, don't give them options to explore the product, contact your company, and so on. Don't include links to other pages; this is too much of a temptation for the customer to click on those links and explore other pages on your site. You want to keep customers singularly focused on the landing page and on taking the desired action.

Landing Pages and Testing Your Campaign

You can use landing pages as a tool to test your lead-generation campaigns and to track the response to your offers. However, you need to make sure that you set up your landing pages correctly, according to the elements of your campaign. You need to remember two points:

1. Each marketing e-mail creative, direct mail piece, or online ad you create must have a corresponding landing page *with content specific to that e-mail, direct mail piece, or online ad.*

2. If you are using more than one online lead-generation tactic (e.g., e-mail marketing, display ads, social ads, etc.) as part of an integrated marketing campaign, you need to use *a separate landing page for each tactic.*

Let's take a quick look at these two points.

USING CONTENT-SPECIFIC LANDING PAGES

Each e-mail, direct mail piece, or online ad you create must have a corresponding landing page with content specific to that creative. For example, if you are testing two online ads with two different offers (e.g., "Buy one, get one free" vs. "Buy now, get 20% off"), you should have a separate landing page for each ad. Each landing page should have language appropriate to the offer in the associated ad. (The landing page for the "Buy one, get one free" ad should reinforce that specific offer, etc.)

And, of course, you should make sure that the destination URLs for each ad take the Web user to the appropriate landing page. You don't want responders to click on the "Buy now, get 20% off" ad and find themselves at the "Buy one, get one free" landing page—or vice versa.

If you are testing offers on different target audiences, or on different groups within a target audience, you may need separate landing pages for each version of the ad or e-mail. For example, say you are marketing products to the alumni of different colleges (e.g., Harvard, Yale, Penn State, etc.). If the language in your ads or e-mails targets college alumni by schools (e.g., "Harvard grads, click here"), you will need a separate landing page for each college (e.g., a "Harvard" ad should take the Web user to a landing page with language aimed at Harvard graduates).

If you are testing different ads or offers on different groups within a target audience, you need to be even more specific. You will need a separate landing page for each offer and for each group that receives each offer. For example, say you're testing a "Harvard grads, get 20% off" offer and a "Harvard grads, get a free gift" offer. You will need a separate landing page for each offer, and the language on each page should describe the corresponding offer as it relates to Harvard grads. If you're also testing a "Yale grads, get 20% off" offer and a "Yale grads, get a free gift" offer, you will need two separate landing pages—one for each offer—with language aimed at Yale grads.

Depending on how many offers you make and how many different groups you are targeting, you may need a great number of corresponding landing pages. For example, if you are targeting an offer to alumni groups from 50 colleges, you will need 50 separate landing pages, each with language directed to the college alumni who received the offer. (Fortunately, it's fairly easy to duplicate landing pages and edit the content on each to suit a particular audience using Web design technologies.)

USING LANDING PAGES WITH MULTIPLE LEAD-GENERATION TACTICS

Many companies that use multiple online lead-generation tactics make the mistake of using a single landing page for all the tactics they employ. For example, they may post search engine ads and display ads, in addition to sending out marketing e-mails to prospective customers. But whether customers click on an online ad or e-mail link, they get the exact same landing page on the company's website, and they see the same generic Web content on that page.

When you use multiple online lead-generation tactics as part of an integrated marketing campaign, you should use separate landing pages for each tactic. Each of your search engine ads, display ads, and marketing e-mails should have a corresponding, separate landing page or a separate set of landing pages (depending on how many ads or e-mail offers you use in your campaign).

There are two good reasons for this. First, as I explained, the content on the landing page should be *specific* to a corresponding creative. If you use generic text on a landing page, it often looks—well—very *generic.* If the language on the page doesn't reinforce the message of a corresponding e-mail or online ad, or if the content is written in bland, nonspecific language, it may disengage customers from the marketing experience. If this happens, customers may not use the landing page to buy your product, sign up as a lead, or perform the desired action.

The second reason for using a separate landing page for each lead-generation tactic is to make it easier to keep track of the response for each tactic. Landing pages are especially important in e-mail marketing (and in direct mail), where the number of visits a landing page receives (e.g., after someone clicks on the corresponding e-mail) allows you to measure the response to the marketing offer.

Note: *It's a bit different with online lead-generation advertising. As we'll see in the next four chapters, search engines, social media sites, and display advertising ads have various technological means (analytics programs, tracking cookies, etc.) to keep track of how many clicks an ad receives.*

Using a separate landing page for each lead-generation tactic makes it much easier to keep track of each tactic's response rate. For example, if you have a separate landing page for your marketing e-mail, direct mail piece, and social ad, you can measure the response rate for each tactic by the number of visitors each separate landing page receives.

If you use the same generic landing page for all three tactics, you can still measure the total number of visitors to that landing page. But it will be much harder to determine which visitors accessed the landing page through the marketing e-mail, the social ad, or the link in the direct mail piece. You will have a harder time measuring the response rate for each tactic and determining how well each tactic is working for you.

> > > *What You Should Know* < < <

To review, here is what you should remember about the basics of online lead-generation advertising:

- When you create an online ad for lead generation—whether it is for search engine marketing, social media advertising, or display advertising—the ad is more functional and less emotional than brand advertising. Your goal is to generate leads through the ad, not to promote your brand.

- The online bid process is used in search engine marketing, social media advertising, and some forms of display advertising. In the online bid process, you bid a PPC or CPM amount that you are willing to pay each time someone clicks on or views your ad. In making this bid, you compete with other advertisers for the top rank or space for your ad. Depending on the tactic, only the ads with the highest bids will be placed either in front of your target audience or in the top spaces on a website or search engine results, where the Web user is most likely to see them.

- You should set a time period of at least one week for testing your ad campaign. In testing your budget, you should set a high daily budget (e.g., $1,000 per day) for each ad for the first week of your campaign. This helps you to determine the maximum number of clicks each ad gets per day.

- You can test different online ads against each other, and test your ads against different target audiences to see which ads get the best response from which audiences. On search engines, you can also test the schedule of the ad to determine the days and times when the ad gets the best response.

- You will use landing pages with all three forms of online lead-generation advertising, and with e-mail marketing and some direct mail marketing. The purpose of a landing page is to reinforce the offer made by the online ad, e-mail, or direct mail piece, and to provide a means for the Web user to sign up as a lead, make a purchase, or take whatever action the tactic is prompting them to take.

- A landing page should provide a soft landing—not a hard sell—for the Web user. Also, the landing page should be focused, and should limit the customer's actions to its intended purpose (e.g., allowing the customer to sign up for a webinar).

- If you are testing different versions of a marketing e-mail or online ad, use separate landing pages for each version. The message on the landing page should be content specific to the message of the creative that brought users to the page. Also, if you are using multiple lead-generation tactics as part of an integrated campaign, each tactic should have its own landing page or set of landing pages.

7

Search Engine Marketing

SEARCH ENGINE MARKETING (SEM) is one of the most cost-effective lead-generation tactics. It's also one of the most accountable, in that the search engines offer in-depth data about the performance of your SEM ads. You can use this data to your benefit to analyze your results and to measure the success of your SEM campaign.

In addition, search engine marketing is one of the most scalable lead-generation tactics. You can start an SEM campaign with as little as $50 and get results very quickly. If your early SEM efforts show promise, you can easily scale up your campaign to post additional ads and increase your results. If search engine marketing isn't already in your menu of lead-generation tactics, you should make it a staple of any future lead-generation campaigns.

SEM enables you to serve up an ad for any search result on a search engine. In general, when someone uses keywords to search for a product or service (e.g., "security cameras," "light industrial staffing services"), the search engine presents them with a list of organic search results. But search engine marketing ads related to that search term also appear in the ad spaces above and to the right-hand side of the organic search results. Usually, two or three ads appear above the organic results list, while another 5 to 10 appear in the right margins of the webpage.

Search engine marketing may help you to attract customers in your target audience who are ready to buy, or who may have a reason to buy soon. A potential customer who accesses your SEM ad on a search engine is *actively searching* for your type of product or service. If you place an ad on the search engine, you may be able to place your product or service in their consideration set. At the very least, you will achieve brand exposure. Potential customers will be aware that your company and its products or services exist.

SEM vs. SEO

SEM should not be confused with search engine optimization (SEO). SEO is the practice of using keywords in strategic places on your website (in the page title, content, headings, etc.), so that the site or webpage gets a higher organic ranking in search results on a search engine. Although SEO can be used for lead generation, you will get quicker results and will generate more reliable leads using search engine marketing ads.

I won't talk much about SEO in this book, because I don't consider it a standard, quantifiable lead-generation tactic. Yes, SEO can be used as a lead-generation tool, just as billboards and TV/radio advertising can be used for that purpose. But the primary function of SEO is to increase your site's ranking in "natural search" results, not to generate leads.

SEO is a very unreliable way to produce leads because the placement of your website in "natural, organic search" is largely out of your control. The goal of SEO is to convince the search engine bots—the programs that index your website—that your webpage is the most relevant one for the keywords being searched. You can work on SEO for months, and your site may still not get the "natural search" traffic you want. Search engines like Google constantly change their algorithms so that search results can't be fixed or manipulated by savvy marketers like us. This makes SEO a cat-and-mouse game that you can never be sure of winning.

Also, it's very hard to quantify SEO as a lead-generation tool because you can't be sure how many leads actually came from your SEO efforts. For example, suppose someone visits your site and signs up as a lead. How do you tell whether that person found you on a search engine thanks to SEO, or visited your site after seeing your latest billboard ad or hearing about your company from a friend? Perhaps a combination of these factors led the person to visit your site. Measuring your lead-generation results with SEO is very difficult, whereas, with SEM, the number of leads you get from the tactic is very easy to measure.

The main element that SEM shares with SEO is the concept of using keywords and keyword phrases to allow a site or ad to rank higher in search results. The difference is, with SEM, you pay for the privilege of having your ad placed in the "ad spaces" at the top or side of the list of natural/organic search results. This way, your ad will be one of the first results that searchers notice when they search for those keywords.

As a marketer, you bid a PPC rate (i.e., $2.50 per click) for any keywords that you think your potential customer will enter when searching for your type of product or service. Of course, you are also competing with other marketers who are bidding PPC rates on the same keywords or keyword phrases. The SEM ads with the highest PPC bids get the highest ranking in search results. Ads with lower bids may be displayed on the second or third page of search results, where they are less likely to be seen. (Or the lower-bidding ads may not even be displayed at all.) So the higher a PPC rate you can bid on a keyword or keyword phrase, the more likely your SEM ad is to be displayed in search engine results.

Google vs. Bing: How It Works

Ten years ago, you could use SEM on a dozen or more search engines. Today, the only ones worth caring about are Google and Bing. In the past 10 years, Google has become so widely used that it has virtually wiped out all of its search engine competitors. When someone wants to search for a product or service on the Web, they say to themselves, "I'll Google it!"

At this point, Google represents roughly 80% of all search engine traffic on the Internet. Bing represents the other 20%, but is growing fast. (We have yet to see if "I'll Bing it!" will become another widely used Internet verb phrase.)

Google's brand name for its SEM advertising program is Google AdWords. The company also uses the AdWords brand to refer to the key-words and keyword phrases that you bid on when posting an SEM or display ad on Google. Microsoft's brand name for its SEM advertising program on Bing is Microsoft AdCenter.

Getting Started

You can open an SEM account on Google or Bing very easily. All you need is $5 (the initial fee for opening the account), and a credit or debit card. (To open an SEM account, click the "Advertising Programs" link at the bottom of Google's main page, or the "Advertising" link at the bottom of Bing's main page. This will take you to either Google AdWords or Microsoft AdCenter, respectively.)

There is not enough room in this chapter to explore all the functions of Google's or Bing's SEM ad platforms. Fortunately, both Google and Bing provide tutorials on their SEM ad platforms that will show you how to build effective ads. These tutorials are extremely easy to understand, and are updated frequently to include the latest features of the platforms. I strongly recommend that anyone who wants to do SEM on Google or Bing should go through the platform tutorials first.

In addition, there are often local classes available, taught by SEM experts or certified Google or Bing partners who will teach you how to create effective SEM ads and campaigns. Search the Internet for SEM ad classes available in your area. (I recently attended a day seminar, sponsored by Google, on how to create effective SEM ads. The seminar was hosted at a local hotel by one of their certified partners.)

One more thing to mention: As with any other online lead-generation marketing campaign, make sure your landing page is ready to go before you start building your SEM ad. Always remember to tie your landing page to the theme that runs through the SEM ad in question. (See the section on landing pages in Chapter 6 for more details.)

Planning Your SEM Campaign

Before you start an SEM campaign, you should take some time to plan it. You should break down your campaign by various ad groups. *Ad groups* are groups of SEM ads that run at the same time on the same search engine for the same products.

For example, if you are selling shoes online, you may have two SEM ads for the same pair of shoes, each with a different offer. You may have a "50% off one pair of shoes" ad and a "Buy one pair, get a second pair free" ad. Both ads will run on the same search engine (e.g., Google) during the same time period (e.g., the first two weeks of your campaign). By running two or more ads simultaneously, you have the opportunity to do various forms of testing, such as A/B split testing, to see which ad gets the better response. (More on testing later in this chapter.)

SEM and Your Target Customer

Unlike social media sites like Facebook, search engines can't collect demographic data from their users. So you don't have the ability to target SEM ads to a specific demographic group as accurately as you can with other online lead-generation tactics like social advertising. For example, you can't target your SEM ad to appear on search results for "unmarried females, ages 35–45, who own their own homes."

In SEM, the search engine user defines the marketing experience, and controls which types of SEM ads will appear with their search results. When they enter a search keyword or keyword phrase (e.g., "inexpensive wireless routers"), the search engine will choose to display SEM ads based on those keywords. The search engine has no idea whether the person searching for "inexpensive wireless routers" is male or female, ages 25, or 35, or 65. It only knows that these keywords represent a particular interest that the user is searching for at that time.

Choosing Your Keywords

You should know which keywords your target audience is most likely to use when searching for your types of products or services. Before creating your SEM ads, make a list of all the relevant search terms that you think your potential customer might use in a Web search.

The SEM ad platforms on Google and Bing provide keyword tools that suggest keywords and phrases, based on your initial inputs and on actual historical search results. In the campaign setup phase, when you start to enter keywords (e.g., "security cameras"), the keyword tools give you a list of additional popular search keywords and phrases that people use when searching for that type of product or service (e.g., "security systems," "business security systems," "business surveillance systems," etc.). Using and bidding on these keywords and phrases allows your SEM ad to appear in a broader range of search results, and allows more search engine users to see the ad.

The number of search keywords you use for a particular SEM ad is limited only by your total budget for PPC rates and by how high you're willing to bid on each keyword. You can attach a thousand keywords and/or phrases to a single ad if you have the budget to bid for that number. In general, the more keywords you bid for, the more your SEM ad will appear in search results, and the better the response to the ad will be.

General keywords tend to command higher PPC rates, because more SEM ads are competing for those search terms. But specific search terms tend to command lower rates, because not every advertiser is bidding for those particular keyword combinations. Therefore, the more specific you get with your keywords and phrases, the lower the PPC rates will be for them, and the lower your bids will need to be.

Specific keyword phrases are called *long-tail keywords*. The longer they are, the more specific they are. The greater the specification, the greater success you will have in attracting potential customers who search specifically for what you offer.

For example, say you are a real estate company in Seattle that specializes in office space and commercial real estate. If you bid on the keywords "office space," "office Realtor," and "commercial real estate," you might need to bid a very high PPC rate (e.g., $4.50 per click) to get your SEM ad displayed in search results for those keywords. Your SEM ad may be competing with ads from hundreds of other office Realtors who are bidding on those same keywords.

However, if you bid on the keywords "office space in Seattle" or "commercial real estate in Seattle," you've narrowed the focus of your target audience to people who are looking for office space in the Seattle area. You can probably bid a lower PPC rate (e.g., $2.50 per click) for these terms. But you will still be competing with other office Realtors in Seattle who are bidding PPC rates to get their SEM ads placed in the search results for these terms.

But let's imagine that your commercial real estate firm specializes in office space for medical and dental practitioners in the Seattle area. If you bid a PPC rate for keywords like "medical office space in Seattle" and "dental office space in Seattle," you may pay an even lower rate (e.g., $1.00 per click). Not as many commercial real estate firms handle medical and dental office space, and therefore not as many firms will be bidding for these keywords.

Don't be afraid to be very specific. When you use long-tail keywords such as "medical office space in Seattle," each keyword you include in the phrase will help to match your SEM ad to a search term used by a potential customer. This allows your SEM ad to rank higher in search results when the customer keys in that specific search term. This is key to making sure your ad appears to the most qualified customers.

Also, the more you specify keyword phrases, the lower your PPC bids will need to be. For example, you may decide to bid on keyword phrases that specify certain cities or districts within the Seattle metropolitan area (e.g., "medical office space in Green Lake," "medical office space in Bellevue," "medical office space on Bainbridge Island"). These phrases might require a PPC bid rate of just 50¢ per click because, again, not as many commercial real estate companies will be competing for these phrases.

If you wish, you can also bid on *related* keyword phrases to give your SEM ad additional exposure. For example, you might bid on the phrases "medical equipment supplies in Seattle" or "dental equipment supplies in Seattle." Medical and dental practitioners often search for these terms, so your SEM ad for "medical or dental office space in Seattle" will still reach your target audience when it appears in the search results for these terms.

But while the bid certainly matters in how the search engines place your SEM ad, so does the relevancy of the ad. Search engines will sometimes put lower-bidding ads above higher-bidding ones if the lower-bidding ads are more relevant. So if a customer is searching for "medical equipment supplies," a medical equipment ad will probably be served before your medical office real estate ad, even if your ad is paying more money.

One more thing: The Google and Bing setup processes give you the option to exclude certain keywords, so your SEM ad won't show up in search results when people search for those terms. For example, suppose your Seattle commercial real estate firm does not sell retail space or restaurant space. In that case, you can enter "NOT: retail" and "NOT: restaurant," using the keyword selection tool. Anyone searching for retail or restaurant space in Seattle will not see your ad.

Designing Your Ad

When you create your SEM ad on Google or Bing, you have a couple of options: a text ad or an image ad.

THE TEXT AD

Like most online advertising venues (e.g., social media sites like Facebook), search engines have very specific constraints for the ads that appear on their sites. All ads on Google or Bing must have the same basic elements:

- *Headline:* The headline for your SEM ad can be no more than 25 characters. Therefore, you want to make the headline snappy! You want the headline to tie in with what the client is seeking. Examples: "Medical offices for lease," "Most durable work shoes."

Note: Your headlines should be as dynamic as possible. Search engines allow you to incorporate search terms into your ad. So if, for example, you sell sports equipment, you can post keyword-specific ads with headlines such as "Tennis rackets 50% off," "Golf clubs 50% off," etc.

- *Description Lines 1 and 2:* You get a total of 70 characters—that's 35 characters on each line—to write your ad. On Line 1, you should give potential customers the basics of what they should know about your company. On Line 2, provide your call-to-action.

> **Note:** *You can insert dynamic keywords in the description lines as well. A good strategy is to pair keywords in the headline with keywords in the description line. For example, you can have a headline that reads "Medical offices for lease" and pair it with description lines that read (1) "Now leasing office space in Seattle," and (2) "Click here to view available spaces." Anyone who is searching for the keywords "Medical offices for lease in Seattle" will be more likely to get your ad in the results.*

- *The Display URL:* This is the URL that will be displayed in the ad. It can be a vanity URL (e.g., "www.seattle-medical-properties.com"), as long as the URL ties into your brand. Google and Bing will check to make sure your vanity URL is appropriate. (They do this to avoid scam ads. For example, a scammer might post an ad with a display URL that reads "workshoes.com." But when people click on the URL, it takes them to a porn site.)

- *The Destination URL:* This is the URL that potential customers actually go to when they click on the ad. It may be different from the display URL, especially for lead-generation purposes. For example, the display URL "www.seattle-medical-properties.com" might appear on the ad. But when customers click the URL, it takes them to a landing page where they must fill in their contact information to become leads before viewing the office properties on the site.

The destination URL is useful if you have different SEM ads with different offers to test. You can have different landing pages for each offer, and attach a different destination URL to each ad. For example, if you sell work shoes, you may be using SEM ads to test two offers: "Buy today, get 50% off one pair" and "Buy 1 pair, get 2nd pair free." You can assign a different destination URL to each SEM ad, so potential customers will be taken to an appropriate landing page on your website for each offer. But you can still use your company's main URL (e.g., "workshoes.com") as the display URL for both ads.

IMAGE ADS

Image ads are like banner ads. In an image ad, your branding message is embedded as an image. You can include your value proposition, brand, call-to-action, and other messages in the image.

Image ads have been around for many years in online display advertising, but they have only recently been added as a feature for search engine ads, and they are not yet as popular on search engines as traditional text ads. They are also more expensive. I recommend that you don't use an image ad on a search engine, because they don't work as well or attract as much lead-generation response. Image ads work better when they are displayed on content pages, which isn't the strength of SEM.

Setting Your Campaign Parameters

Once you create your ad, you need to set parameters for how you want to run the ad campaign on a search engine.

YOUR SCHEDULE

Google and Bing give you tremendous control over your ad schedule. You control the days and times when your ads run. This is called *dayparting*. For example, if you are running an SEM ad targeted at businesspeople, you can schedule the ad to run on the search engine Monday–Friday, 8 a.m.–5 p.m. If you are targeting consumers, you might have the ad run Monday–Friday, 5 p.m.–1 a.m. and Saturday–Sunday, 8 a.m.–11 p.m.

The Google and Bing dayparting tools can be extremely useful when you are testing two SEM ads against each other (e.g., a "50% off" ad and a "Buy one, get one free" ad), to see which gets the better response. For example, you can apply the same search term (e.g., "comfortable work shoes") to two ads. But you can use the dayparting tools to control how and when search engine users who enter that search term see each ad.

You might set up a dayparting schedule so that the ads alternate in rotation. (Ad #1 appears in search results when one person searches for "comfortable work shoes," and Ad #2 appears the next time someone searches for that same term.) You can schedule the two ads to run independently on different days and times (e.g., Ad #1 runs Monday–Friday, 8 a.m.–5 p.m., and Ad #2 runs Friday–Sunday, 5 p.m.–1 a.m.).

You can pause one ad while the second ad continues to run. Or you can pause both ads if you need to, until you decide to resume the campaign. Also, after your ads have been running for a while, Google or Bing will give you suggestions on which ad to run at which times, based on historical data about how each ad performed.

You can also use the Google and Bing ad platforms to self-optimize your ad campaign over time. If you post multiple ads, you can create a schedule that runs the ads in rotation. Eventually, the search engine will start to serve your best performing ad over the others. For example, if you run two separate ads for "comfortable work shoes" in rotation, after a designated time period (e.g., one week), the search engine examines the click rates for the two ads. If one ad has received only 100 clicks, but the second has received 500, the search engine will start serving the second ad more often as the better performing one. During the second rotation, the second ad may be served for 15,000 impressions, while the first one is served for only 5,000.

GEOGRAPHIC TARGETING

Google and Bing allow you to target your ads geographically, based on an estimate of where searchers reside. But geo-targeting in SEM is not as accurate as geo-targeting in some other forms of lead-generation marketing. For example, you can get very specific with geo-targeting tools in social media advertising, where users often enter their location (e.g., "Hometown: Atlanta, Georgia") on their Facebook pages. (I'll cover this in detail in Chapter 8.)

But Google and Bing can't track users' locations when they search for a specific search term. (For example, you may be a Boston-based CEO who searches for "Los Angeles office space" from an airport computer terminal in New York.) The search engines can only "guess" about which part of the country the user is located, based on the IP address they use when they do a search.

Google and Bing provide geo-targeting tools where you can enter a city and state (e.g., "Beverly Hills, California"), a metro area (e.g., "greater Los Angeles area"), or a zip code (e.g., "90210"), and you will receive a map of the geographic area. You can then target your SEM ad to appear to users within that geographic area. Google's geo-targeting tool also allows you to create bundles of cities to geo-target your SEM ad. For example, you can create a bundle of cities for Southern California (e.g., Los Angeles, San Diego, Santa Barbara), and your SEM ad will appear to search engine users within the geographic areas of those cities.

If you want to geo-target an SEM ad more effectively, I recommend that you bid for keyword phrases that specify the geographic locations where you are targeting customers (e.g., "Office space in north Los Angeles," "Office space in Canoga Park"). This guarantees that your SEM ad will appear in search results for users in those geographic areas.

YOUR BUDGET

Google and Bing ask you to set a daily budget for each SEM ad you post, based on how much you are willing to pay per day on each ad. Your SEM ad will appear daily in search engine results until it receives the number of clicks equal to your daily budget. For example, if you enter a daily budget of $300 and a PPC bid of $2 per click, the ad will appear in search results until it reaches 150 clicks for that day.

If you wish, you can assign a lifetime budget. Your SEM ad will appear in search results until the number of clicks it receives equals that budget, regardless of how much time it takes. For instance, if you enter a lifetime budget of $1,000 at $2 per click, your ad will appear in search results until it receives 500 clicks. Your $1,000 budget can be spent in one day, 10 days, or 30 days, depending on the popularity of the ad.

Testing Your SEM Ad Campaign

As I explained in Chapter 6, I recommend setting a time period of one week for an SEM test campaign. This gives you an adequate time period to monitor the response to each SEM ad, and to measure and understand the collected data. Also, I recommend setting a high daily budget (e.g., $1,000 per day) for the first week of your campaign, to truly test the effectiveness of your ads. This is expensive, but it will give you an idea of the maximum number of leads you can obtain each day with your ad.

The good news is, after your ads have been up for a week, search engines give you a ton of information about how the ads are performing. The data collection tools used by search engines to measure the results for SEM ads are more mature than those used to measure results for display or social media ads.

The data that the search engines collect for each ad includes:

- *The Number of Clicks Your Ad Has Received:* This is a great indicator of whether you're getting the volume of clicks you want, based on the available budget. For example, if you're getting only a dozen clicks per week but were expecting hundreds, then something is not working with your campaign.

- *The Number of Impressions Your Ad Has Received:* This is the number of times your SEM ad appeared in search engine results and was seen by searchers. Impressions have value in building your brand, even though you don't pay for them with SEM.

- *Average CTR:* The number of times searchers clicked on your ad, divided by the number of times the ad appeared in search engine results.

- *Average CPC:* This is the average of what all marketers in your category of search results are paying per click. Average CPC can help you understand if you gave a decent bid for your SEM ad. For example, if you bid a PPC rate of $1.00, but the average CPC is $2.00, it means other marketers are bidding higher for your SEM ad keywords. You might consider raising your bid to $2.50 per click, so that your ad will place higher in search engine results.

- *Total Cost:* The total amount you've paid so far for this particular ad.

- *Average Ad Position:* The average position at which your ad is being shown in search results, in relation to other SEM ads, based on your bid. For example, if your ad normally appears in second or third position in search results, your average ad position may be 2.3. A 2.3 average may be good, because you might not want to bid for the top position in search results. (I'll explain why shortly.) But Google and Bing will give you advice on how much you need to bid to get that top position, if that's your goal.

In analyzing your results, this information can help you to determine how well each SEM ad is working, and how well the overall ad campaign is working. You can use the data provided by the search engines to determine how efficient and cost-effective each ad is in terms of bringing new leads to your organization.

TESTING YOUR SCHEDULE

The days and times when search engine users view your ad will make a difference in your response rate. A large part of success is knowing when your target audience is most likely to be online, as well as most likely to see your ad on a search engine and click on it. Fortunately, search engines also give you information about the days and times when your ads get the best response.

For example, if you are marketing a business product, you may find, after running the ad for a week, that you get the highest response rate on weekdays between 9 a.m. and 5 p.m., when businesspeople are more likely to be searching for your type of product. If you are marketing family vacation packages, you may find that you get your highest response on weekends, or even on late weekday mornings (e.g., after 9 a.m.), when parents are online.

I recommend, for the first week, you should run your search engine ad on a 24/7 schedule. This will give you an idea of the days and times when your ad gets the highest response. Once you know those days and times, you can use the search engine's dayparting tools to adjust your ad schedule. You can turn off advertising for the days and times when you get the lowest response and save budget during those low periods.

> **Note:** *The longer you run an SEM ad campaign, the more information the search engines will give you to help you improve your capability. Google and Bing give you a series of tools to help you measure data such as your CPL and your goal conversion rate. (On Google, these tools are called Google Analytics.) Although I don't have room in this chapter to explore these applications, I strongly recommend that you learn how to use them through the online tutorials provided on the search engines.*

A Second-Place Winner

One side note about SEM is worth mentioning. SEM is one of the few areas where finishing second place or even third place can be just as beneficial as finishing first. For example, say you have an SEM ad on Google, and you've bid a PPC rate of $2.50 for it. After a week, your average ad position is 2.3. This means your ad is consistently showing up in search results in second or third position when somebody searches for the search keywords you used. Google advises you that, to gain first position for your SEM ad, you need to bid a $6.00 PPC rate. This will put your ad ahead of the top bidder's SEM ad, which is normally appearing in first position in search results.

However, you may not want to spend extra money just to gain that top spot. The fact is, search engine users will often consider clicking on the second- or third-position ads in search results just as seriously as they would consider the first-position ads. Often, an SEM ad works on the basis of how well the ad is written, or how good the offer or call-to-action is to the potential customer who is looking for that type of product or service. If you have a good SEM ad or a great offer, you can often save money by bidding for second or third position and still get a great result.

Look at your average CTR. A rate of 2.1% is a very good rate. (Two out of every 100 customers who see your ad in search results will click on it.) You may be getting some quality leads from this SEM ad, enough to eventually provide you with a significant ROMI. Therefore, you might not want to bid a higher PPC rate to obtain first position in the search results. You may get just as many leads if your ad appears in second or third position, without having to spend additional money.

About AdChoices and the Google Display Network

Google has created an ad network—a network of advertising partnerships with numerous independent websites—called the *Google Network*. This network allows Google to expand the number of sites where it can post SEM and display ads.

The Google Network is divided into two components: The *Google Search Network* includes partner search engines such as Ask.com. When a user searches for keyword search terms (e.g., "new video games") on the partner search engines, Google supplies the search results with search engine ads—the same ads that would appear if the Web user were searching for that term on Google.

The *Google Display Network* (formerly the Google Content Network) allows Google to run SEM and display ads on thousands of independent websites. Google has agreements with website owners (who are part of Google's AdSense program) to run content-related ads on their sites. For example, a number of blogs and chat sites run by video game enthusiasts display SEM or display ads for video game products in the margins of their web pages. The ads usually appear in a small menu window with the label "AdChoices" (formerly "Ads By Google").

Note: *Microsoft has two content networks, the Bing Content Network and the Microsoft Media Network, which they use to post SEM and display ads on partner websites. However, Microsoft and Bing do not currently have the large volume and range of partner sites that you get with the Google Display Network.*

When you set up your SEM ad, Google's ad creation platform will ask if you want the ad to appear on the content-related websites of publishers in the Google Display Network. An AdChoices ad can bring you additional leads or sales by placing your ad on a webpage where the content is aimed at your target audience. For example, if you have a video game product, and you choose to have your SEM ad displayed on video game blogs and chat rooms, your ad may get a good response. The people viewing the ad on those websites are video game enthusiasts who may be looking for your product.

However, I strongly recommend that you do AdChoices ads as a separate ad campaign from your regular search engine ad campaign. The bidding strategies for AdChoices websites are completely different. Whereas you might pay a $2.50 PPC rate to place your ad on the search engine, you may pay only a 50¢ PPC rate to place an ad on a content-related site. Therefore, you should treat search engines and publishers' websites as two different venues, and have *separate SEM ads* for each venue (e.g., one set of ads for the search engine and one set for the content-related website). By keeping AdChoices ads as a separate campaign, you protect yourself from overpaying, and have the ability to sharply hone your PPC bid.

You should test two or more different ads on the AdChoices websites, just as you might test two or more ads on the search engine, to see which ad gets the best response. And measure the results of your AdChoices website ads *separately* from the results of your search engine ads, so you can see how well each set of ads performs on each venue.

A Final Word

For SEM ads, a best-of-breed CTR is around 2.5% of all your ads served to the customer in search engine results. If your CTR is lower than that, you might need to make adjustments to your campaign.

Fortunately, SEM is a very flexible tactic. You can pause your ads on the search engines, and either replace them with new ads or try bidding higher on certain keywords, so your ad appears higher in the search results. Also, the search engines give you a large amount of data on each ad to help you analyze and improve your results. So it's very easy and inexpensive to adjust your SEM ad efforts if you need to do so.

> > > *What You Should Know* < < <

To review, here is what you should know about SEM:

- Search engine marketing (SEM) is one of the most flexible, scalable, and cost-effective lead-generation tactics. In SEM, you place ads for your products or services in search results on search engines. When a potential customer searches for your types of products or services, your ad is placed in the ad spaces at the top of the list of results or in the margins to the side of the page along with other SEM ads.

- SEM ads use search keywords or keyword phrases. As a marketer, you bid a PPC rate for each keyword you wish to use with your SEM ad. The higher your bid for a certain keyword, the higher your ad will be placed in search engine results when searchers use those keywords.

- In planning your SEM campaign, you should divide your campaign into ad groups, that is, groups of multiple ads that run at the same time on the same search engine for the same products.

- In choosing your keywords, you can bid for as many keywords or phrases as your budget will allow. Search engines have tools to help you choose specific keywords in relation to your SEM ad. In general, the more specific the keyword phrase is, the higher your SEM ad will rank in the results when potential customers search for that term, and the lower your PPC bid for that phrase will need to be.

- In designing your SEM ad, be aware of the parameters that all ads on Google and Bing must follow. All ads must have a headline (up to 25 characters), two description lines (up to 35 characters each), a display URL, and a destination URL.

- The search engines allow you to set a schedule for days and times when your SEM ads will run, and a daily or lifetime budget for how much you want to spend on the ad. If you have a location-specific ad, you can also do some limited geographic targeting.

- The search engines give you a large amount of data about the performance of your SEM ad, including the number of clicks and impressions the ad received, your total cost for the ad, and the average ad position in search results. This data can be very useful in evaluating the success of your SEM ad campaign.

- You have the ability to refine the schedule of your SEM ad so that the ad runs only on days and times when it gets the best response. This is called dayparting. You should run your ad 24/7 for the first week to determine the days and times it will get the most clicks and then adjust your schedule to take advantage of peak days and times.

- You may not wish to bid for the first position in search results for your SEM ad. If you have a good SEM ad or a great offer, you may save money by bidding for the second or third position and still get a great result.

- You can choose to have your SEM ads displayed on affiliate websites that have appropriate content for your products or services. However, you should treat SEM ad campaigns on affiliate websites as separate campaigns from your ad campaigns on search engines so you can provide separate bids, measure your results on each venue separately, and understand how well each campaign and venue work for you.

8

Social Media Advertising—Part I:
Facebook and LinkedIn

TO BEGIN with, I need to make a distinction of sorts: In this chapter, and in the next chapter, I will focus on social media *advertising*, which is a subset of social media itself. You should not confuse social media advertising—or "social advertising," for short—with the use of social media as a customer engagement tool.

Social media has been around for over a decade; its origins go back to the online communities of the 1990s, such as Geocities and Tripod. But in the past few years, social media has become a full-fledged phenomenon, used by millions of people around the world. Many companies are now embracing social media as a useful tool to reach out to consumers. Advertisers and marketers use social media tools to generate buzz and activity about companies and their products and services. The most common tools used for marketing are blogs, Twitter, and social media sites like Facebook and LinkedIn.

For example, in social media, marketers make regular blog posts to keep their audiences in touch with the company and to drive traffic to the company's website, thus increasing their organic ranks on the search engines. Companies use tweets to make special offers and announcements to their Twitter followers, and they post special offers to their Facebook Fans on the company's Facebook page.

However, social advertising is a component of social media that is specifically designed for lead generation. In *social media advertising*, marketers post banner ads on social media sites in order to generate leads. These ads target potential customers with specific demographics, as defined by the social media users themselves. Companies pay for these ads on a PPC or CPM basis.

What's the difference between social media and social advertising? Simply this: In social media, you are "preaching to the choir," or at least to the congregation. The people who follow your blog posts, Facebook posts, Twitter feeds, etc., are already your leads or customers. They are your Facebook Fans, LinkedIn contacts, Twitter followers, blog followers, and other types of supporters. Even if they haven't made a purchase from you yet, they know your company and have a definite interest in what you offer. You hope they will share your blog posts or Facebook posts or that they will retweet your Twitter tweets to other social media users.

In this chapter and the next one, I won't talk about how to use blogs, company Facebook pages, or the social aspects of Twitter to generate leads (although some companies have used them for this purpose). In general, when you use Facebook posts, tweets, and blogs as social media, they are not traditional lead-generation tools. They are more like buzz-building tools, similar to public relations or word-of-mouth marketing.

But the purpose of lead-generation marketing is to acquire new leads, and that's where social advertising comes in. In a social ad campaign, your ads will be posted to anyone on Facebook, LinkedIn, or Twitter who falls within the demographics you select. As a quick example, say you are a travel company and you post an ad on Facebook for Honeymoon Cruises. Your ad will be seen by Facebook users who list their marital status as "engaged."

Social advertising allows you to reach out to potential customers who are not already your Facebook Fans, LinkedIn contacts, or Twitter followers, and convert them into new leads or drive them to sales. The most popular social media sites—Facebook, LinkedIn, and even Twitter—have all embraced social advertising.

In this chapter, I will talk about Facebook and LinkedIn, which are Web-based social media networks. I'll talk about the components that go into building a compelling lead-generation campaign on these two networks. I'll also talk briefly about advertising on MySpace and other social media sites. In the next chapter, I'll talk about Twitter, which is primarily a mobile-based social media network, and which has developed a slightly different model for social advertising.

Planning Your Social Advertising Approach

As you plan your approach for a social advertising campaign, you need to understand how social media sites like Facebook and LinkedIn work, as well as how advertising works on each site. Each social media site has its own parameters and policies for posting ads. Before you design your campaign, you need to research each site where you plan to post an ad campaign and understand the parameters and policies for each site.

This chapter gives you a short overview of the parameters and policies of online advertising for Facebook and LinkedIn. However, be aware that social media sites change their advertising platforms from time to time. Some features I describe in this chapter (and in the next chapter) will probably be out-of-date by the time this book is published. I have little doubt that, as time goes by, Facebook, LinkedIn, and Twitter will introduce new features to their ad platforms.

When you plan an ad campaign on a social media site, you should research the site's current parameters and policies for online ads. And if you regularly use social advertising for lead generation, you should keep yourself up-to-date as ad parameters and policies change over time on each social media site.

Researching Your Target Audience on Social Media

Social media networks offer a huge advantage to lead-generation marketers. They enable you to define and reach out to your target markets and customers with more precision and accuracy than most other advertising venues.

Networks like Facebook, LinkedIn, and Twitter provide social media communities for people with similar interests, backgrounds, and goals. People log on to Facebook to talk about their preferences, hobbies, needs, family activities, and choices. They share their personal likes and dislikes with each other. With LinkedIn, employees of different companies log on to make connections with other businesspeople, to search for jobs, to promote their company and its services, and to trade business ideas and information. Twitter (which I'll explore in the next chapter) allows people to share short snippets of information. Twitter users can follow conversations about topics of interest to them, and communicate with friends, business executives, and subject-matter experts.

The more these people talk about and share their interests in online communities, the more marketers know about who they are. We know their demographics, psychographics, and buying behavior. We know what they like or dislike, where they work, and what they do during their free time. Social media makes it easier than ever to research and understand our target audiences and their wants and needs.

The best part is that all this information *is provided by the community members themselves, free of charge to marketers.* As a result, the information provided by Facebook, LinkedIn, and Twitter users is probably more accurate than any other type of profile data you can get.

For example, when you fill out your first Facebook profile, the site asks you for your date of birth, marital status, and whether you have any brothers or sisters. The site then links you to your spouse and siblings. This is great for you as a social community, because now you can create links to family and friends. But what most users don't realize is that Facebook and other social media sites use this information to understand certain attributes about you.

For example, say you click "engaged" under "marital status" on your Facebook page. Every company that deals in wedding accessories (gifts, cards, shoes, etc.) and every travel company that sells honeymoon packages now knows that you're in the market to buy their types of products or services. If you say you "like" Pepsi-Cola on Facebook, Pepsi and other soft drink companies know that you're in the market to buy soft drinks or related merchandise.

Social media sites like Facebook don't sell the personal data they collect from you and other users. But they do profile users and their behavior in order to provide ads and information that will be more in line with the users' likes and dislikes. Facebook and other social media sites utilize the information they collect from users to offer ad space to marketers. This way, the marketers can easily identify the people most likely to buy their products, and can then post PPC ads that will appear exclusively on the social media pages of people within their target market.

This is a big improvement over traditional marketing methods, where advertisers must commission a large billboard ad and put it out on the highway where everyone can see it. Chances are their intended audience will see it, but so will a lot of other people who have no interest in that company's products.

Of course, even if you put an ad in front of your target audience on Facebook or LinkedIn, there's no guarantee you will get the response rate you want or the number of leads you need. But social media sites certainly give you the ability to segment and target your audience with more accuracy than ever before. This allows you to spend less time and effort identifying and locating your target audience, and focus on targeting your social media ad to a particular concept to attract that audience.

Advertising on Facebook and LinkedIn

Facebook and LinkedIn (and Facebook's competitor, MySpace) have set the standard for social advertising. They were the first social media sites to allow companies to advertise to users who were *not* in the company's regular group of Facebook Fans or LinkedIn contacts.

Facebook and LinkedIn had it relatively easy because they are Web-based social media sites. They were able to develop an advertising model based on a previously used tactic (banner ads) and a payment method (PPC) that had been used before in search engine marketing. Other social media tools—like Twitter, which works best on mobile devices—have had trouble developing an effective social advertising model.

Three Essential Steps of Web-Based Social Advertising Campaigns

There are three essential steps in planning and creating a successful lead-generation ad campaign on Facebook, LinkedIn, or any other Web-based social media site. (These steps also apply to Twitter, but in a slightly different way. See the next chapter for details.)

1. Research and define your target audience.

2. Create your ad.

3. Set up your campaign on the social media site.

Let's take a look at each step.

STEP 1: RESEARCH AND DEFINE YOUR TARGET AUDIENCE

You should research your target audience on the social media site where you plan to post your ad campaign, and define your audience in as much detail as possible. Each social media site allows you to select a *specific set of parameters* for your target audience, so that only users who match your criteria will see your ad.

STEP 2: CREATE YOUR AD

You create your ad and its call-to-action (CTA) to drive results and leads from the social media site. Social media ads need to fit within a certain paradigm in order to be properly displayed within the content and context of the social media site. Each social media site has certain parameters that you must follow in creating your ad.

As I mentioned in Chapter 6, online ads must be very short and functional. You have a limited number of characters for each ad (25 for the title, 70 for the message). Your goal is to create quick, compelling copy—including a value proposition, CTA, and offer—that will prompt your target audience to click on the ad.

STEP 3: SET UP YOUR CAMPAIGN ON THE SOCIAL MEDIA SITE

After creating your online ad on the social media site, you set up your campaign so that it will work to your best advantage and have the best chance of reaching your target audience. This is a very important step because it defines how you will spend your money on the campaign and how effectively you will reach your target customers.

In general, you set up your campaign on a social media site according to three parameters:

1. *Your Bid:* You must bid your PPC rate for how much you're willing to pay each time someone clicks on your ad (e.g., $2 per click). The higher you bid, the more likely it is your ad will be presented to the target audience on the social media site, over other ads with lower bids aimed at that target audience.

2. *Your Budget:* You must set a budget (e.g., $1,000 per day) for the maximum amount you wish to pay on a daily basis. The ad will run on the social media site until it receives enough clicks (e.g., 500 clicks at $2 per click) to reach that budget. (Some sites also let you set a lifetime budget for the ad.)

3. *Ad Schedule:* As of this writing, Facebook and LinkedIn allow you to set only a general schedule for your ad. If, for example, you wish to run the ad for 30 days, you can set a start date (e.g., April 1) and end date (e.g., April 30) for the time period when it will run. (I'll talk more about schedules for social media ads later in this chapter.)

Understanding the Ad Campaign Setup Tools

Facebook and LinkedIn each have their own *ad campaign setup tool* that allows you to create and set up your social ad campaign on that site. Although each setup tool has a slightly different set of options, they follow the "Three Essential Steps of Web-Based Social Advertising Campaigns" that I list above. They allow you to define your target audience, create your ad, and set up your campaign on that social media site.

In the following pages, I will take a *brief* look at how the ad campaign setup tools work on Facebook and LinkedIn. I won't go into too much detail because the options that the setup tools give you may change before this book is published. But when planning a social media ad campaign, you should first familiarize yourself with the ad campaign setup tools, and the parameters and policies regarding online ads, for each social media site you plan to use.

Defining Your Target Audience

Facebook and LinkedIn give you a set of demographic and psychographic search tools that allow you to define your target customers. You can search for specific features of the audiences you are targeting with your ad. Once you post the ad, it will appear only on the pages of users or groups that meet your defined criteria.

Some of the common categories that the search tools give you include:

Location Facebook, LinkedIn, and other social media sites allow you to do geo-targeting. You can target your audience according to a specific geographic location. If you know how to use them, these options can provide a significant advantage.

If you have a global or national product or service, you can choose to display your ad to every Facebook or LinkedIn user in a certain country (e.g., United States) or continent (e.g., North America). But if you have a more localized product or service (such as industrial cleaning or janitorial contracting services), you can set up your ad so that it will appear to social media users only within a certain state or city (e.g., Facebook users in the Atlanta, Georgia, metropolitan area). This is a major advantage for local marketers, because you know your ad is reaching Facebook users only in your area of service, who are close enough to buy your product.

But if you're a national advertiser, you can also use the "location" option to your advantage. You can customize your social media ad with special offers according to each location. For example, you can run one Facebook ad with a special offer for California residents and another Facebook ad with a different offer for New York residents. You can use different messaging and copy for the two ads to target them to users in each location.

Demographics Facebook and LinkedIn provide a series of demographic search options in their ad campaign setup tools. Setting these demographics ensures that your ad will be displayed only to people within your target audience.

For example, if you're marketing beauty products or spa treatments, you can set the "demographics" option so that only female Facebook users will see your ad. Or if you're marketing products or services related to colleges and student loans on Facebook, you can set "demographics" so that only high school or college-age students will see the ad. On LinkedIn, if you're marketing a product aimed at recent college graduates who are just entering the workforce, you can select "Ages 20–25."

Subcategories On Facebook and LinkedIn, the ad campaign setup tools include a series of filters that let you define a more specific target audience. You can narrow down the number of users or user groups who will see the ad by choosing specific demographic and psychographic subcategories.

Facebook provides the most detailed set of filter options for locating and targeting specific customers. For example, if you choose "education" as a basic category for defining your audience, you can target alumni from certain high schools, colleges, or professional schools (e.g., graduates of the Wharton School of Business). You can also target people who have earned certain types of degrees (e.g., people with MBAs).

You can target your ad to appear on the Facebook pages of employees of a certain company, such as General Electric. (If you are a nonprofit organization like United Way, this is a great way to target companies that match employee donations.) Using the demographic options in the advanced filters, companies can even target ads to their own employees who are on Facebook.

You can target your ad to people on Facebook according to their interests, birthdays, relationships, languages they speak, or any other demographic provided by the ad creation tool. You can target your ads to certain Facebook groups (e.g., Star Wars fans) based on their likes and dislikes.

LinkedIn lets you narrow your target audience according to several business-related options. You can target employees of specific companies (e.g., "General Electric"), or certain industries (e.g., "accounting," "electronics"). You can also target LinkedIn members with specific job titles (e.g., "CEO"), job roles (e.g., "accountants"), or job categories (e.g., "accounting," "sales," etc.). Also, you can target members of certain LinkedIn Groups (e.g., "Software CEOs' Group") or outside trade organizations (e.g., members of the Direct Marketing Association).

Creating Your Ad

Facebook and LinkedIn have very specific constraints for the ads appearing on their sites. All ads must follow the same four basic parameters:

1. *Title:* Each social media ad must have a title with a maximum of 25 characters (24 on Facebook), including spaces.

2. *Body Text:* Facebook and LinkedIn give you 135 characters, including spaces, for body text in each ad, to express your value proposition, CTA, and offer.

3. *Image:* You can create and upload your own ad image. In general, it must be a .PNG, .JPEG, or .GIF file. The image will be extremely small, but visible on the ad. Each social media site will shrink your image down to their preferred size (Facebook: 35 × 35 pixels; LinkedIn: 50 × 50 pixels).

> **Note:** *Social media ads give you very limited space for images, so whatever image you use should be related to the ad itself (e.g., a picture of the product). You shouldn't use your brand in a social media ad, since the point of the ad is to drive people to the product or offer.*

4. *Destination URL:* When people click on the ad, this URL takes them to your webpage of choice. If it's a lead-generation ad, you should provide a URL to a landing page on your external website that lets them buy the product, sign up for the webinar, etc. (You shouldn't use this URL to send them to your Facebook Fan page or company LinkedIn page, since this won't drive them to a sale or help you to collect them as a lead.)

Setting Up Your Campaign

In setting up your campaign, Facebook and LinkedIn ask you for several criteria:

1. *Your Bid:* Facebook and LinkedIn ask you to set a bid amount for your ad. Each site gives you suggestions on the amount you should bid. (See next section for more information.)

2. *Payment Method:* Facebook and LinkedIn both use the PPC method; you pay every time someone clicks on the ad. However, LinkedIn also offers a CPM option, where you pay each time the ad is posted on a LinkedIn website, whether or not people click on it.

3. *Your Budget:* Facebook and LinkedIn both ask you for a daily budget. Your ad will run daily on the site until the number of clicks equals your budget. For example, if you enter a daily budget of $1,000 and a PPC bid of $2 per click, the ad will run on Facebook until it receives 500 clicks for that day.

4. *Your Schedule:* As I mentioned, Facebook and LinkedIn allow you to set start and end dates for your ad. The end date option is useful for testing. For example, you can run an ad on Facebook or

LinkedIn for seven days, and test the response to the ad for that time period.

The Bid Process and Web-Based Social Media Ads

As I explained in Chapter 6, social media sites use a bid process for online ads. You can bid any PPC or CPM amount you wish to pay for your Facebook or LinkedIn ad. But, in general, if the social media site is displaying more than five different ads toward a target demographic, the site will serve *only the ads that represent the five highest bids.*

Fortunately, you don't have to guess. The ad campaign setup tools on Facebook and LinkedIn give you *bid suggestions.* When you post an ad on either site, you'll get a bidding range of the top five bids for your target audience, based on what other marketers are posting to that demographic. This bidding range gives you an idea of the PPC rate you need to bid in order to make sure site members in your target audience see your ad.

For example, say you are posting an insurance ad on Facebook, aimed at retiree homeowners who live in the Atlanta, Georgia, area. Any ads targeted toward those demographics will be displayed during the time those users are on Facebook. But Facebook will display only the ads with the highest PPC bids because, of course, Facebook wants to get paid the greatest amount of money. The cutoff will be the PPC cost for the lowest of five bids. If you bid a PPC amount lower than the fifth bid, chances are that your ad won't be displayed.

But Facebook's ad tool may suggest a bid range of $2.08–$2.54 for your insurance ad. So the highest bid for ads to your demographic is probably about $2.54, and the lowest is about $2.08. If you can afford to enter a PPC bid that is higher than the highest suggested bid (e.g., $2.60), you will almost guarantee that your ad will be the first one shown to users in your demographic.

If you enter a PPC bid that is only slightly higher than the lowest suggested bid (e.g., $2.15), chances are still good that your ad will be displayed to users in your target demographic. But it may be the last ad served to those users. Obviously, the higher you bid, the better you will position your ad to your target audience.

Testing Your Social Advertising Campaign

Social media sites make it easy to test the various elements of your ad campaign. Like search engines, each social media site has a set of data collection tools that give you feedback and analysis about the response to your ad (although the data analysis tools on social media sites are less sophisticated than those of search engines).

You can use the data analysis tools on social media sites to test the interest of different target audiences for your products or offers. You can get some feedback about the days when your ad gets the best response (even though your options for using this information are more limited with social media). Testing also provides insight on how to spend your daily budget for an ad, depending on the response it gets.

Also, although the ads themselves are limited to certain parameters (e.g., only 24–25 characters for the title), Facebook and LinkedIn allow you to create variations on your ads. You can post three or four different versions of an ad (with different titles, CTAs, etc.) to one social media site, and test which version or offer gets the best response.

Again, I recommend setting a time period of one week for a test campaign. A week gives you adequate time to monitor the response to each ad, and to measure and understand the data you collect. Also, I recommend assigning a *significant budget* (e.g., $1,000 per day for each ad) to the test campaign, to truly test the effectiveness of each ad.

TESTING ADS AGAINST EACH OTHER

If you have two or more versions of an ad, and you're not sure which one will generate the most leads from potential customers, you can test variations on the ad. Run all versions of the ad on the same social media site (e.g., Facebook) for a week, and see which ad gets the best response. You can also test various offers or CTAs to see which are most attractive to potential customers. For example, you can test a "Buy one, get one free" offer against a "Buy for 20% off" offer.

TESTING YOUR TARGET DEMOGRAPHICS

If you're not sure which target group will be the most interested in your ad, you can run variations on it for each group. For example, if you're not sure which age group would be most interested in your offer, you can create four variations of an ad, with messages targeted to people in their 20s, 30s, 40s, and 50s. After the four ads run for a week, you'll know which age group gives you the best response.

If you think people in various cities or states might respond differently to your ad, you can create ad variations targeted at different geographic locations. For example, you can create one version of an ad to target New York residents and another version for Los Angeles residents. You can test numerous combinations of target demographics to find out which groups of potential customers give you the best response. Since social media allows you to display your ads directly to people with certain target demographics, I encourage you to do as much demographic testing as possible.

TESTING YOUR SCHEDULE

Testing your schedule gets a little tricky with social media ads. Facebook and LinkedIn currently don't offer dayparting tools for scheduling specific days and times (e.g., Monday–Thursday, 5 p.m.–11 p.m.) when your social media ads will run. (Facebook *did* offer a dayparting tool in beta form a couple of years ago, but has since withdrawn it.) However, I think this will likely change in the near future, as social media sites follow the lead of the search engines, and adopt dayparting tools.

As of this writing, Facebook and LinkedIn both give you a daily response graph that measures each day's CTRs for your ad. But these graphs don't give you any information about the specific times on any given day when your ad gets the most clicks. However, you can still do some limited scheduling for your social media ads.

After your ads run continuously for the first week of your campaign, you can check the daily response graphs to see which days give you the best response. If you see that your ads are getting a minimal response (e.g., fewer than 50 clicks) on certain days (e.g., Monday through Thursday), you can manually pause the ad on the social media site so it doesn't run on those days. This saves your budget for days (e.g., Friday through Sunday) when you get a better response.

Or, if the daily response graphs show some fluctuation in your daily CTRs—if, for example, you average 500 clicks on Friday through Sunday, but average only 200 clicks on Monday through Thursday—you can adjust the daily budget for your ads on the social media sites. If you are bidding a PPC rate of $2 per click, you might set a daily budget of $1,000 for Friday through Sunday, and a daily budget of $400 for Monday through Thursday. Just remember that you will need to *manually* reset the daily budget, or re-start the ad on the social media site, every few days.

A Word About MySpace and Other Social Media Tools

A few years ago, MySpace was one of the three leading social media sites. It still offers a social advertising platform, but not many marketers post ads on MySpace anymore. In the battle for social media users, MySpace has been eclipsed by Facebook. It's possible, but somewhat unlikely, that MySpace will stage a comeback in a few years. Unless MySpace can reinvent itself as something better than Facebook Lite, it will probably never have the high number of users it once had. (Yes, I know. Apple was once declared "dead" and came back, but Apple came back because it developed new and innovative products to sell. As far as I know, MySpace currently has no products in development.)

But you shouldn't dismiss MySpace as a social advertising option just because it doesn't have as large a community of social media users as it once did. If you follow the indirect marketing theory (see Chapter 13), you should try to extend your marketing efforts into places where your competitors are not marketing. If all your competitors are marketing on Facebook, you may have success marketing to social media users who are still on MySpace. You will face less competition for ad placement than you would on Facebook, and you'll be able to pick up potential customers on MySpace that your competitors are ignoring.

MySpace is proof that, like lead-generation tactics, the social media business is in a constant state of flux. Currently, social media sites like Tumblr, Foursquare, and Pinterest are still trying to work out their social advertising platforms. If these sites develop innovative ways for companies to reach out to potential customers—or if some new social media phenomenon comes along—who's to say that Facebook, LinkedIn, or Twitter won't be eclipsed as one of the top three social media sites, the way MySpace has been eclipsed?

But even if new forms of social media and social advertising come along, the tactics provided in this chapter and in this book will continue to be useful for you. Even if a social media site comes up with a slightly different model for social advertising—as Twitter has done—you will be able to adapt the three steps of social advertising campaigns that I mention earlier in this chapter to work with the new model.

> > > *What You Should Know* < < <

To review, here is what you should know about social advertising on Facebook and LinkedIn:

- Social media advertising involves using social media sites to generate leads by posting PPC ads on the sites that target potential customers in specific demographics.

- Social media sites provide valuable insight on the demographics and buying behavior of your target customer. The customers themselves supply most of the information.

- In planning a social media ad campaign, you should first familiarize yourself with the social media sites, with their ad campaign setup tools, and with the parameters and policies for advertising on each site. You should also research your target customers thoroughly on each site.

- In general, Web-based social media ads must have (1) a title, (2) a limited amount of body text, (3) an image, and (4) a

destination URL to take people who click on the ad to a landing page.

- All social media sites will ask you to bid an amount that you
  are willing to pay (e.g., $2 per click). On Web-based sites, the
  ads with the top bids have the best chance of being posted to
  the intended target audience.

- You will be asked to set a daily budget for the amount you are
  willing to pay every day (e.g., $1,000). Your ad will run until it
  receives enough clicks at that bid rate to meet that budget
  (e.g., 500 clicks at $2 per click).

- You will be asked to set a general schedule, including start and
  end dates for when your ad will run. Currently, social media
  sites do not offer dayparting tools, but on Web-based sites, you
  can manually pause and restart your ad during periods when
  you know you will get a low CTR.

- Test your social media campaign for a week. The Web-based
  social media sites allow you to run variations on your ads to
  see which ad or offer will get the best response. You can also
  test ads to different target audiences on Web-based sites.

9

Social Media Advertising—Part II:
Twitter Advertising

LET'S TALK about Twitter, the social media platform that everyone is, well, twittering about.

Since its creation in 2006, Twitter has become one of the most widely used social media networks ever. According to Twitter itself, over 1 billion people now have Twitter accounts. Over 140 million people use it regularly (e.g., within the last 30 days), and about 30 million people use it daily, generating over 300 million tweets and 1.6 billion search queries per day.

Twitter applies the concept of *microblogging* to a social media platform. When you tweet and retweet on Twitter, you share text messages with a circle of Twitter followers, instead of one-on-one with individuals. You can send out quick thoughts or opinions (of 140 characters or less), get updates from people you are following, and follow Twitter Trends to see the most popular subjects that people are talking about.

You could say that Twitter's rapid success is due to its being the right medium, created for the right venue at the right time. Its development as a social media tool coincided with the skyrocketing use of mobile devices, and Twitter became the ideal platform for on-the-go social media interaction. Although it can be used on the Web, most people prefer to use Twitter on their iPhones, iPads, Androids, and Blackberries. Twitter makes it easy for people to share thoughts and have quick-snippet conversations with their peers, without getting too distracted from the things they need to do today (which can happen sometimes when you log on to Facebook).

Twitter has proven itself valuable in spreading the word on news and events. For example, the 2011 Arab Spring revolution in Egypt is sometimes referred to as the "Twitter Revolution." During the uprising, the Mubarak government shut down all traditional news sources. The revolutionaries were cut off from normal sources of information that could tell them what was happening in the country, and whether their protests were having an effect. But people were still able to get their news from Twitter. They relied on tweets to figure out what was going on from minute to minute, to organize protests, and to send word about where the next rallies and events would be held. Twitter became a recognized vehicle for communication and was cited as a major factor in the success of the revolution.

In the business world, you can use Twitter to spread news about your company much faster than you can by e-mail. For example, say your company has created a new application for the iPhone or iPad. You can send out a tweet, and everyone who follows you will get the news instantly, and may retweet that information to all their friends. You can also use Twitter to follow the feeds of CEOs and executives at other companies, to track emerging trends in various industries, and to get advice from industry experts.

But since Twitter came out, people and companies have been struggling with the idea of how to use it as a lead-generation marketing tool. It's easy to send out tweets with special offers to people who are *already* following your company's Twitter feed. But how do you use Twitter to reach out to potential customers who aren't yet subscribers?

The Beginnings of Twitter Marketing

At one point, many companies thought they could use Twitter for marketing simply by setting up a company Twitter account, or by having their CEO set up a Twitter account. If they could get a million people to subscribe to their company Twitter feed, or to follow the CEO or other executives' Twitter feeds, they could use that network to market their products or services.

The problem is, unless you're a multibillion-dollar company like Apple, which is continuously coming out with new, innovative products that everyone wants, it's very hard to get millions of people to follow you on Twitter. And unless you have a world-famous industry leader like Bill Gates or Steve Ballmer on your team, it's hard to build a huge Twitter following for your CEO. Even if they have a need for your types of products or services, most potential customers are not that interested in the inner workings of your company, or in the everyday activities of your executives. They don't feel the need to follow you on Twitter, unless they know you're going to continuously offer new products or deals that they will want or can use.

It's funny, but Twitter is still considered an entertainment tool by most people who use it. The people with the most Twitter followers are celebrities, and some celebrities have figured out ways to profit from their high following. When Ashton Kutcher learned he was the first person to have 1 million Twitter followers, he started a company to sell his influence through Twitter. For $25,000, he would tweet his endorsement of products, businesses, or trends (e.g., "Just bought a pair of NextHotBrand sneakers. I totally love these shoes!" "Just ate lunch at FastBreak Burgers. Love their Triple XXX Cheeseburger Deluxe!")

These celebrity tweets work the same as celebrity endorsement commercials or ads. Unfortunately, they work best with broad appeal, nationwide-brand consumer products from companies like Coca-Cola who have lots of money to blow on Twitter endorsements. For companies like Motorola, New York Life, or John Deere, celebrity tweets aren't going to be very effective in marketing your products or services. (Although I personally think it might be funny to see Ashton Kutcher send out a tweet—"Just bought a John Deere wheat thresher. I think everyone should have one!"—and then watch his millions of followers stampede to their local John Deere dealership to buy one.)

Twitter for Business and Promoted Products

As I explained in the previous chapter, when companies use tweets to advertise their products or services to Twitter followers, it's not really lead-generation marketing. It's more like a high-tech form of word-of-mouth marketing, where you're sending out special offers to circles of people who are *already* your customers or leads.

But just before finishing this book, I discovered that Twitter actually has an advertising program—Twitter for Business—that you can use for lead-generation purposes. This program uses an advertising model that is very different from the model used by Web-based social media sites.

Twitter for Business has been offered since 2010, but is not widely advertised, so many advertisers haven't heard about it. The program offers Promoted Products, a series of marketing tools that enable your company to reach out to Twitter users outside your regular group of Twitter followers, and to turn them into followers and possibly into leads.

Twitter's Promoted Products include:

• Promoted Twitter Accounts

• Promoted Tweets

• Promoted Trends

In general, Twitter's Promoted Products works something like SEM, where you bid a PPC rate to have your SEM ad placed at the top of search results when users search for certain keywords (e.g., "boat insurance," "accounting software"). With Twitter, you bid to have your Promoted Accounts, Promoted Tweets, or Promoted Trends placed where Twitter users will see them. (Where they will appear on Twitter depends on which type of Promoted Products you use.)

Let's look at each of the Promoted Products, how they work, and how they can be used for lead-generation marketing.

PROMOTED ACCOUNTS

If you're a regular tweeter, you know that, when you log on to your Twitter home page, your "Who to Follow" column gives you suggestions about which Twitter feeds to subscribe to, based on your interests.

Twitter's Promoted Accounts lets you promote your company Twitter account, or a CEO's account, or other innovative executives' accounts. (For lead-generation, a company Twitter account is probably your best choice.) Your Promoted Account will be displayed at the very top of the "Who to Follow" columns of Twitter users who are not yet your subscribers, but who may have an interest in your company or its products or services. Your goal is to increase the number of subscribers to your company account, and thus increase the number of Twitter followers who will follow you regularly in order to take advantage of your tweeted special offers.

Once Twitter users click the "Follow" link to subscribe to your Promoted Account, it should be fairly easy to turn them into actual customers or leads. You might send them a personal tweet with a special offer (e.g., "Buy today, get 20% off accounting software"), or with a link to a landing page where they can sign up to receive e-mail offers from your company. Or, if they are now following the Twitter feed of your CEO or other executive, you can send out invitations to a webinar starring that executive.

PROMOTED TWEETS

Promoted Tweets are the social media ads of Twitter. You send out a Promoted Tweet with a special offer (e.g., "Buy today, get 20% off accounting software"), and it goes not only to subscribers to your Twitter feed, but also to unsubscribed Twitter users who may have an interest in your offer.

Your Promoted Tweet will appear at the very top of a Twitter user's timeline, so it will be the first thing they see when they log on to check their account. It will also appear on their Twitter profile page. Also, Promoted Tweets appear at the top of search results when people search for keyword terms (e.g., "accounting software") on Twitter, just as SEM ads appear at the top of search results on Google or Bing.

PROMOTED TRENDS

You need a brief explanation of Promoted Trends, just so you know what they are. A Twitter Trend is something that many people are tweeting and retweeting about. When you log on to Twitter, you get a list of Top Trends for the day.

A Promoted Trend is a one-day promotion of a special event that the advertising company wants everyone on Twitter to tweet or retweet about. For example, if Apple releases a new version of the iPhone or iPad, they may pay for a Promoted Trend to run on the release day, so everyone on Twitter will know about it. Or a movie studio may pay for a Promoted Trend to run on the day their latest blockbuster movie comes out.

Who sees a Promoted Trend? Everyone on Twitter sees it. And I mean *everyone*! All of Twitter's 30 million regular, everyday users will see the Promoted Trend tweet at the top of their Twitter timeline on that day, accompanied by a link to "Follow the Trend."

Promoted Trends are extremely expensive. For a one-day Promoted Trend, Twitter charges a set fee of $120,000. (That's right!) And it accepts only one advertiser per day for the Promoted Trend of the day. So you should use a Promoted Trend only if you have major money to spend and a very special wide-appeal event coming up, one that you think will produce a very significant ROMI for you.

Promoted Trends are not a form of lead-generation advertising; they are more like a form of brand advertising. In digital terms, a Promoted Trend might be the equivalent of hiring an airplane to fly over a city trailing an advertising banner. Yes, you'll get wide exposure, but you probably won't get many leads from it. Therefore, you shouldn't use it as a lead-generation tool, even if you have the $120,000 budget for it.

Getting Started with Twitter for Business

To use Twitter for Business, you must first apply for the program. Go to Twitter's home page (www.twitter.com), click the "Twitter for Business" link at the bottom of the page, and fill out the Web application. A Twitter representative will contact you to talk about your company's eligibility for the program.

Unlike advertising on Facebook or LinkedIn, Twitter for Business is not open to all businesses (although that may change in the future). It's more of a "Members Only" club. Twitter keeps a tight control of the program, and has very strict criteria for accepting companies as clients.

For example, Twitter requires that all companies that apply to Twitter for Business must have a *minimum* of 500 subscribers to their Twitter feed to be accepted. In fact, they prefer you to have *more than 500*. I would say that if you have 1,000–5,000 subscribers, Twitter would start to take you seriously as an advertising client. If you have 10,000 or more subscribers, Twitter would consider you a major client who could truly benefit from Promoted Products.

Twitter is selective, because the *targeting* of Promoted Accounts and Tweets is based on who your current Twitter subscribers are and their interests. (I'll get to how this works shortly.) But the more subscribers you have on your company or CEO Twitter account, the better Twitter is able to assess the demographics of the Twitter users outside your circle of subscribers who will be most interested in Promoted Accounts and Tweets from your company.

The Three Essential Steps and Twitter Marketing

As I mentioned in the previous chapter, Twitter's advertising model is different from the one used by Web-based sites like Facebook and LinkedIn. Although you can apply the "Three Essential Steps of Web-based Social Advertising Campaigns" to lead-generation advertising on Twitter, they are not a perfect fit. But it's important to understand how these steps apply (or don't apply), because they may affect whether you *really* want to use Twitter's Promoted Products as marketing tools.

TARGETING BY INTEREST ON TWITTER

Step 1 of the three essential steps—researching and defining your target audience—applies to Twitter, but in a *different way* than it does on Facebook or LinkedIn. Before you even contact Twitter to talk about Promoted Accounts or Promoted Tweets, you need to research your current Twitter followers. You need to know what kinds of people are subscribed to your company's Twitter feed, what their interests are, and, most importantly, *how well they represent the demographics of the target customers you're trying to reach.*

Twitter is an unusual case in lead-generation advertising venues. When it comes to defining audiences for Promoted Accounts or Tweets, *Twitter controls the entire targeting process.* As an advertiser on Twitter, you have almost no control over targeting. Outside your circle of subscribers, you can't target your Promoted Accounts or Tweets to groups of Twitter users based on their demographics, as you can with social media ads to users on Facebook or LinkedIn. For the most part, Twitter does that targeting for you.

Twitter uses what it calls "targeting by interest." They look at your current Twitter subscribers and their interests, and they place your Promoted Accounts and Promoted Tweets on the pages of Twitter users who are not among your current subscribers, but who have similar interests to those of your subscribers.

For example, say you're a major airline like Southwest Airlines. You decide to send out a series of Promoted Tweets, promoting special offers for discount air fares to various destinations (e.g., Las Vegas, San Francisco, Cancun, etc.). When you submit your Promoted Tweets, Twitter looks at the list of subscribers who currently follow your Southwest Airlines company account. Chances are that a large number of your Twitter followers will list travel as an interest, and will be subscribers of Twitter feeds for other airlines and hotel chains. Twitter then looks for other Twitter users outside your list of subscribers who subscribe to other travel-related feeds, and targets your Promoted Tweets to those users.

This is why your Twitter account should already have a large following (e.g., 1,000 or more subscribers). The more subscribers you have, the better Twitter can assess your subscribers' interests, and the more accurately it can target your Promoted Account to other users who have those interests.

However, Twitter's demographic targeting can also work against you, especially if you have too diverse a range of followers with different interests, or your target customers are not among the majority of your current Twitter subscribers. For example, say you're a nationwide marketing agency that services Fortune 500 companies. You decide to send out a Promoted Tweet offering marketing services. But about half of the 1,000 current subscribers to your company Twitter account are other marketers who follow your account in order to track trends in the marketing industry. The other half of your subscribers are from industries that you service as clients (retail, restaurant chains, auto, food and beverage, energy, etc.). Among your subscribers from these client industries, no one group of followers from any one industry has a real majority.

Based on this makeup of your subscribers, Twitter's demographic targeting system may end up placing your Promoted Tweet in the timelines of marketers who are not among your subscribers. Most of those marketers won't need your services because they are already marketers themselves. At the same time, the Twitter users you were hoping to pick up as new clients—people in the retail, auto, energy industries, etc.—may not see your Promoted Tweet, because Twitter's targeting system did not recognize them as being a majority group of subscribers to your Twitter feed.

Twitter's Promoted Products isn't the best marketing option for every company. If you don't think your current list of Twitter subscribers is a good representation of the types of potential customers you're trying to reach, you might turn to other options for online lead-generation advertising. But if the subscribers to your company Twitter account are regular customers, and if they subscribe to your account specifically to get your special offers, then Twitter marketing could work very well for you.

CREATING YOUR TWITTER ADS

Step 2 is to create your ad on Twitter. This step doesn't really apply with Promoted Accounts because there is no ad to create. When you promote your company account, Twitter creates the ad for you using an image you select (such as your company logo) and a "Follow" link that allows Twitter users to subscribe to the account.

For Promoted Tweets (and for any special-offer tweets that you post for subscribers to your company Twitter account), you should apply the same principles that you would to any other type of ad, within the usual Twitter parameters. For each Promoted Tweet, Twitter gives you the usual 140 characters, including spaces, to express your value proposition, call-to-action, and offer. You must also include a destination URL link to a landing page on your website. Twitter will automatically convert the destination URL into a "bit.ly" URL (e.g. http://bit.ly/offer1) to keep it short for you.

SETTING UP YOUR AD CAMPAIGN ON TWITTER

When you are accepted to the Twitter for Business program, you get access to a series of tools on Twitter's website that enable you to set up campaigns using the Promoted Products. Most of these tools are very simple. For example, a "Promoted Tweet" check box will appear underneath the regular field that you use to enter tweets for your company website. When you enter a tweet for a special offer, simply check the check box to mark it as a Promoted Tweet, and Twitter will target and place it for you.

> **Note:** As I explained, Twitter gives you very little control over which Twitter users outside your company account subscribers will see your Promoted Accounts or Tweets. However, Twitter's ad campaign setup tool gives you some limited targeting ability. For example, you can do limited targeting by location, targeting your Promoted Account or Tweet to users only in certain cities (e.g., Atlanta, Georgia) or in certain countries (e.g., the United States, Canada). You can also target a Promoted Account or Tweet to appear only on certain devices (e.g., iPhones, iPads, Androids).

A few other things you should know about setting up an ad campaign on Twitter:

Payment Methods Twitter has actually developed new concepts of payments for its Promoted Products. These concepts are similar to PPC, but are designed for how Twitter users interact with tweets.

- For Promoted Accounts, you pay a cost-per-follow (CPF) rate. In other words, you pay a rate every time a Twitter user clicks on the "Follow" link and subscribes to your Promoted Account.

- For Promoted Tweets, you pay a cost-per-engagement (CPE) rate. You pay a rate every time a Twitter user clicks on your Promoted Tweet, retweets it, replies to it, or marks it as a favorite.

The good news is, with Promoted Products, you don't pay by impression. You don't have to pay each time a Twitter user sees your Promoted Account or Tweet. You pay a rate only when a Twitter user *interacts* with the Promoted Product, which makes these marketing tools very cost-effective.

The Bid Process Like Facebook and LinkedIn, Twitter uses a bid process for Promoted Accounts and Promoted Tweets.

- With Promoted Accounts, you are bidding against other companies to see which Promoted Account will be placed in a Twitter user's "Who to Follow" column. Currently, Twitter recommends a competitive bid of $2–$3 for Promoted Accounts.

- With Promoted Tweets, you are bidding against other companies to see which Promoted Tweet will be placed in a Twitter user's timeline. Twitter currently recommends a competitive bid of $0.50–$1.50 for Promoted Tweets.

Your Budget As with Facebook and LinkedIn, you must set a budget (e.g., $7,000 for one week) for the maximum amount you wish to pay for your Twitter campaign. Your Promoted Account or Tweet will appear on Twitter pages or feeds until it receives enough clicks (e.g., 7,000 clicks at $1 per click) to reach that budget. You can also set a timeline (e.g., one week) for how long the Promoted Account or Tweet will run on Twitter.

Testing Your Twitter Campaign

Like Facebook and LinkedIn, Twitter gives you a set of robust analytical tools so you can measure the response to your Promoted Accounts and Tweets. The features of Twitter's analytics tools are:

- *Timeline Activity Dashboard:* You can measure the activity of your Promoted Accounts and Tweets on a minute-by-minute basis. You can track how many impressions you've generated, how many retweets, how many clicks, how many replies, and how many follows your promotions have done.

- *Followers Dashboard:* This useful dashboard gives you insight into your followers' interests, geography, gender, level of engagement, etc.

- *Conversion Dashboard:* Twitter has integrated conversion tags into their advertising platform, allowing you to track the activity of your Promoted Tweets all the way to conversion. You can track each click to your landing page, and which of those clicks converted to leads, transactions, or sales. This is very helpful in tracking your CPA on Twitter.

Again, Twitter controls the targeting process for Promoted Accounts and Tweets, and the scheduling of when those Promoted Products appear to Twitter users. So while you get great information from the analytics tools, you can't really use that information to improve your Twitter marketing campaign, the way you can use analytics to improve your campaigns on Facebook and LinkedIn. About the best you can do is to use the analytics tools to determine if Twitter advertising actually works for you.

You might run two or three test campaigns on Twitter to see how successful they are. If your campaign has a good conversion rate, and your Followers Dashboard shows that your Twitter ads are reaching the right demographics, you might continue using Twitter as an advertising venue. If you have a low conversion rate, and your ads don't seem to be reaching the Twitter users whom you'd like to have as customers, you might want to think about using other online advertising venues.

The one aspect of Twitter marketing that you do have control over is your campaign budget. As always, set a significant budget (e.g., $1,000 per day for each ad) for the test campaign to truly test the effectiveness of your ads. Also, let the test campaign run for one week, so you have adequate time to monitor the response to each ad and to measure the collected data.

A Final Word About Social Media Sites

You don't have to limit your use of these sites to social advertising campaigns. As I explained in the previous chapter, social media sites provide a unique and valuable research tool that enables you to tap into your target customer's mindset. By studying the people who respond to your social ads on Facebook, LinkedIn, and Twitter, you can gain valuable insight into the demographics, wants and needs, and buying behaviors of your target customers. You can use this research to your benefit in planning and executing lead-generation campaigns using other tactics, such as direct mail, trade shows, etc.

> > > *What You Should Know* < < <

To review, here is what you should know about social advertising on Twitter:

- Twitter has a program called Twitter for Business that you can use for social advertising. Currently, you must apply to Twitter in order to be accepted into this program. Twitter requires that you have a minimum of 500 followers of your company account to be accepted.

- Twitter offers several Promoted Products, including Promoted Accounts and Promoted Tweets. Promoted Accounts lets you promote your company's account. Promoted Tweets lets you send out special offers in the form of tweets to your Twitter subscribers, and to non-subscribers who have similar interests.

- In general, your Promoted Tweet must have a value proposition, offer, and call-to-action, and must be no more than 140 characters. You must also include a destination URL to take people who click on the tweet to a landing page. Twitter uses bit.ly to shorten your destination URL.

- Twitter controls the targeting process and determines which Twitter users will see your Promoted Accounts and Tweets, based on the interests of your current Twitter subscribers. Twitter's Promoted Products will work best for you if the subscribers to your company account are a good representation of the kinds of target customers you are trying to reach.

- For Promoted Accounts, you pay a cost-per-follow (CPF) rate every time a Twitter user subscribes to your account. For Promoted Tweets, you pay a cost-per-engagement (CPE) rate every time a Twitter user clicks on your tweet, retweets it, replies to it, or marks it as a favorite.

- As with Web-based social media sites, Twitter will ask you to bid an amount that you are willing to pay for each Promoted Account or Tweet. You will be asked to set a budget for the amount you are willing to pay (e.g., $7,000 for one week). Your Promoted Account or Tweet will run until it receives enough clicks at your bid rate (e.g., 7,000 clicks at $1 per click) to meet that budget.

- You should test your social media campaign on Twitter for a week. Twitter gives you a set of robust analytics tools to monitor the response to your Promoted Accounts and Tweets.

10

Display Advertising

DISPLAY ADVERTISING is the use of online display ads (also known as banner ads) to generate leads by posting them on websites that are frequented by the ad's target audience or that have content related to the ad.

Display advertising is the most widely used form of digital marketing. As I mentioned before, display advertising is the next step in evolution from print ads and outdoor advertising. The popularity of display ads is a direct result of the popularity of print ads. Many companies have shifted their advertising focus from print and outdoor ads to online display ads because their target audience is spending more time online. Today, display advertising represents the largest percentage of marketing budget that is spent outside of traditional advertising.

Display advertising is also the oldest form of online advertising. Online display ads first appeared in the mid-1990s with the creation of Web browsers and graphical user interfaces. What's interesting about display advertising is how it has evolved over time, just as the Internet and the digital world have evolved. Display advertising was originally used as an online brand-building tactic, but it has gradually evolved into a lead-generation tool. This makes display advertising unique among the tactics discussed in this book. All the other tactics (such as direct mail, e-mail marketing, etc.) have always been lead-generation tactics.

As I explained in Chapter 5, it's very hard to measure the effect that print ads (such as magazine ads) or outdoor ads (such as billboards) have on a customer. You can never be sure how many people have seen the ad, or how many bought the product as a result of seeing it. But in the Internet age, advertisers have combined online display ads with technologies that allow viewers to have an interactive experience with the ad. In addition, advertisers have added new technologies that track the number of clicks an ad receives. This gives advertisers a *measurable result* for each display ad. Thanks to this combination, online display ads have evolved into a powerful lead-generation tactic.

Adding More to the Ads

Display advertising is the most innovative form of lead-generation marketing. The ads themselves, the technologies they use, and the ways that advertisers present the ads to customers have also evolved over time. When the Internet began, display ads were limited to image ads with static images or brand logos. The ads had to follow restrictive guidelines: They could be placed only in certain areas on a webpage, the images had to fit into a certain box or profile, and Web users had very limited interaction with the ads.

But then, advertisers and Web developers started to introduce new technologies to display ads. They added features like Flash animation, audio, and embedded video, and created ads that can *expand on rollover*. (The ad expands to page size when Web users roll the cursor arrow over it, using their mouse or touchpad.) Web developers also created *pop-up ads* that pop up in a new window or as a page overlay whenever someone accesses a certain site. (These are now called "modal ads." Many advertisers don't use them anymore because Web surfers find them annoying. But they are still in use on some websites.)

Also, Web developers now have the ability to place a display ad virtually anywhere on a webpage. A good example is Pandora, an Internet music/radio site, where the background of the webpage displays video/animation ads for online games and products like Sobe drinks. Developers can customize ads to reflect the theme or content of any webpage so they will appeal to the site's regular audience of users. Display ads are now using advanced programming languages such as HTML 5, which allows webpages to better support audiovisual features within the ads.

In addition, advertisers are adapting display ads to serve new and emerging online mediums. The advent of smartphones and tablet computers has created new opportunities to exploit display advertising even more. You now have interactive experiences based on taps and touches instead of clicks, and new ways to create an interactive experience on the iPhone or iPad that happens from the time users see the display ad to the time they interact with it.

For example, Cadillac has teamed up with a website called Cool Hunting that promotes the latest trends and fashions in art, clothing, jewelry, electronics, etc. The Cool Hunting site offers an interactive app that promotes the Cadillac CTS and CTS-V coupes. Procter & Gamble's Pampers brand offers a "Hello, Baby" app that allows pregnant women to chart the development of their baby. Users can interact with life-sized images of a developing baby, plan events and doctor's appointments with a pregnancy calendar, and provide pregnancy updates to friends on Facebook. I'm positive that, in the years to come, we will continue to see further innovations and technologies that provide us with new and exciting ways to experience a display ad.

The Internet Advertising Bureau

A number of industry standards have been designed around display advertising. The Internet Advertising Bureau (IAB)—a nonprofit organization made up of 500 media and technology companies that are leaders in online advertising—has created a series of standards, guidelines, and best practices for how to set up and deliver display ads.

The IAB has standardized many elements of display advertising, including the different types of display ads (image ads, video ads, Flash animation ads) and the different pixel sizes, file sizes, and dimensions. They have also created standard contracts for setting up display ad campaigns, with specifications for how advertisers pay for display ad campaigns, and how website owners get paid for displaying ads on their site.

IAB standards have tremendously simplified the process of creating a display ad campaign, which could have been very complicated for advertisers. Often, websites that provide space for display ads base their standards for ads (in terms of what types of ads, pixel sizes, file sizes, etc., they will accept) on the IAB guidelines. Also, many websites and companies that specialize in display advertising campaigns use IAB standard contracts or variations of them. IAB standards change over time, and will continue to change as display ads evolve and adopt new forms and technologies. To get the latest version of the IAB standards for display advertising, visit their website at www.iab.net.

Five Steps of a Display Ad Campaign

Planning and executing a display ad campaign has five major steps:

1. *Research target websites:* You begin by researching websites where your display ads are most likely to be seen by your target audience.

2. *Choose how to approach your target sites:* There are several ways to approach target websites about purchasing ad space. In general, you can approach the websites directly or go through a placement agency. (I'll give you examples of the different types of placement agencies in this chapter.)

3. *Create your ad.*

4. *Deploy your campaign.*

5. *Test your campaign.*

Step 1: Research Target Websites

When you plan a display ad campaign, your first step is to research where and how to reach your target audience. Once you have determined the demographics of your target customers, you should research the websites, blogs, and independent "special interest" community sites (e.g., sites outside of Facebook) where your target customers spend time online.

Usually, of course, you develop a display ad (its branding, message, etc.) to appeal to the type of customer you think will be a frequent visitor to the site. (For example, if your target audience is financial investors, you develop a display ad for financial investment sites.) So it makes sense to study the sites where your target customers are spending time, and where your ads will be most appropriate.

I recommend you make a list of target sites—that is, sites that are frequented by your target customers, where you think your display ads will get the most coverage. How many target sites you have on your list depends on how general or specific your products or services are, and how many sites are frequented daily by your potential customers.

If your company offers general consumer products, such as auto insurance, you may find hundreds of general content websites where your display ads will get regular views from your target customers. If your company offers more specific products (e.g., plumbing pipes and fixtures) to a more specific target audience, your list of target sites will be shorter (e.g., home builders sites, do-it-yourself fix-it sites, trade organization sites, and industry news sites for the construction industry).

The best way to find the details of a target site and its audience is to download the site's media press kit. Go to the site, and click the advertising link that is usually located at the bottom of the home page. The site's advertising page usually includes a download link to the media kit.

A traditional media kit has four sections:

1. *A Site Profile:* This section describes the purpose of the site, how the site is structured, and what content sections exist on the various pages.

2. *The Audience:* This section gives information on what types of people visit the site and their demographics. It usually describes the typical age group, sex (male, female, or both), occupations, and other characteristics of people who spend time on the site. It may also have details about their buying behavior. (Many websites do surveys or polls to gather information about the people who visit them.)

3. *Specifications:* This section provides specifications for the kinds of display ads the site is willing to accept. It specifies the "ad space" locations on the pages (top of page, right-hand margin, etc.) where display ads can appear. It also tells you which content pages or sections on the site are available for display ads.

4. *Advertising Rates:* This section lists rates for display advertising.

THE DETAILS OF THE SITE

When examining a target site, there are a few things you should pay special attention to on the site itself, and in the media press kit. (I recommend you take notes for each site where you plan to buy advertising space.)

The Home Page and Other Pages Look at the content not only on the home page, but on the other pages of the site as well. Some pages may have content that is specific to your target audience. Your display ads may get a better response if they are served on these content-specific pages than if they are served on the home page.

For example, a "home builders" site may have a plumbing page that offers advice on home plumbing. If you sell plumbing pipes and fixtures, your display ad may get a better response on this page. If you are selling financial management software for 401K investors, and your target site is a business news site, your display ad might get a better response on the personal finances page than it would on the marketing news page. If you are selling laptops, your ad might get a better response on the technology news page.

The Current Display Ads Look at the display ads currently on the target site. Look at their size, shape, and special features (animation, video, audio, etc.). Note their content, branding, and message. You can get a sense of what types of ads work best for the site. This can give you insight into how to plan and develop your own display ads, so they will fit with the content and standards of each site.

Also pay attention to the locations of the ads (top of page, side margins, etc.). When buying advertising space from a target site, you may want to choose the location on a page where you wish to display your ad. For example, you may want to display your ad in the most prominent places, such as at the very top or in the right-side margins of the home page. (Advertisers sometimes call this "premium space," and it is usually more expensive to buy.)

Another option for choosing the location of your display ads is called "*run of site.*" In effect, you let the site owners choose the pages where your ads will appear and their placement on the pages, based on their unused ad space inventory. The run-of-site option is becoming more popular because it allows advertisers to take advantage of unused ad space on the websites, usually at cheaper rates. The site owners prefer to have ads running on any page, instead of blank space, so they will often offer discount rates to advertisers to place their ads on pages that currently don't have any ads.

The Pricing Structure The pricing structure of the website is usually listed in the "advertising rates" section of the site's media kit. CPM is the most dominant form of pricing. Many sites charge a flat CPM rate for every 1,000 times your ad is served on their site. In placing display ads on different pages, some sites may charge higher CPM rates for pages that get more visitors. (For example, a display ad on the home page may command a higher rate.)

Other websites sell display advertising space based on CPA pricing structures, such as PPC. Some sites may use an auction-based method, similar to the bid process in SEM and social advertising. On these sites, space for display ads is auctioned off to whoever bids the highest PPC rate. Other sites may use a pay-per-performance model; ads that get the most clicks get served in the best locations on the site.

Sometimes, the pricing structure you encounter depends on how you choose to approach your target sites. We'll talk about this in the next section.

Step 2: Choose How to Approach Your Target Sites

Before you approach your target sites, you need to make a decision on the question of "high-traffic vs. low-traffic sites." This question depends on how you want to spend your budget and where you think you can get the best response to your ad.

For example, you may decide to "go big" by displaying your ads on 5–10 high-traffic sites, where you know your target customers are likely to see them. Advertising rates on these sites will be more expensive, but you will probably get a good response. Or, you may decide to "go small" by displaying your ads on 40–50 websites with lower traffic that serve the same target audience. Advertising will be less expensive, but the response rate will be less for each site. However, you can maximize the overall response to the ad by deploying it on more sites. (You can also, of course, do a mixture of, say, 5 high-traffic sites and 25 low-traffic sites.)

You can approach your target sites in several ways:

1. Work directly with websites.

2. Work with content networks.

3. Work with ad networks that offer ad-serving tools.

Let's take a look at each of these options.

Working Directly with Websites and Content Networks

You can work directly with a website or a content network to deploy your ads. A content network is a network of websites owned by the same company. A single parent company may have a content network made up of hundreds of sites.

For example, InterActiveCorp (IAC) owns one of the largest content networks on the Internet, with over 50 websites dedicated to various online themes. IAC has cornered the market on online dating with sites like Match.com, OKCupid.com, and LoveandSeek.com. IAC also owns search engines like Ask and Excite, game sites like IWON! and Retro Gamer, and e-commerce sites like ShoeBuy.com and OutletBuy.com. All these sites are supported by display advertising.

Again, when you work directly with a website or content network, the cost of display advertising is usually based on a flat, non-negotiable CPM rate. If you spend some serious money, a well-connected website or content network may throw in some freebies that only they can provide. They may offer a free e-mail blast to promote your company, or put an article about your company in their monthly e-newsletter. Often, the more you spend, the more the website or content network owner is willing to give you.

Ad Networks and Ad-Serving Technologies

Ad networks are companies that have developed a network of advertising partnerships with numerous websites across the Internet. Ad networks give you access to a series of sites, and let you post your display ads on sites where the audience meets your target demographics.

Of the hundreds of ad networks, the most prominent are 24/7 RealMedia, Atlas Solutions, and DoubleClick (a subsidiary of Google). Also, the Google Display Network (formerly Google Content Network) allows you to post content-related display ads on websites owned by independent publishers. For example, if you're marketing video games, they can connect you with video game blog owners who will post display ads for your games on their sites. Visit www.google.com/ads/displaynetwork for more information on posting display ads through Google's ad networks.

Microsoft is currently offering placement of display ads on partner websites through two separate ad content networks. The Bing Content Network places display ads on commercial partner sites such as MSNBC and WSJ.com. The Microsoft Media Network places display ads on smaller, independently owned partner sites. Visit advertising.microsoft.com for more information.

Ad-serving platforms give you a lot of management and control over your display ads. The platforms include various ad-creation tools that enable you to create new display ads, store multiple ads in an online library, and post your ads on multiple target sites that have a partnership with the ad network. The ad-serving platforms also provide you with valuable analytics, so you can monitor the number of impressions and the CTR for each display ad you post.

On the business end, contracts with ad networks are often very easy to manage. You only need to sign one contract with an ad network. That contract then applies to every site that has a partnership with that network where you want to post a display ad. You don't have to sign separate advertising agreements with each content site.

DIFFERENT TYPES OF AD-SERVING NETWORKS

There are several types of ad-serving networks that I should mention here:

Affiliate networks connect advertisers with independent website publishers who wish to be affiliate marketers. An affiliate marketer will post a content-related ad on their website for a company with an eCommerce site. If someone clicks on the ad and buys something from the eCommerce site, the affiliate marketer gets paid a commission.

For example, an affiliate marketer may post an ad for Best Buy on their website. If a visitor to their website clicks on the ad and buys something online from Best Buy's e-commerce site, the affiliate marketer gets a percentage of the sale. Some of the largest affiliate networks include CommissionJunction, LinkShare, ShareASale, and ClickBank.

Lead-generation networks connect advertisers with a network of companies that provide ad space and promotions for products and services that complement their own. For example, LeadFEED (owned by TKL Interactive) has agreements with multiple publishers of industry and trade publications (e.g., *Aviation Week, Marketing Weekly, ITPro*) and with multiple advertisers in the same industries served by those publications.

When a consumer signs up for or renews a subscription to an industry or trade publication, the publication's website presents them with display ads that are targeted to subscribers within that industry (e.g., an *Aviation Week* subscriber may get an ad for a company that produces airplane parts). The subscriber has the opportunity to sign up, or opt in, to receive special offers from the advertised company, thus becoming a lead. The lead-generation network's interactive technology then sends the subscriber's contact information (which they have provided to the publisher for their subscription) to the advertised company. There are also consumer-based lead-generation networks, such as MyPoints, Point.com, and Swagbucks.

Trading desk agencies focus primarily on websites that use an auction-based payment model. These agencies act as a go-between to help you place your ads on sites offering the lowest advertising rates. Trading desks have created automated arbitrage software tools that continuously monitor a group of sites, based on the demographic criteria of your target audience. When the software finds an appropriate site offering the cheapest rate (i.e., a $1.00 PPC rate), it immediately posts your display ad on that site. If the rate goes up on that site (i.e., it is raised to $2.00 per click), the trading desk software will automatically transfer your ad to another site with a lower PPC rate (e.g., $1.25 per click). The goal of a trading desk is to find the cheapest site where they can post your display ad at any given time.

Campaign optimization agencies (COAs) are ad-serving networks that allow you to track the interaction and buying behavior of website users *after* they see your ads. COAs have developed tracking technologies that allow them to track a Web user's online movements after they view your display ad. This allows the advertiser and the COA agency to do "smart targeting," to post display ads that are better suited to a user's interests, even on websites that are not related to those interests.

For example, if a Web user views your Republican-targeted display ad on RedStates.com, the COA tracking technology targets them as (probably) being a Republican. Using cookies and IP address tracking, the COA platform can then serve Republican-targeted ads to them on nonpolitical sites. If the user visits a consumer site (e.g., Flowers.com, Gifts.com) where the COA agency has an advertising partnership, they may see the same Republican-targeted ad that they saw on RedStates.com.

Step 3: Create Your Ad

When you create a display ad, you need to be aware of not only the marketing aspects of the ad (the branding, CTA, etc.), but also its physical dimensions. You will need to create your ads so they meet the specifications of the websites where you plan to post them. Each website has its own preferences and guidelines for the kinds of ads they will and won't accept. These preferences and guidelines are usually listed in the site's media kit, and they usually follow IAB standards.

The good news is, ad-serving software tools allow you to use multiple versions of the same display ad. You can create different versions of an ad (e.g., a top-of-page banner ad, a side box ad, a logo ad, etc.) using the same images, message, call-to-action, and other elements in each version. You can then match the versions of the ad to different websites, according to the websites' dimensions and guidelines.

You must pay attention to five dimensions when creating a display ad:

1. *Ad Placement:* This is the type of ad you want, based on its location on the webpage. A few examples of ad placements are:

   - *Leaderboard Ads:* Vertical rectangles that serve as the full-length header or footer of a webpage.

   - *Banner Ads:* Vertical rectangles about half the length of leaderboard ads.

   - *Side Boxes or Skyscraper Ads:* Tall, horizontal rectangles that fit in the side margins of a webpage.

   - *Ad Boxes or Rectangles:* Box-shaped or rectangular ads that fit in the side margins of the Web content.

   - *Logo Ads or Button Ads:* Small ads that also fit in side margins.

2. *Ad Style.* The ad may be an image ad, text ad, video ad, rich media (Flash animation) ad, or mobile ad. Table 10.1 contains basic information on the different ad styles.

TABLE 10.1. Ad Styles for Display Ads

Ad Style	Accepted File Formats	Accepted File Sizes	Important Things to Consider When Creating the Ad
TEXT ADS	n/a	n/a	• You only have a limited amount of space to work with in text ads. Try to maximize the word count as best you can. • It's tempting to try to add phone numbers to your ad, but they rarely work and are considered skirting around the system.
IMAGE ADS	.JPEG .GIF .PNG	Max. 25–35 KB	• People have become desensitized to flat banner ads. Make sure your ad stands out.
VIDEO ADS	.MPEG2 .WMV	Typically 100 K	• What user action starts the ad video? Does the video run automatically when the user loads the webpage in their browser? Does it start on rollover (i.e., when the user rolls the mouse cursor over the ad)? When the user clicks on the ad? • Does the ad expand to a higher resolution when the video plays? If so, what user action by the user (rollover, clicking on the ad) will expand the ad?
RICH MEDIA ADS (typically use flash animation)	.SWF	Typically 100 KB, with the subsequent download adding another 200 KB	• Animation in Flash ads is typically limited to 30 seconds. • Average animation speed is 25 frames per second. • Does the ad expand to higher resolution when the animation plays? If so, what user action (rollover, clicking on the ad) will expand the ad? • Does the animation have sound? If so, what action (rollover, clicking on the ad) is needed to start the sound?
MOBILE ADS (for smartphone or tablet devices)	.JPEG .PNG .SWF (accepted by Android devices) HTML-5 (accepted by Apple devices)	Max. 45 KB	• For Tablet ads, you need to decide if you want to design an ad for Android or Apple. iPad and iPhone do not accept Flash animation videos, but Android does. • Apple devices support HTML-5 files, but Android devices do not. • What is the behavior of the ad? When someone taps on it, what happens?

3. *Ad Size:* The physical dimensions of the ad measured in pixels. A few examples of typical sizes are:

- *Logo Ads:* 125 × 50 pixels

- *Side Boxes:* 120 × 320 pixels

- *Ad Boxes:* 300 × 250 or 336 × 280 pixels

4. *File Size:* Measured in kilobytes, display ad file sizes usually have to be very small, so the ad can load quickly on the page.

5. *File Type:* This depends on the ad style. (Common file types are .JPEG, .GIF, .PNG., .SWF, etc.)

TRACKING YOUR CTR AND CONVERSION RATE

When you create your ads, you need to determine how you will track the response to each individual ad you post. In other words, if you post exactly the same ad on five different webpages, you need a way to track the performance of each of them. This enables you to measure the performance for each ad, and tells you which websites are giving you the best response.

For each ad, it's essential that you track (1) the CTR and (2) the conversion rate. Your CTR, in this case, is the number of clicks each individual ad receives on *each* webpage where it is posted. Your conversion rate is the number of people who take an action after clicking on each individual ad.

You can track your CTR and conversion rate in two ways. The most common way is to attach a tracking pixel to each individual ad and landing page. Many ad-serving companies will supply this functionality for you. For each individual ad, the tracking pixel reports back to the ad-serving software how many times the ad was viewed on the website where it was posted, and how many clicks the ad received.

Every time a potential customer clicks on the ad, the tracking pixel follows their click trail once they reach the ad's landing page. It then reports how many customers were converted into leads, sales, etc. You can view this information using the tracking software's analytics tools, and use the data to analyze the performance of each ad.

The second way to track CTRs and conversion rates is to create an individual, corresponding landing page for each ad you post. You can then attach an analytics program, such as Google Analytics, to each page. By tracking the number of visits each landing page receives, you can estimate the CTR for the corresponding ad. The analytics program will also tell you how many people clicked on or used the "special offer" conversion tools that you provide on the landing page for them to buy your product, sign up as a lead, etc. This allows you to measure your conversion rate.

Creating individual landing pages for each ad you post may be necessary if you are dealing directly with individual independent websites, or if you are working with a content network that doesn't provide analytics tools to track the response to individual display ads. If you create individual landing pages, each ad you post should have its own separate destination URL, which corresponds to its own separate landing page.

Of course, if you're posting the same ad on 60 different websites, you will need 60 duplicate landing pages, one for each individual ad. Fortunately, Web technology makes it easy to duplicate a landing page 60 times and assign a separate URL to each duplicate. (See Chapter 6 for more information on landing pages.)

Step 4: Deploy Your Campaign

As I said before, you should decide early on whether you want to deploy your ads to a small number of high-traffic-but-more-expensive sites, to a large number of low-traffic-but-less-expensive sites, or to a mix of both. How you execute your campaign depends on the method you use to deploy the ads on websites. If you're working directly with the websites or content networks, you will probably send them the ads so that they can post them on the assigned pages for you.

If you're working with an ad network, you will probably send them the ads (or they may help you to create the ads), and the network or agency will use their ad-serving software to post your ads on different websites. In some cases, the ad network may have full-service ad-serving software that lets you automatically post your own ads on their different partner websites.

Some websites and ad network companies require a hard copy for certain types of ads. For example, for video, rich media, and some mobile files, the company may require you to deliver your ad on a CD disk, instead of sending it to them by e-mail.

WHAT KIND OF CLICK-THROUGH RATE CAN YOU EXPECT?

The biggest problem that advertisers face with display ads is consumer indifference. Over the past decade, even as display ads have become more innovative and more fun to look at, the economics of display advertising have actually gotten worse. In the early days of the Internet, display advertising was new and interesting and rich. People had never seen these ads before and were curious about them, so they clicked on them quite often. You could sometimes see a *phenomenal* 15% CTR on an ad!

Now, if you're lucky, your display ad may get a CTR of between two-tenths of 1% to half a percent. In other words, for every 1,000 people who see your ad, only two to five people will actually click on it. As everyday Internet users, we've become so used to seeing display ads on websites that most people just ignore them. (I personally haven't clicked on a display ad in the last decade or so.)

In the early days of the Internet, it might have taken a hundred views of a display ad on a webpage to get one click on the ad. Today, it might take a thousand views. The good news for marketers is, people are spending more time online, and a popular website may have a million or more visitors every day. Therefore, an ad featured on a popular site may receive the million views per day that it needs to gain a CTR that makes it a cost-effective lead-generation tool. (Even if Web users don't click on it, they still gain some awareness of your brand or product just by viewing the ad.)

The other good news is, with the introduction of mobile devices, marketers are now creating innovative and fun-to-use display ads for iPhones, iPads, and Androids. These ads provide interesting and engaging interactive experiences for mobile device users. In addition to video and animation, marketers are now serving mobile ads that allow smartphone or tablet users to watch a movie, run a sample application or mini program, or even play a game. Mobile ads are now getting the same high response rates that regular display ads received in the early days of Internet browsing. Today, an innovative mobile display ad may get a 10–15% CTR!

Step 5: Test Your Campaign

Once again, I recommend a test period of one week for your ad campaign. Again, today's ad-serving platforms offer highly detailed analytics that allow you to see the response rate to your ads on different websites. You can use these analytics to improve the performance of your ads and your campaign.

TESTING YOUR ADS AGAINST EACH OTHER

As with the other online lead-generation advertising tactics, you should test ads against each other to see which gets the best response. For example, if you have a "Buy for 50% off" ad and a "Buy one, get one free" ad, try putting each ad on five target sites to test which offer gets the higher CTR.

TESTING CONTENT SITES AND YOUR TARGET AUDIENCE

Also, you should test various content sites to see which sites give you the best response. If you find an ad on one site is not giving you the response you need, compare the click rate for that ad with the click rates for the same ad posted on other websites. If the same ad is getting a better response on other sites, it probably means that your target audience is not visiting the underperforming website in great numbers. But if the ad is underperforming on *all* websites, you may need to redesign the ad, or provide a better offer, CTA, etc.

If you're not sure which target audience will give you the best response to your display ads, try testing them on sites that attract different target audiences. For example, if you have a product that you think might appeal to both married adults ages 40–50 and retirees 65 and over, you might pick five websites frequented by each target audience (10 sites total), then post your ad on those sites. Perhaps your ad will get a good response from both target audiences.

TESTING YOUR BUDGET

As with other forms of online lead-generation advertising, I recommend that you set a high test budget for your display ad campaign—$2,500 to $5,000 per campaign, if you can afford it. This allows you to find the maximum CTR, and the maximum number of leads, you can get from each ad. Again, a high test budget gives you room to test the true effectiveness of your ads, and to determine how many clicks each ad will get on each website.

Once the ads are deployed, the degree of control you have over your budget will depend on your approach. If you are working directly with websites, you usually negotiate a fixed price for posting your ads on the site, and a fixed time period for the ad campaign. (For example, you will pay $5,000 to have your ad on the site for six weeks.)

If you work with an ad network, you may be able to use their ad-serving tools to set and control budgets for each ad on each website, just as you do with search engine and social media ads. You can set a daily budget, a weekly budget, or a campaign budget, and your ad will run until your set budget amount has been reached on that site. (In reality, because pricing is usually on a CPM basis, you're setting a budget for the number of impressions the ad will receive.)

Some major ad networks give you the option to start or stop running an ad when you feel like it. However, on most ad networks, your ad will keep running until the set budget has been fulfilled or the agreed-upon end date of the campaign has been reached.

> > > *What You Should Know* < < <

To review, here is what you should know about display advertising:

- Display advertising involves placing online display ads on websites that are frequented by the ad's target audience, or that have content related to the ad. Display ads are the most widely used form of digital marketing and the oldest form of online advertising.

- Technology innovations have allowed display ad developers to add special features to the ads, such as video, audio, and Flash animation. In addition, display ads on mobile devices have provided fresh opportunities for marketers to reach their target customers with new and innovative ads.

- The Internet Advertising Bureau (IAB)—a nonprofit organization made up of leading online advertisers—has created a series of standards, guidelines, and best practices for how to set up and deliver display ads. Most websites that offer space for display ads have adopted the IAB's standards and guidelines, and use standard IAB contracts.

- In researching the sites where you want to post display ads, you should make a list of target sites where you know that members of your target audience are frequent visitors. Download the media press kit available on each target site for information on the site and its target audience, the site's specifications for ads, and the site's advertising rates.

- There are several ways to approach target sites where you wish to post your display ads. You can work directly with the websites themselves or with content networks that own a series of sites. You can also work with ad networks that have partnerships for advertising with various websites.

- When creating your display ads, you must pay attention to the dimensions of the ads in order to make sure they fit the specifications of the sites where you plan to post them. These dimensions include the ad product (e.g., a logo ad, a side tower ad), ad style (e.g., image, video, mobile), file size and type, pixel size, and any special ad features (e.g., audio, Flash animation).

- In deploying your campaign, you should decide whether to deploy your ads to a small number of high-traffic sites, a large number of low-traffic sites, or a mix of both.

- When testing your campaign, keep track of the response to your display ads on different websites to see which sites give you the best performance for your ad. You should also test different versions of ads to see which ads or offers get the best response.

11

Selecting and Targeting a Mailing or Contact List

THIS CHAPTER provides a short overview of some concepts that apply to *list-based lead-generation marketing tactics*, such as direct mail, e-mail marketing, and cold calling. I'll show you how to define your target audience for each of these tactics so you have the best chance of reaching potential customers with a need for your types of products or services. I'll also show you how to select a reliable *list owner*—a vendor who can sell or rent you a list of potential customers who meet your target criteria.

Both e-mail and direct mail marketing campaigns are based on mailing lists. For both tactics, a *mailing list* is a list of target customers who meet certain demographics. An e-mail mailing list includes the e-mail addresses of potential customers on the list, and a direct mail mailing list contains the mailing addresses of the potential customers.

Cold calling, on the other hand, is based on a *contact list*, which is similar to a mailing list. Because cold calling is primarily a B2B tactic, a contact list will typically include the name, company name, job title (e.g., CIO, CEO), and phone number of each contact. It may include other information, such as the mailing address of the company, the number of employees there, or the e-mail of the contact.

Defining Your Target Audience

When you begin a direct mail, e-mail, or cold-calling campaign, you first need to fully define the specifics of your target audience. This is a *crucial* beginning for any e-mail, direct mail, or cold-calling campaign. Your campaign will not be successful unless you reach the *right target customers* who have a definite interest in your products or services. Therefore, you need to define your target customers with as much precision and demographic detail as possible.

Once you define your audience, you give these specifics to a list owner, who compiles a list of names and contact information based on your target criteria. A list owner may have an initial list of, say, 500,000 names for a certain category (e.g., pet owners). But when you give them specific demographic criteria (e.g., higher-income cat owners who own expensive breeds of cats), they will apply those specifics to their initial list and give you a targeted list of, say, 50,000 names that match your criteria. (Some list owners may add a surcharge for targeting.)

E-mail and direct mail marketing allow you to get very specific in defining your target audience. For example, let's say you're planning an e-mail campaign to market a new gourmet cat food. You've determined your best target customers will be cat owners who want to give their cats the highest-quality food.

Which type of e-mail mailing list would get the best response for you: (1) a general list of pet owners, (2) a list of cat owners, or (3) a list of purebred Siamese cat owners? If you use the general list of pet owners, you may end up sending your e-mail offer for gourmet cat food to *thousands* of people who have no need for it (e.g., dog owners, fish owners, etc.). Using a list of cat owners will get you a better response, but you will still send your offer to many lower-income cat owners who don't spend a lot of money on luxury items for their pets.

However, when you buy or rent an e-mail list of cat owners, you can ask the list owner to give you a targeted list of cat owners who own more expensive breeds. Siamese cats are a high-class breed that usually sell in the $100–$1,000 range. Therefore, Siamese cat owners probably have a higher household income, and are more likely to spend extra money on their cats and their health. A new brand of gourmet cat food might be of interest to them.

Here's another example: Let's say you are sending out an e-mail offer advertising memberships for an exclusive tennis club. Do you want an e-mail list that targets (1) athletes in general, (2) tennis players, or (3) tennis players with $100,000 household incomes? When buying or renting a list of tennis players, I would ask the list owner to target that list to $100,000 income recipients. There may be many tennis players on the initial list who have household incomes of less than $100,000, but who would still be interested in the tennis club membership. But by targeting your first campaign to tennis players with incomes of $100,000 or more, you're increasing your chances of business.

With cold calling, your targeting is not quite as specific as it is with direct mail or e-mail marketing. But you can still define certain demographics for the potential customers you want to call. Again, cold calling is primarily used for B2B marketing. If you have a software product for accountants, for example, you might define your audience as CEOs of accounting firms with 100 or more employees.

Psychographic Targeting and Geo-Targeting

You can use other forms of targeting to narrow your audience on a mailing or contact list. You can use psychographic targeting to target customers according to their interests and buying behavior. For example, if you are marketing vacation packages, you might rent a subscribers list from a travel magazine. The demographics of the subscribers may be varied (they may be young or old, male or female, etc.), but the psychographic (they like to travel) is the same.

You can also use geo-targeting to narrow your audience by city, state, or zip code. Using zip codes, you can target it according to neighborhoods or ier routes. For example, say you own a regional chain of nail salons—— operates 200 stores across several states. You're planning an e-mail campaign to send out discount coupons specific to each local nail salon. You might rent a list of prospects from a national beauty magazine. For each local nail salon in your chain, you can establish a five-mile radius based on zip codes. You can then send out e-mail coupons to people on the list who live within the zip code radius for each local nail salon.

You can use geo-targeting in cold calling as well, especially if you want to break into a certain local market for your product or service. For example, say you want to target business owners in the Seattle metropolitan area. In addition to other demographics for the type of business you are targeting, you might ask the list owner to limit names and phone numbers on your contact list to businesses with area codes that operate within a 100-mile radius of Seattle (e.g., 206, 425, 253, 360).

Try to select as many different filters as you can for a mailing list or contact list. For example, if you are marketing a small business product, you might select one city (e.g., Los Angeles), one group of potential customers (e.g., CEOs and company founders), and one company size (e.g., companies with 500 employees or less). You should have these filters ready when you contact the list owners to buy or rent e-mail lists. The more targeted you are, the better response you will get, and the more cost-effective your campaign will be.

Expanding Your Target Universe

You need to make sure that any list you buy or rent will give you a large enough target universe to be meaningful to you. For example, say you are planning an e-mail marketing campaign for a business software product. You decide to rent a list of subscriber e-mail addresses from a well-known software magazine. You want to target large companies, so you ask the list owner (in this case, the magazine publisher) to give you a targeted list of e-mail addresses for chief marketing officers (CMOs) at companies with 250,000+ employees.

But after the list owner applies your target audience filters to their complete list of 500,000 subscribers, they come back to you with only 500 subscribers who are CMOs of companies of that size. E-mail marketing (as I'll explain in Chapter 12) is a large numbers game, and 500 addresses is usually not a large enough universe to run a successful e-mail campaign (or even a test of one).

In this case, you can do several things. First, you can widen your scope to include other types of executives. You can ask the list owner to create a new targeted list for you that includes not only CMOs, but also vice presidents and directors of marketing, marketing managers, and even vice presidents of sales (who often influence marketing decisions). You can also expand your criteria by asking the list owner to target executives at mid-sized companies (e.g., with 50,000 or more employees), as well as large companies. This might double or even quadruple the number of names on your list.

You can also increase your target universe by seeking out other lists. You might contact other software magazines or other list owners to rent additional names of executives who match your target criteria.

In some tactics, such as cold calling, you can take steps to improve the accuracy of your list. You can research contact names, addresses, e-mail addresses, and phone numbers to see whether they are still accurate or in use. I'll talk about how to do this in Chapter 14.

Buying vs. Renting a List

In direct mail and e-mail marketing, you have the option to buy or rent a mailing list. Each option has its advantages and disadvantages. You can buy a mailing list from a list owner. The advantage of buying a list is that purchased lists are often less expensive than rented lists. Companies like ZoomInfo, Spoke, and Hoover's have gone through the trouble of compiling lists of contact information for people in certain demographics. Once you give them a set of criteria, they can create a list of target customers for you based on information they have collected.

> *Note: A* list owner *is a company that specializes in compiling mailing lists for e-mail and direct marketing and/or contact lists for cold calling. A* list manager *is a company that sells or rents these lists on behalf of the*

list owner. It used to be that list owners always turned their lists over to list managers to handle the sales or rentals, and marketers dealt exclusively with list managers. But now, some list owners are handling their own list sales or rentals. So you may deal with either a list owner or a list manager when buying or renting a mailing or contact list.

The main disadvantage of buying a list is that purchased lists are often less accurate than rented lists. A purchased list will often have more invalid or out-of-date mailing addresses, e-mail addresses, job titles (if it's a list of businesspeople), and other information than a rented list will contain. The reason is that the owner of a purchased list usually has no direct relationship with the people on the list. Often, the people on the list don't contribute their contact information directly, and they don't know that the list owner has collected that information.

For example, let's say a list owner chooses to compile a list of executives in various positions at software and high-tech companies, ranging from Fortune 500 companies down to small startups. They will build a "crawler" program that will search websites and extract the names of major executives, along with their contact information. But there are so many software and high-tech companies that it may take the list owner a year to map enough data to be useful to marketers who buy their lists.

Two years later, you ask the list owner for a list of 1,000 e-mail addresses of sales executives at software companies with 500 or more employees. They will give you a list based on information that was gathered two years ago. But during that time, some of the sales executives on the list are likely to have moved on to other companies. Or they may have left the sales department and taken on other positions at the company. Usually, the list owner has no way of knowing of such changes at each company on your contact list. Some phone numbers or e-mail addresses on the list may turn out to be inaccurate, or some contacts may no longer fit your criteria as target customers.

Instead of buying, you can also *rent* a mailing list. When you rent a list, you pay a fee to use an existing list for a single campaign in order to reach your target audience. Often, the owner of a rented list has a relationship with your potential clients, and therefore has a sense of their demographics and buying behavior. For example, Nike may rent out the list of subscribers to *Tennis* magazine, an obvious target audience for athletic gear. Dell may rent the *Forbes* subscribers list to high-tech marketers who want to reach small-business owners. Marriott Rewards may rent the *Conde Nast Traveler's* list to marketers who are targeting people interested in traveling.

A rented list is usually more expensive, but it also tends to be more accurate and more targeted to the right demographic. For this reason, a rented list is often more cost-effective in the long run. It gives you a better chance of getting your message to your target audience.

> **Note:** *In cold calling, you can only buy a contact list; you don't have the option to rent one. I'll explain why in Chapter 14.*

Negotiating Prices for Lists

Mailing and contact lists are usually rented or sold by CPM, at a given variable price per 1,000 e-mail addresses, mailing addresses, phone numbers, etc. B2C lists usually range from $20 to $100 CPM. B2B lists range from $80 to $500 CPM, depending on the perceived value associated with the information on the list. Be aware that CPMs for business-related lists will usually be higher than CPMs for consumer-related lists, because business-related lists are worth more and provide better ROMI to the companies that buy them.

Be aware that CPMs tend to be negotiable. List owners know there are flaws in the techniques they use to compile their mailing and contact lists. They will often price a list according to how accurate they think it is. There's a lot of flexibility in list pricing, so try to take advantage of that when you negotiate a price for buying or renting a mailing or contact list.

You should know your target CPA when you approach the list owner, estimate your ROMI based on the CPM rate the list owner is offering, and use your target CPA to negotiate. For example, say you're selling a $250 product using e-mail marketing, and your target CPA is 10% of the price (e.g., $25 or less). If a list owner is offering a list at a $500 CPM rate, you pay $500 for a list of 1,000 e-mail addresses. If only 10 people on the list of 1,000 end up buying the $1,000 product, your actual CPA is $50, which is double the target CPA you wanted to spend.

But you can then go back to the list owner and *negotiate a better CPM for the next list of 1,000 e-mail addresses* that you buy from them. You can ask for a $200–$250 CPM, which (if you get the same response to your e-mail with the next list of 1,000 names) will put you within your projected $25 target CPA.

Also, be aware that you can negotiate lower prices for high-volume lists. For example, you may be able to rent a list with 25,000 e-mail addresses at $100 CPM ($2,500 total). But a list with 100,000 e-mail addresses might be negotiated down to $50 CPM ($5,000 total) due to volume. The price is doubled, but you get four times as many names, so the 100,000 list may have a higher value for you.

Choosing a Reliable List Owner

The real trick to building a reliable mailing or contact list is to find a *trustworthy list source*—either a list owner or a list manager—and buy or rent an initial list from them. List owners like ZoomInfo and Hoover's have reputations for building more reliable mailing and contact lists for their clients. Their lists are usually 60–70% accurate (meaning 60–70% of the names and contact information on the list will be valid), and they will give you a list that is *specifically targeted* to the criteria you give them.

The problem is that many "charlatan" list owners on the market will try to sell you a bogus list, full of names of people who do *not* match the criteria for your target audience. Or the list will be five years old and filled with outdated contact names, or out-of-service mailing addresses, e-mail addresses, phone numbers, and other information.

For example, if you are marketing a new brand of cat food, you may ask a charlatan company for a list of 1,000 e-mail addresses of people who are cat owners, but they may give you a list of pet owners in general. About one-third of the people on the list will be cat owners, but the rest will be dog, fish, bird, and other animal owners—or some may not even have pets at all. And when you try to send out an e-mail creative with a special offer to people on your list, you discover that half the e-mail addresses on the list are no longer in use.

Your best strategy to avoid working with these types of companies is to do research on list owners before you buy their lists. Ask other advertisers who do direct mail, e-mail marketing, or cold calling to recommend a reliable list owner, someone who has provided them with accurate, on-target lists. Also, if you've never worked with a certain list owner before and want to know if you can trust them, you might research them online and see what other advertisers have to say about them.

If you decide to give a list owner a try, ask them to provide a sample list that you can test for accuracy. For example, if you are targeting CEOs at small companies with 50 employees or less, you might ask a list owner for a test list of 100 names and e-mail addresses of CEOs who meet that criterion. If you test the list and discover that it doesn't match your criterion (e.g., most names on the list are mid-level executives at companies with over 500 employees), you might not want to do business with that list owner.

The key quality you should look for in a list owner is *cooperation*. A good list owner will consult with you to make sure they understand the demographics of the target audience you seek, and will make sure you receive the best possible list of contacts that match those demographics.

The Make-Good

It's a standard practice for most reliable list owners to credit their clients for dud names, or names whose essential contact information (e.g., the mailing address) is out-of-date. This practice is called a *make-good*. When you do business with a list owner, make sure a make-good policy is written into their contract before you sign it.

You can request a make-good for one of two reasons: (1) The contact information on the list was out-of-date, or (2) the campaign didn't perform as expected because the target names provided by the list owner didn't match the target criteria you provided. (In this case, you will need to demonstrate that the flaws were in the mailing or contact list, not in your own creatives.)

When you request a make-good, the list owner will either (1) provide you with additional names that match your target criteria, to make up the difference, or (2) give you a partial refund for names on the list where the contact information was out-of-date.

As the client, it's usually your responsibility to request the make-good. Therefore, you need to keep careful track of the results of your campaign, and of how many duds you get. There are some slight differences in the ways to keep track of duds for direct mail, e-mail marketing, and cold calling. I'll talk a bit more about keeping track of them and how to request credits for them in the chapters on individual tactics.

> > > *What You Should Know* < < <

Here is what you should know about selecting and targeting mailing lists:

- Defining the demographics of your target audience in as much detail as possible is an essential first step for any direct mail, e-mail marketing, or cold-calling campaign. The success of your campaign depends on getting your offer in front of the right people, who have a need for your types of products or services.

- After you define your target audience, you will give a list of demographics to a list owner, who compiles a list of contact information for you based on your criteria. In some cases, you may need to expand your target criteria in order to get a larger target universe.

- You can either buy or rent a mailing or contact list from a list owner. A purchased list will be less expensive, but the information on it will typically be less accurate. If you rent a list, the list will be more expensive, but the information will usually be more accurate. A rented list is usually more cost-effective in the long run.

- When you work with a list owner, you should do research to make sure they are a legitimate organization before you do business with them. If possible, request a sample list of target customers to make sure they match your criteria.

- A reliable list owner will offer a make-good as a standard practice. After they give you a list of potential customers, they will credit you for names on the list that don't match your target criteria, or whose contact information is out-of-date. It is your responsibility to keep track of the duds on the list and request a credit for them.

12

E-Mail Marketing

E—MAIL MARKETING is an *active* form of marketing. It gives you a unique opportunity to contact people who are not yet familiar with your products or services, or who haven't placed your products or services in their consideration set. If you send the right e-mail to potential clients at the right time, it may prompt them to make a transaction, or to request more information from you. Or it may simply give them a new awareness that your products or services exist. This may pay off for you in the future, when potential clients realize you can provide a solution they need.

Other forms of online marketing are more passive. With SEM, social media advertising, and display advertising, the *customer* has to be actively in the market for your products or services. You must wait for the customer to contact you. (In SEM, they must be actively looking for your product or service in order to find you.) With e-mail marketing, you are reaching out to the customer.

Also, e-mail marketing gives you more control as a marketer over the experience your customers receive. You can control the brand, the e-mail's look and feel, and the amount of text your recipient has to read. You can control the day and time when they receive the e-mail in their inbox, the subject header, what happens when they open the e-mail, and what happens when they click through and take action.

E-mail marketing is also a persistent form of marketing. The target customer can save the e-mail and refer back to it at a later time, or easily pass it on to a friend or colleague.

With social advertising or SEM, the website or search engine controls the customer's experience, and your ad must fit within a restricted framework that the medium provides for you. For example, in posting a PPC ad on a search engine like Google, you are limited to using a set number of characters (25 for the headline, 70 for the description), and you can't use images or company logos for ads that appear in the right-hand margin of the user's search results.

Spam vs. E-Mail Marketing

Unfortunately, e-mail marketing has gotten a bad rap, thanks to the phenomenon of spam. I'm sure you're familiar with spam in its many forms—the offers for pornographic sites, bogus male enhancement products, low-cost medications, the letter from a businessman asking you to invest in Nigerian oil stocks, etc. But you might not be aware of how significant the problem of spam is.

Think about this: The amount of spam that you get in your e-mail inbox is only about *one-half of 1%* of the amount of spam that *tries* to enter it. About 99.5% of the spam messages that are sent to your e-mail address every day do not get through. Most ISPs (including Web-based e-mail services such as Gmail and Yahoo) do a good job of protecting you from spam, but occasional pieces slip in. So if you get only 5–10 spam messages per day, that means between *1,000 and 2,000 spam messages* were sent to your e-mail on that day but didn't get through!

Many marketers shy away from e-mail marketing, afraid that any e-mail offer they send out will be viewed as spam. But in doing so, they miss out on an effective marketing tool. A 2011 survey by CSO Insights found that 55.2% of all companies surveyed listed e-mail marketing as their most effective lead-generation tool, in terms of generating the best quality and quantity of leads.[1]

The reality is that many people *do* buy legitimate products from unsolicited e-mail offers. A 2009 study by ExactTarget found that over 50% of all Americans have made a purchase as a result of an e-mail message they received.[2] Also, in 2011, the Direct Marketing Association reported that e-mail marketing brings an average ROI of $40.56 for every $1 spent. The same report predicted that e-mail marketing will bring in $67.8 billion in sales for 2012.[3]

E-mail marketing can be a very useful tool for lead-generation marketers. If you know the right ways to use it, it can provide you with a high number of actionable leads.

The CAN-SPAM Act

In 2003, the U.S. government passed the CAN-SPAM Act, a law intended to reduce the amount of spam on the Internet. The CAN-SPAM Act sets national standards for the sending of commercial e-mail, and requires the Federal Trade Commission to enforce those standards. (CAN-SPAM is an acronym for Controlling the Assault of Non-Solicited Pornography and Marketing.)

The CAN-SPAM Act provides certain guidelines for legitimate e-mail marketing ventures, including unsolicited e-mail marketing offers and e-newsletters. As a marketer, you need to be aware of and follow these guidelines. The CAN-SPAM Act states that each marketing or advertising e-mail you send out must include the following features in order to be considered legitimate:

1. You must *clearly identify yourself and your company* in the e-mail. In other words, you must say who you are and what your company does.

2. You must *provide a physical address* for yourself or your company. If someone wants to write to you to be taken off your mailing list, they should be able to do so as an alternative.

3. You must give recipients *an easy opt-out* for your e-mail list if they don't want to receive e-mails from you. This can be a link to an "unsubscribe" page (e.g., "If you no longer wish to receive e-mails from this company, please unsubscribe here") or just simple instructions (e.g., "If you wish to unsubscribe from this newsletter, please send us a reply with unsubscribe in the subject line").

4. You must promise to no longer send e-mails to those who have opted out.

As a marketer, I would also recommend that you use only *permission-based e-mail mailing lists*, on which the potential customers have actually opted in to receiving e-mails from you. With permission-based lists, customers must either sign up to receive offers directly from you (e.g., through your website) or elect to receive third-party offers from you through another marketing organization they trust. For example, a potential customer may have subscribed to a magazine where the signup form included the option for them to receive third-party offers through the magazine's subscription list.

The Five Steps of E-Mail Marketing Campaigns

You must follow five steps in every e-mail marketing campaign. These steps correspond to the five steps of lead-generation tactics discussed in Chapter 4:

1. Define your target audience.

2. Select and target your e-mail mailing list.

3. Design your creative assets.

4. Test your e-mail campaign.

5. Measure your results.

Step 1: Define Your Target Audience

Your first step in an e-mail marketing campaign is to define your target audience in as much detail as possible. You should have this information ready when you contact a list owner about buying or renting a mailing list. See Chapter 11 for an in-depth look at how to define your target audience.

Step 2: Select and Target Your List

Again, e-mail marketing gives you two options to acquire a permission-based mailing list of potential customers. You can buy a list from a list owner like ZoomInfo or InfoUSA. These companies will compile a targeted list of customers for you, based on target demographics that you provide. Or you can rent a list from a company or publication that services or is associated with your target market.

A purchased list will often be less expensive, but the names, contact info, and targeting on the list will often be less accurate. A rented list will be more expensive but may be more cost-effective in the long run. The people on a rented list usually have a more direct relationship with the company or publication that owns the list, and therefore the names and information on the list will be more accurate.

For example, if you rent a list of subscriber e-mail addresses from *Tennis* magazine, you can be reasonably sure that most of the people on the list will be interested in an e-mail offer for tennis or athletic gear. In most cases, the people on the list have ordered their subscription to *Tennis* magazine online. When they filled out the online subscription form, they opted in to receive special offers from *Tennis* and its affiliates.

When you contact a list owner to buy or rent a list, you give them a set of specific demographics for your target audience. The list owner then targets your list according to those demographics. For example, if you are renting a list of subscribers from *Tennis* magazine, you might ask the list owner to target your list to subscribers with annual household incomes of $50,000 or more.

See Chapter 11 for more information on buying or renting a list, as well as how to select a reliable list owner.

Step 3: Design Your Creatives

You should create two pieces of creative for your e-mail marketing campaign: (1) the e-mail itself and (2) a landing page on your website. This page allows customers to perform the intended customer action (e.g., buy the product, sign up for a webinar, etc.) after they click on the call-to-action in the e-mail.

If you don't already have an e-mail creative or landing page, it's worth the cost to hire a creative professional or consultant to drive the development of these elements. A graphic designer will have numerous suggestions and techniques for designing both the e-mail and the landing page, so your creatives will have the best chance of getting a positive response from recipients.

Also, it may be worthwhile to hire a professional copywriter to write copy for the e-mail and landing page. The better you can explain the benefits of your product, service, or offer to potential customers, the more likely they will be to respond to the e-mail, and to follow through on the landing page.

Additionally, there is plenty of material available on the Web for best practices for building an e-mail creative or landing page to maximize deliverability and conversion rate. eMarketer and Marketing Sherpa are two especially good websites that provide e-mail and landing page tips and techniques.

CREATING YOUR E-MAIL

You need to understand and consider a number of elements when generating your e-mail creative:

HTML vs. Plain Text You should create two versions of your e-mail creative: an HTML version and a plain-text version. Some e-mail readers don't render graphics, which will revert back to the plain-text version of the e-mail. This is particularly true on mobile devices like Blackberries, where e-mail programs will usually choose to display the plain-text alternative.

Typically, you can design your e-mail creative in HTML. (At this writing, HTML 4.01 is the only markup language that renders the same across all e-mail and Web clients.) For more information on guidelines for e-mail deliverability, visit the Interactive Advertising Bureau (www.iab.net), and download their free white papers.

Text vs. Graphics Many marketers would love to do e-mails as text only. But it's often very difficult to persuade potential customers of the worth of your product using text alone. You need a good mixture (e.g., 70% text and 30% graphics) in your e-mail for it to be effective and deliverable.

Make sure you have *some* text, but don't try to overload your e-mail with it. People don't like to read huge blocks of text in an e-mail. Use just enough text in your primary message to tell your story; explain the value of your product, service, or offer; and establish your identity as a legitimate brand.

The same principle applies to graphics. An e-mail overloaded with graphics will be unappealing to the target customer, especially if you don't supply enough text to explain why they should care about your offer. Also, most ISP spam filters will flag an e-mail with too many graphics, and block it from being delivered to the target customer.

Even when inboxes do accept e-mails with graphics, sometimes they won't render those graphics right away. On some devices (such as a Blackberry), recipients may have to click on the e-mail to acknowledge it as safe before graphics can appear. Therefore, your e-mail needs to be well written so the message is clear and so it still looks like a reasonable and legitimate e-mail, even without the graphics.

Your Brand Make sure your brand is well represented in the e-mail. Use your logo and/or your tag line. Even if recipients don't click through the e-mail for lead-generation purposes, you will still win some brand awareness when they view it.

Your Call-To-Action The CTA is the most important element of the e-mail. What do you want recipients to do after reading the e-mail? Do you want them to click through to a landing page? Make a purchase? Call an 800 number? Sign up for a webinar?

You want to create a strong, action-oriented call-to-action (e.g., "Sign up for your account today!" "Join our webinar today!"). Make it *urgent* that recipients should take action from this e-mail as soon as they read it.

> **Note:** *In writing your CTA, try to stay away from "salesy and sleazy" words like* free, all new, act now, *etc. There are two reasons for this: First, many "salesy" words like* free *are considered spam triggers, and ISP spam filters will often block e-mails with too many of these words. Second, your CTA should focus on the value of your product, service, or offer. You don't want to sound too much like a salesperson, or potential customers may decide they don't trust you enough to respond.*

Your Subject Header Your subject header—the phrase in the subject line of the e-mail—is *extremely* important. It is a key factor in whether recipients will actually *open* your e-mail, once they see it in their inbox. Therefore, you want your subject line to be as compelling as possible (e.g., "Buy today and get 35% off"; "Control your calorie burn with the Body Bugg"; "Increase weight loss by 40%").

If potential customers are not familiar with your product, don't name the product in the subject header. Instead, describe the *benefits* of the product, and focus on its value. For example, say you have a brand new software named QuickNix that helps people to organize their daily lives and schedules. If you send out an e-mail advertising this software, your subject line should not be, "Introducing QuickNix software." Instead, you should describe how this software will help the people who use it. A good subject header line might be, "Organize your life with just a few clicks."

Your subject header should be 50 characters or less: short and punchy, not long-winded and confusing. Recipients should be able to read it; easily identify with your product, service, or offer; and want to click on the e-mail.

Also, be very careful about how you phrase your subject header and about what you put in it. A badly written subject line could alert anti-spam programs, and your legitimate offer might wind up in the recipient's Junk folder.

For example, you should not use more than one punctuation mark or symbol in your subject line. Also, avoid using ALL CAPS. "Buy today and get 35% off" is a good subject line, but "Buy TODAY and get 35% off!!" will almost certainly cause your e-mail to be flagged as spam.

> **Note:** *Avoid using acronyms in your subject header as well. Even legitimate acronyms like* MP3 *or* DVD *can cause your e-mail to be flagged as spam.*

Your "From" Line Be specific about who appears in the "From" line. Will it be from your company name? From your CEO? From one of your sales representatives? Or from "Customer service at [company name]" or "Sales at [company]"?

You should be as transparent, legitimate, and brand-worthy as you possibly can with your e-mails. Use your brand name in the "From" line, either your company name or product name. (If you must choose between the two, I recommend using the product name. For example, if your company name is Johnson Enterprises and you are selling the QuickNix Software, use "QuickNix Software" in the "From" line.)

You might want to use your CEO's name in the "From" line, but only if the CEO has some name recognition. On the other hand, you should stay away from using department names in the "From" line for lead-generation e-mails, because they are too impersonal. Who wants to receive an e-mail offer from the sales department or customer service? (Department names are best used in transactional e-mails, such as customer support interactions.)

Whatever brand name you use in the "From" line of your marketing e-mails, you should use it consistently throughout the text and graphics of the e-mail creative. Also, make sure you use the same brand name in the "From" line of every subsequent e-mail you send out after the first one, so that recipients will recognize that brand name whenever they receive an e-mail from you. For example, if you send out an e-mail offer from QuickNix Software, and 500 recipients sign up as leads, make sure every subsequent e-mail you send out to those 500 recipients is from QuickNix Software.

CREATING YOUR LANDING PAGE

Again, landing pages are an essential companion piece to an online lead-generation creative, such as a marketing e-mail or online ad. See Chapter 6 for an overview of how to create a good landing page.

DEPLOYING YOUR E-MAIL

Deployment is the sending-out or mailing of your e-mail creative to your prospective customers. This works in one of two ways. If you buy a list, the list owner sends you a targeted list of e-mail addresses, and you handle the actual deployment of the e-mail campaign yourself. Technically, once you own a list of prospects, you can send out as many e-mails to the people on that list as you wish, unless they choose to unsubscribe or opt out from receiving e-mails from your company.

But if you rent a list, you usually do so on a one-time-only use agreement, meaning you agree to send out only one e-mail creative to the names on the list. When you do your deployment, you give your e-mail creative to the list owner, and they deploy the marketing e-mails for you. In other words, the list owner will send out your e-mail creative to all the names on the rented list.

With rented lists, the list owner usually has a more direct relationship with the people on the list. For example, a magazine may rent out a list of e-mail addresses of subscribers who have opted in to receive special e-mail offers. But the magazine also wants to protect its subscribers from receiving spam. For this reason, list owners who rent you a list usually insist on doing the e-mail deployment for you, as a means of enforcing the one-time-only use agreement. (If you get a good response from the list, you can always rent the list again to send out additional e-mail offers to the same people.)

Step 4: Test Your Campaign

You need to consider numerous factors when testing an e-mail marketing campaign:

IDENTIFYING YOUR TESTING AUDIENCE

You need to identify a portion of your target universe that you will use as a testing audience for your e-mail campaign. I recommend testing *at least 25,000 names* for any given set of target demographics. You need a decent amount of scale to see some success from it. Anything smaller than 25,000 addresses is really too small for you to determine whether your campaign is working for you.

E-mail marketing works best when you work with a *larger universe*. A strange phenomenon occurs in e-mail marketing, which I often refer to as the "law of large numbers." Basically, the law is: "The larger your target universe, the better your response will be. The smaller your target universe, the worse your response will be." I've seen the law at work many times in e-mail marketing. One day, you might send out a marketing e-mail to only 500 target customers and get no response. The next day, you send out the same e-mail to 50,000 customers in exactly the same target market and get a 10% CTR.

There's no way to explain why this happens, but the implications for testing e-mail marketing should be clear. The larger your testing audience is, the better your response will be, and the more data you will receive that will enable you to accurately test your results and make improvements to your campaign.

YOUR TEST BUDGET

When you test an e-mail marketing campaign, you should put enough money into the test to make it meaningful. I recommend setting a budget of $2,500 to $5,000 per individual test. A high testing budget will give you a reasonable sample representative of the actual target universe.

I also recommend that you test and measure your e-mail creatives four to eight times (at least four times). This will help you to understand how well your creatives work, and how well e-mail marketing works for you in general. Testing your campaign multiple times allows you to try different messages, test the response of audiences with different sets of demographics, test the days and times when your e-mail gets the best response, etc. You should divide your total testing budget into small but equal amounts, so you can stretch it over several tests. For example, if you have a testing budget of $10,000, you should do four $2,500 tests.

Many companies take a "minimum budget" approach to testing e-mail marketing campaigns. They budget only $500 or $1,500 per test. Using smaller budgets for testing is a legitimate practice, but you should understand its limitations. If your test budget is too small, you won't have a large enough sample size to run an accurate test of your e-mail creatives, your target audience, and other aspects of your campaign. With too small a sample size, you cannot collect enough data to determine whether e-mail marketing is working for you as a tactic.

Let's say you spend $100 to rent 1,000 names, and you get eight clicks from your marketing e-mail to your landing page. How much can you really learn from only eight clicks? Was the low response due to problems in the e-mail creative? Is the problem in the e-mail subject header, or with the offer, or the CTA? Did you send the e-mail to the wrong target audience? With only eight responses, it's hard to determine what the problem is and how to fix it.

By contrast, if you rent 100,000 names and your e-mail receives 200 clicks, you can learn a lot more about who clicked on the e-mail, why they clicked, etc. For example, if you are testing two e-mail creatives, you will have a better sense of which e-mail creative gets the best response, and the days and times when it gets the best response.

Also, with a larger response, you can collect more information about the people who clicked on the e-mail. If, say, your e-mail invites people to sign up for a webinar, you can include questions on the landing pages where they sign up (e.g., "What is your job title?" "How many employees does your company have?"). A larger response will help you to get a better idea of who your target customers are, and what their interests are in terms of your types of products or services.

TESTING YOUR E-MAIL CREATIVES

I recommend that you do A/B split testing on two elements of your e-mail creatives: the subject header line and the e-mail creative itself. For example, you might test two offers using two e-mails with different subject headers (e.g., "Buy one pair of shoes, get one free" and "25% off best-quality work shoes"). Or if you have two e-mail creatives for the same offer—one that is all text with a single graphic, and one that has a few additional graphics and less text—you might test them using the same subject header (e.g., "25% off best-quality work shoes") to see which creative gets a higher response.

You never know what kinds of subject headers or creatives will get the best response from your customers. On a recent A/B split test, one of my clients mistakenly sent out a test e-mail with only the word "Webinar" in the subject line. To their surprise (and mine), the "Webinar" e-mail got three times the response of the other test e-mail with the well-crafted subject header.

However, you should be careful not to make your testing too complex. Don't try to test five versions of the same creative, each with different graphics, background colors, etc. If you try to test too many elements in your e-mail creative at one time, it will be harder to measure the response to those elements, and harder to determine whether any of them are giving you any real advantage.

TESTING YOUR SEND SCHEDULE

The key to testing your schedule is experimentation. For each campaign, you need to determine what you think will be the best days and times to send out e-mails to your target audience. Then you need to test different days and times to figure out when your audience will give you the best response.

You may be surprised by the days and times when your e-mails get the best response. For B2B campaigns, a long-held belief is that e-mails sent out between Tuesday and Thursday of any given week will give you the best response. This strategy also holds that you should send e-mails only in the morning, so that people will see them in their inbox when they get to work.

But because so many e-mail marketers use this strategy, I think there's room to be more flexible. I've seen B2B campaigns succeed when the e-mails were sent out on Sunday afternoons. Businesspeople tend to check their e-mail on Sunday evenings or very early on Monday mornings, just to make sure they don't have to address any emergencies before going into work. And I've seen successful campaigns where the e-mail was sent out at noon, instead of in the morning. Many businesspeople handle all their major business deal-ings in the morning hours. They often check their e-mail during their lunch hour, and have more time to think about offers in the afternoon.

For B2C offers, your schedule will depend on your target audience and when you think they are most likely to be reading their personal e-mails. I've seen e-mail campaigns for different target audiences get good responses at different days and times. The more you test your schedule, the better you'll be able to pinpoint the days and times that give you the best response.

Step 5: Measure Your Results

The key to measuring your success is to understand your CPA for an e-mail marketing campaign. Determine your target CPA before the campaign begins, and measure it against your actual CPA when you get the results of the test campaign. You can then work backward in terms of figuring out what CPM rate will generate the best return for you.

One important thing to understand: If your test campaign is not success-ful—if you feel as if your CPA was too high—it doesn't mean e-mail mar-keting is a bad channel for you. The next time you rent the list you used in the campaign, you need to negotiate a lower price. A list doesn't need to have the highest-performing conversion rate if the CPM is low enough. As I explained in the previous chapter, CPMs for various lists are often nego-tiable. So, for example, if your target CPA is $40, you might spend $1,000 to rent a list of 10,000 names and e-mail addresses at $100 CPM. If you get only 12 or 13 purchases from customers on that list, your actual CPA for that campaign is $80, which is double your target CPA.

But you can then go back to the list owner and negotiate a lower CPM for a list of new names with the same targeting criteria. If your price for renting the original list was $100 CPM, you can negotiate for a $50 CPM to rent a list of new names from the same vendor. When you use that list in your next e-mail marketing campaign, your actual CPA should be closer to your target CPA of $40, and you should meet your ROMI.

Also, you need to be aware of the average open rates, CTRs, and con-version rates for e-mail marketing. For B2C campaigns, open rates are usually 2–10%. For example, if you send out 1 million e-mails, between 20,000 and 100,000 recipients will open it. For B2B campaigns, open rates are usually 5–15%.

For B2C campaigns, your average CTR is usually 0.5–2%. If you send 1 million e-mails, between 5,000 and 20,000 recipients might actually click through. B2B campaigns usually have a CTR of 2–5%.

The other component is your *conversion rate.* In other words, calculated from your CTR, how many people take the desired action once they get to the landing page? A 15% conversion rate is a good rate. That means 15 out of every 100 people who visit the landing page after clicking on your e-mail convert to a lead or sale. If your conversion rate is lower than 15%, you might want to think about changing your offer or optimizing the text on your landing page. If your conversion rate is higher than 15%, you have a very good campaign going.

For B2B campaigns, the average CTR can be as high as 2%. A conversion rate can be as high as 25% if your product and offer are properly targeted and if you have a good landing page.

> > > *What You Should Know* < < <

To review, here is what you should know about e-mail marketing:

- E-mail marketing is an active form of marketing that involves reaching out to your potential customer. Although it has something of a bad reputation due to spam, many marketers have a high success rate with it.

- To avoid your e-mail creative being identified as spam, follow the guidelines for effective e-mails, as outlined in the CAN-SPAM Act of 2003. Your e-mail must clearly identify your company, have sufficient contact information, and have an opt-out for customers who no longer wish to receive your e-mails.

- You should also use a permission-based e-mail mailing list, where the recipients have opted in to receive e-mails from you.

- You can buy or rent an e-mail address list. Purchased lists are usually cheaper, but the demographic targeting and contact information is not as accurate. Rented lists are usually more expensive, but more targeted to your target customers, and therefore usually more cost-effective in the long run.

- When you buy or rent a list, you should give the list owner a set of demographic filters for your target audience. The list owner will give you a targeted list of e-mail addresses for potential customers who fit your audience.

- Your e-mail should have a 70/30 mix of text and graphics. You should have both an HTML version and a plain text version of the e-mail. Your e-mail should include your brand, a call-to-action, a subject header that prompts the recipient to open the e-mail, and a "From" line that is transparent, legitimate, and brand-worthy.

- You should also create a landing page on your website that reinforces the e-mail offer and allows the customer to take action (e.g., to make a purchase, sign up for a webinar, etc.).

- You should identify a portion of your list to use as a testing audience for your e-mail campaign. You should test your e-mail creatives at least four times, using a large number of recipients (e.g., 25,000 per test). You should test the response to your e-mail creatives. You should also test your schedule to see which days and times you get the best response to your e-mail.

- When measuring your results, measure your target CPA against your actual CPA to determine the cost-effectiveness of your campaign. If your actual CPA is higher than your target CPA, you can often negotiate a lower CPM rate with the same list owner when you buy or rent a list for your next e-mail marketing campaign.

13

Direct Mail Marketing

IN RECENT YEARS, there has been a lot of debate about direct mail marketing. Some say direct mail is a "dead tactic," and that it has been (or should be) replaced by newer forms of lead generation. Direct mail is certainly an expensive tactic, whereas other lead-generation tactics can be done more cheaply. Some marketing experts say it is silly for companies to spend $50,000 to create, print, and ship 25,000 direct mail pieces, when they can send out the same number of promotional e-mails for about $5,000, roughly one-tenth the production cost.

But direct mail is far from dead. In fact, it's more alive than ever. In 2010, according to the U.S. Postal Service, U.S. businesses spent about $171 billion in advertising. Of this, approximately 12%—or about $20.5 billion—was spent on direct mail. U.S. households received 83.5 billion pieces of advertising mail in 2010. And although overall spending for direct mail advertising fell sharply during the 2008–9 downturn, it had a modest increase of 2.1% in 2010.[1]

Like all lead-generation tactics, direct mail always has a varying response rate. Although most people will throw a direct mail piece away when they receive it, direct mail pieces still get more consideration than marketing e-mails. The 2010 U.S. Postal Service study also found that 81% of all people either read or scanned direct mail pieces sent to their address.[2] Meanwhile, a separate study by the E-Mail Experience Council of the Direct Marketing Association found that only 17%–18% of all e-mail recipients will actually open and read an e-mail marketing piece before deleting it.[3]

Unlike unwanted e-mail marketing pieces, people tolerate junk mail in their mailbox. People have a negative, visceral reaction to getting unsolicited e-mail, but they tend to think of receiving unsolicited postal mail as part of being a homeowner. Depending on what you are offering the potential customer, you may get a better response with traditional direct mail than you would with e-mail marketing. This is one reason why direct mail can still be an effective lead-generation tool. It can still work well in many different situations.

When Should You Use Direct Mail?

You should use direct mail if you sell a product or service that you think will get a good response with this tactic. Direct mail is very effective for products or services where the target customers need to take time to think seriously about whether to take advantage of a certain offer. It is also effective if you are marketing a complicated product or service where the offer has to be spelled out in great detail, or if you are presenting several detailed offers at once.

E-mail marketing, on the other hand, tends to work best for products that can be sold online, where the target customers can make a quick decision and take immediate action on the offer. In e-mail marketing, the product or offer needs to be explained very quickly and with a minimum of detail, or the target customers will become disengaged from the e-mail and lose interest in it.

Direct mail can also work very well if you have a brand-new, first-of-its-kind product or service that you need to explain in detail to the target customer. For example, since 2009, Clearwire has had tremendous success with their direct mail campaign to introduce their new WiMAX-based, 4G wireless Internet service for mobile users (which it now sells under the Clear label). Direct mail is a very effective way for Clearwire to introduce and explain the new WiMAX technology to potential customers.

B2C DIRECT MAIL

Certain business-to-consumer industries use direct mail very effectively. For example, credit card companies, mortgage brokers, and insurance companies have more success with direct mail than they do with e-mail marketing.

A financial, credit, or insurance offer is a serious decision to make, and people need time to think it over before they take advantage of it. Direct mail allows a financial, credit, or insurance company to give the customer an offer *in writing* in its entirety, including the fine print, so that customers know what they get if they sign up for it. It's more reassuring for the customer to have a physical letter in front of them that outlines the offer in detail. Customers find this a better approach than a marketing e-mail, which asks them to make a snap decision to commit to a serious financial obligation.

Also, customers want to make sure a financial, credit, or insurance offer is genuine and legitimate before they commit to it. E-mail marketing doesn't work as well for credit card, mortgage, or insurance companies because phony offers for these types of products are among the top spam e-mails. A legitimate promotional e-mail from such a company is likely to be mistaken for spam and deleted immediately. For offers from financial businesses, people would rather have a physical letter as proof that the offer is legit and the company is trustworthy.

Direct mail works well for selling vehicles. The auto, recreational vehicle, and recreational boating industries continue to spend billions each year on direct mail marketing because it helps them to increase sales and provides a significant ROMI. Direct mail is also effective for businesses that offer technical services for the home, such as lawn care, storm windows, or driveway paving. People need to consider these services carefully, because a technician has to come to their home to install or hook up a product.

Finally, direct mail works well for cable services because it allows them to add dimensionality to an offer. For example, Comcast can send out a direct mail envelope that includes one-sheet flyers for several different offers, such as high-speed Internet; basic cable service; and premium channels like HBO, Showtime, and so on. This kind of presentation allows the customer who opens the envelope to look at each flyer and consider each offer separately. (Also, using direct mail gives cable companies more control over their branding.)

B2B DIRECT MAIL

With a direct mail package, you can take time to fully explain a B2B product, service, or offer to customers, so they will understand the benefits of it. You can also include a gift, a catalog, a coupon, a visual aid, or any number of physical components in the package that may spark your potential customer's interest in the offer.

By adding dimensionality to your B2B offer through a direct mail piece, you increase the chances that your target customers will at least consider the offer. CEOs or other executives are more likely to delete an e-mail offer without reading it. But if they receive a large envelope or dimensional mailer in the mail, they are more likely to open it just to see what it is. (Or their secretary or assistant will open it, and, because they assume it is important, will often walk it over to the executive's office so that the executive can consider the offer.)

THE INDIRECT MARKETING THEORY

You might use direct mail as a "change-up" from your regular lead-generation marketing tactics. There's a notion among marketers called the *Indirect Marketing Theory*, which states that marketers often flock to the most popular tactics of the day. When this happens, you can sometimes give yourself an edge by switching to less popular tactics where you have less competition. So if all your competitors are using e-mail marketing, you might try using direct mail as a way to get more attention from your customers. They may be more responsive to a direct mail package from you than they would be to another marketing e-mail from one of your competitors.

Calculating the Costs

One challenge of direct mail is that it's fairly expensive. Like trade shows, direct mail requires a huge, up-front investment. Therefore, you want to engage in direct mail only in scenarios where your ROMI will be very high.

In terms of ROMI, direct mail works best if you are selling (1) a very expensive product, such as a car or recreational boat, or (2) a product or service that will provide a significant annuity to your company over a long time, such as insurance or a credit card service. If you are selling a very inexpensive product (e.g., a one-time-purchase product for $10 each), direct mail may not be the best tactic for you to use.

You need to be able to justify the expense of using direct mail. The key reasons for using direct mail are (1) you think your target audience will respond well to the tactic, and (2) the response to your campaign will be high enough to give you a significant ROMI over the initial expense of creating it. *Both of these must be true* for you to use direct mail successfully.

The principal expenses of direct mail are:

- Buying or renting a mailing list

- Printing the direct mail piece

- Paying for the shipping costs

With direct mail, the expense of renting or purchasing a list is typically the same as with other tactics that require mailing or contact lists. The real expense comes with the printing and mailing of the piece.

Direct mail is similar to e-mail marketing in that the larger your target universe, the higher the response you will get. For example, you will get a higher response if you ship a direct mail piece to 5,000 potential customers than you will if you ship the piece to only 500 customers. But where you can create an e-mail marketing campaign virtually (e.g., on the computer) for very little money, a direct mail campaign requires the production and ship-ping of a large number of physical mail pieces.

A CASE EXAMPLE

Let's look at a case example for calculating costs for a direct mail campaign. Say you decide to produce and send a six-page, 8 × 11-inch brochure on your product or service. This brochure is small enough that it can be shipped in an ordinary mailing envelope.

You might pay a list owner $500 for a mailing list of 5,000 target cus-tomers and their addresses. Then it may cost you $3.00 apiece to print 5,000 copies of the brochure, for a total of $15,000. To ship each brochure, it may cost you a bulk mail postal rate of 25¢ per envelope, for a total of $1,250. (Keep in mind that you can often save money over the standard postal rate by shipping in bulk.) Your total expenses for this direct mail campaign amount to $16,750.

Now let's say you get a 1% response rate to the campaign. Out of 5,000 tar-get customers, 50 respond to the brochure to become leads. Of those 50 leads, maybe half (25) convert to become customers. This means your cost-per-action (CPA) for the campaign is $670 per customer ($16,750 ÷ 25 = $670).

Will this direct mail campaign provide a significant ROMI? It depends on what you're marketing. If you're marketing a one-time-only home ser-vice like driveway repavement, which costs only about $400–$500, this cam-paign would produce a negative ROMI. Your expenses were too high. (A less expensive campaign, such as printing a one-sheet mailing flyer, might have provided a better ROMI.)

On the other hand, if you are marketing an insurance package, the monthly insurance premiums that each converted customer pays will justify the $670 CPA in a very short time. If the customer stays with your company over several years, you will earn a significant long-term ROMI for the direct mail campaign. If you are marketing very expensive products, like BMWs or recreational speedboats that sell in the $100,000 range, one sale will be more than enough to justify the expense of your direct mail campaign. Twenty-five sales will produce an excellent ROMI.

as you wish. The size and shape of your mailing piece depend only on your imagination and on the size of your budget for printing and shipping it.

The most common types of mailing pieces are:

- *Postcards:* Can be 3 × 5 inches or larger, with a special offer printed on it.

- *Flyers:* Usually one-page, 8 × 11-inch, folded-without-envelope flyers outlining your business or special offer.

- *Sales Letters:* One- to two-page sales letters mailed in a 4 × 9-inch envelope, of the kind you might get in your mailbox from Comcast or Geico Insurance.

- *Brochures:* Can be mailed as two- to three-page stand-alone mailers, or as multiple-page brochures enclosed in large envelopes.

- *Dimensional mailers:* Direct mail packages that may be shipped in an oversized envelope or box. They may include multiple pages of sales materials advertising a special program, a set of products or services, etc. They may even include a tchotchke or toy (e.g., a ballpoint pen, gift card, USB stick, T-shirt, gift basket, etc.) that comes as a free gift with the package.

CREATIVITY IS AN ASSET

Direct mail is a lead-generation tactic that can benefit from creativity. As I mentioned in Chapter 1, some lead-generation tactics, such as e-mail marketing, can be less effective when marketers try to be too creative with the creative assets. But with direct mail, it helps to use some creativity in designing and creating your mailer, brochure, or sales letter. How much creativity you need depends on what you are marketing, and how elaborate you want to be in attracting your client. Some fancy direct mail packages can provide very unusual and effective customer experiences. Here are just a few examples:

The Bank of America Truck Promo   One of the best direct mail campaigns I've ever heard of came from Bank of America. The campaign targeted financial decision makers (e.g., CFOs) at commercial businesses. Bank of America sent out a dimensional mailer package containing radio-controlled toy trucks with the Bank of America logo painted on the truck trailer. Each dimensional mailer included the toy truck but not the remote control device that you needed to control the truck and make it go. To get the remote control device for the truck, the direct mail package explained, all you needed to do was to have a "no obligation" meeting with a Bank of America representative.

In this package, Bank of America had several elements that helped to make the mailer a successful lead-generation tool: It had a great creative (the highly branded truck), a great CTA ("Call us today to set up a meeting"), and a great offer ("Take a meeting with us and we'll give you the remote control for your toy truck, with no obligation").

The Vacation Package I received a dimensional mailer from the Via Luna Group (www.wefightboredom.com), a marketing agency in Plano, Texas, that creates interactive Web experiences. They sent a direct mail package targeted to people like me, who might have a use for interactive Web-based marketing promotions.

The direct mail package had only two things in it: A hotel key card—the kind you use to unlock your room door at a hotel or resort—and a table napkin with a circular stain from a Mai Tai or Piña Colada glass. A handwritten note was on the napkin: "Hey, Dave! Wish you were here!" Also written on the napkin was a website URL. It was supposedly the website of the resort hotel where the card key and napkin had come from, but the URL was personalized to me (e.g., "www.name-of-resort.com/davescott").

I went to the personalized URL on the Web and found an interactive experience waiting for me. It was a series of Web animation pages giving me a tour of the imaginary hotel from which the enclosed key card came. I clicked through various rooms in the hotel—my suite, the lobby, the hotel bar, the pool, the tennis courts. At the end of this interactive tour, I received a webpage with a message: "Do you realize that you just spent 27 minutes on this website? Let us do the same for you and your lead-generation efforts."

Just for the record, I almost never spend 27 minutes on any website (except maybe Facebook), so the fact that this personalized website was able to hold my attention for so long is pretty impressive. By sending me this demonstration, the agency proved to me how an effective direct mail piece, coupled with an interactive Web experience, could be a great source for attracting potential customers.

DIRECT MAIL ON A BUDGET

You don't need to spend a lot of money and construct an elaborate direct mail creative to have a successful campaign. You can make creativity work to your advantage even if you're on a tight budget.

The trick is to create a document that is compelling enough to prompt your potential customer to take a close look at your offer and evaluate it. For example, credit card companies and auto dealerships often send out direct mail offers that resemble a bank check, usually in a business envelope with an address window. The words "Pay to the order of [name of recipient]" are visible through the address window. Recipients will often open the envelope just to see whether an actual check is inside.

In fact, the document inside is not an actual check, but a voucher for a refund or reward that you get when you sign up for the special offer. If it's a credit offer from a department store, you might get a $500 gift certificate when you sign up for their credit card service. If it's an offer from a local car dealership, you may get $2,000 cash back if you purchase a car from them by a certain date.

Airlines and other travel companies sometimes send out direct mail offers that resemble airline tickets or a cruise ticket. When potential customers open the envelope, they may find a voucher for free airline miles or a free all-expenses-paid cruise. The voucher is redeemable only if the potential customer signs up for the company's Frequent Flier or Frequent Traveler program.

PERSONALIZING THE DIRECT MAIL PACKAGE

A direct mail package can be very effective if you can provide a personal experience for the potential customer. Again, the direct mail package I received from Via Luna Group had a great creative element that was personalized to me: a hotel key card, a cocktail napkin with a handwritten message ("Hey, Dave! Wish you were here!"), and a URL personalized to my name (www.name-of-resort.com/davescott). This made me just curious enough to go online and check out the URL, to see the "place" (in this case, the interactive hotel animation) where someone "wished I was." By personalizing the direct mail package and product demonstration for me, the agency was able to provide a more intimate and effective online experience. This went a long way in selling the effectiveness of their services to me.

If you use a landing page or online product demonstration, you should use personalized landing pages for each potential client who receives the direct mail piece. Some interactive marketing agencies specialize in creating personalized URL landing pages (also known as PURLs) for direct mail pieces. This is fairly inexpensive because the interactive marketing agencies have automated tools to create duplicate landing pages that are customized to each client.

A personalized landing page also provides a way for you to collect individual analytics on a lead source. You can measure the response to your direct mail package by attaching an analytics cookie to each landing page, to let you know whether the page was accessed. And you can measure your conversion rate by the number of customers who signed up for the offer. You can also attach a lead form to a personalized landing page that allows you to collect relevant information about the prospect.

There are other ways to personalize a direct mail package. For example, if you have a small product or toy that you can easily manufacture and ship at a low cost, you might include a personalized version of it, with the potential customer's name or company logo on it. I recently received a direct mail package from a pen manufacturer that included a personalized ballpoint pen with my company name, address, and logo printed on it. The message in the direct mail package said, "We can give you 1,000 of these pens for 25¢ apiece."

This struck me as a pretty impressive direct mail effort. This company probably went to several thousand websites for individual companies, pulled logos from each website, and created an individual logo pen that they included in each direct mail package sent to every company. It was an extremely compelling way to get me to consider a product (personalized pens) that I might not have been in the market for until I received the direct mail package.

INTRODUCING THE QR CODE

The Quick Response (QR) code is a technological innovation, developed in Japan, that has been around since the 1950s. For several years, it has been used extensively with Blackberries, specifically for scanning PIN numbers with Blackberry Instant Messaging. But during the time I've been writing this book, the QR code has been adopted into widespread use in marketing and advertising in America.

The QR code is a small, box-shaped, 2D-matrix code, sort of like a bar code, except that it can hold thousands of alphanumeric characters of information. You can scan a QR code with your smartphone and use it to access webpages, online video, online coupons, etc. You're probably already familiar with QR codes. For example, you might see a QR code on a magazine ad for a popular singer's latest album. If you scan the QR code, it runs the singer's latest music video on your smartphone video screen, or gives you a promotional ad for the singer's upcoming tour. Also, major airlines are now using QR codes on their digital boarding passes.

Direct mail printers are now adopting QR codes, which gives marketers a great opportunity to use this new technology to their advantage. As I mentioned in the chapter on display ads, marketers are now creating interactive, fun-to-use ads that allow mobile users to run a movie, a commercial, a sample application, or even a game on their iPhones, iPads, or Androids. Today, mobile ads sometimes get a better response than Web-based display ads, because the technology is new and innovative.

It's too soon to tell, but using QR codes in direct mail might bring about a similar increase in response to direct mail packages. By attaching a QR code to your direct mail creative, you can link your prospective customer to an interactive experience via their smartphone. For example, say you have a direct mail piece advertising cruise packages. You might attach a QR code that lets smartphone users access an interactive application that takes them on a virtual tour of one of your cruise ships. At the end of the virtual tour, they can use their smartphone to sign up as a lead in order to receive e-mails about upcoming cruise packages. As a special offer, they might get a 20% discount on their first cruise, just for having viewed the online virtual tour.

The QR code makes it easy to personalize the online experience for the customer. You can create a PURL landing page for each customer, and attach the personalized URL to the QR code. When customers scan the code, they can access their personalized landing pages through their smartphones.

Even if you don't use personalized landing pages, you can still use the QR code to your advantage. For example, if you are offering a financial, credit card, or insurance package, it's best to keep the bulk of marketing information in the direct mail package itself. (Again, for these kinds of offers, customers prefer to have it in writing.) But you can attach a QR code to the direct mail package that will take customers to simple landing pages on their smartphones, where they can sign up for your offer or request more information.

QR codes also make it easy to track the response to your direct mail package. You can attach a tracking cookie to each landing page (whether it's personalized or not), and track the number of times your customers access the landing page through their smartphone by scanning the QR code.

PRINTING AND SHIPPING

The real expense of direct mail comes with the printing and mailing of the actual piece. For example, it may cost $10 to print an individual mailing piece. If you send your direct mail piece out to 30,000 potential customers, the overall printing costs will be $300,000. (If you add a branded or personalized tchotchke to it, the cost of producing each individual mailing piece might go up to $20. So the overall production costs will then be $600,000.) The cost of shipping a direct mail piece might be a $1–$5 bulk rate, depending on the size of the package. For a 30,000-piece mailing, the shipping costs would be between $30,000 and $150,000.

The good news is that many sophisticated printing houses have figured out ways to print large-volume direct mail campaigns while saving the client money. Some printers will handle both printing and mailing. Also, if a national printing company has printing facilities in New York, Atlanta, St. Louis, Seattle, etc., they can print and ship your direct mail packages from those locations. (For example, the New York office ships to addresses in the Northeast, the Atlanta office ships to addresses in the South, etc.) This saves you money over having to print and ship your direct mail packages nationwide from one location.

Step 4: Test Your Direct Mail Campaign

Direct mail is probably the hardest lead-generation tactic to test effectively, for several reasons. First, direct mail is such an expensive tactic that it needs to be done in bulk. You need to print and ship a large number of direct mail pieces (e.g., 5,000 or more) in order to get a measurable response to your campaign. Also, unlike online tactics such as search engine marketing and social advertising, once you've started a direct mail campaign, you can't instantly stop it in order to rework your creatives or change your target audience.

It's easy to measure your delivery rate with direct mail by the number of returned envelopes. If you send out 5,000 envelopes, and 500 of them are returned to you (due to incorrect address, change of address, etc.), you can assume the other 4,500 were delivered. So you have a delivery rate of 90%. But measuring an open rate for a direct mail campaign is next to impossible. You have no way of knowing how many recipients actually open the envelope, and how many just throw it away without opening it.

Your best strategy for testing and measuring the effectiveness of a direct mail campaign is to do it on a market-by-market basis. For example, if you have a national campaign, pick three regional markets (e.g., Cincinnati, Phoenix, and Kansas City), and do test campaigns to measure the responses to your offer in those markets. If the direct mail package performs well, you can then roll it out to other markets.

Step 5: Measure Your Results

It's easy to measure the success of a direct mail campaign. To get your conversion rate, divide the number of mailers you sent out (e.g., 30,000) by the number of people who responded to the mailer and became an actual lead (e.g., 1,000). To get your CPA, divide the total cost of the campaign (e.g., $50,000) by the number of leads obtained. (In this case, if you obtain 1,000 leads at $50,000, your CPA is $50 per lead. If 200 of those leads convert to customers, your cost-per-sale is $50,000 ÷ 200 = $250.)

You should run several test campaigns to see whether direct mail will work as a marketing tool for your types of products or services. You need to measure the response rate you get from direct mail to see whether it produces a significant ROMI for you. The more expensive your product—or the more money you plan to make from the client using a long-term service like insurance—the higher your ROMI will be, and the more you will be able to justify the cost of using direct mail.

> > > *What You Should Know* < < <

To review, here is what you should know about direct mail marketing:

- While direct mail marketing is an old-school tactic, it can still be a highly successful lead-generation tactic. People have a more positive reaction to receiving direct mail pieces in their mailbox than they do to receiving marketing e-mails in their inbox.

- Direct mail is very effective for selling products or services where customers need to think seriously about the offer before accepting it. It is also effective for selling complicated products or services that require a good deal of explanation.

- Direct mail often requires a large, up-front investment in printing and shipping. Therefore, you should engage in direct mail only if you are selling an expensive product, or a product or service that will provide a significant ROMI over the long term.

- When you obtain a targeted mailing list for your direct mail campaign, a rented list will be more expensive but more accurate than a purchased list. However, when you use a rented list, you usually do so with the understanding that you will send only one mailing to each recipient on the list.

- Direct mail pieces can include postcards, flyers, sales letters, brochures, and dimensional mailers. Usually, some creativity helps in reaching out to your potential customer. The more personal you can make a direct mail package and its accessories (e.g., a landing page, a personalized tchotchke or toy), the better your chances of catching your potential customers' interest and turning them into actionable leads.

- Direct mail is very difficult to test because it is so expensive, and because you must print and ship a large number of creatives to get a measurable response. A good strategy for testing your direct mail campaign is to target regional markets and measure the response to your offer in those markets.

- When measuring your results, measure the overall cost of the campaign against the number of products or services sold to determine your cost-per-action. Then compare the CPA against the purchase price of your product (or the long-term income that results from your product or service) to determine whether your ROMI justifies the use of direct mail.

14

Cold Calling

COLD CALLING is a traditional, "old school" tactic, and some marketers might say that it's more of a tool for generating sales leads than marketing leads. But I actually think it's a good idea to talk about cold calling as a marketing tactic. If you and your marketing department use it right, you can turn cold calling into a very effective tool for generating marketing leads.

Cold calling works very well as a lead-generation tactic for certain types of businesses. It's particularly effective if your business has a small, well-defined purchasing audience. For example, say your company sells exclusively to government agencies and departments, or you have a product that you sell only to hospitals or medical establishments. In most cases, you know who the decision makers are at these companies, or at least you know which people in which positions are most likely to need your type of product or service. It's just a matter of getting in touch with them. In this case, cold calling may be a very effective option for you.

The Five Steps of Cold-Calling Campaigns

The five steps of cold-calling campaigns correspond with the five steps of e-mail marketing and direct marketing campaigns:

1. Define your target audience.

2. Select and target your cold-calling list.

3. Design your creative (in this case, your cold-calling script).

4. Test and execute your campaign.

5. Measure your results.

Step 1: Define Your Target Audience

You define your target audience for cold calling the same way you do for e-mail marketing or direct mail. See Chapter 11 for an in-depth look at how to define your target audience using demographic, psychographic, and geographic targeting.

Step 2: Select and Target Your Cold-Calling List

Once you've defined your target audience, the next step is to create a targeted list of contact and demographic information for your potential customers. This list should provide you with their phone number, job title, and any useful information about the company and where they work.

As I mentioned in Chapter 11, for cold calling, you need to buy a contact list. You don't have the option to rent one. The reason is simple: With cold calling, there's no way for a list owner to enforce the "one-time-only" use agreement that you normally agree to when renting a mailing list for e-mail or direct mail marketing. Once you have a list of phone numbers, technically you can call the people on that list as many times as you wish. In fact, you may have to call a contact more than once, especially if you get the contact's voice-mail on the first call. List owners know this, so with cold calling, they only offer lists for purchase, not for rent.

To buy a list, you should contact a list owner that specializes in creating contact lists for cold calling. These companies will build a list for you based on the information you provide about your target demographics. See Chapter 11 for information on how to pick a reliable list owner.

IMPROVING YOUR LIST

Once you have purchased an initial list, your goal should be to improve it before you start making calls. Even if you buy a list from a reliable list owner, you still need to research the names on it and verify the accuracy of the contact information. Even the best contact list will often have some dud names and other inaccuracies. (I'll talk about how to handle these shortly.) Also, although a contact list will give you the names and phone numbers of people in your target demographic, it won't give you much more information. You will still need to do research to find additional data about the people you are calling.

You want to make your contact list as accurate and as far-reaching as possible. By researching your contact names, you can expand the list to include additional people at your target companies who might have a need for your products or services. You can also cut names from the list if you think certain people might not be the right ones to contact (e.g., the person has moved on to another position, left the company, etc.). But you want to find out as much context as you can about the people on your contact list, beyond just their name and phone number.

You can research and improve your contact list in several ways. First, you should decide who will handle the research. You can, of course, do the research yourself if you have the resources. But this type of research is time-consuming, and it may tie up your lead-generation staff if you ask them to handle all the research themselves.

You also have the option to use third-party organizations to verify names and research contacts on a list. A number of offshore companies in India will do this research for you, for pennies on the dollar. Or you can use online crowd-sourcing tools such as Amazon's Mechanical Turk (available from Amazon Web Services) to outsource this research to hundreds of part-time individuals. If you can reduce the number of dud names on your contact list by 20%, then it's certainly worth spending a little money to have someone research and verify your contacts for you.

USING LINKEDIN

Whether you improve your contact list yourself or assign the research to a third-party company, it will help you to know some tools that you can use for this type of research. Even if you let an outside company handle the verifying of names on your list, it may help your lead-generation team to do a bit of personal research on the contacts before they make the calls.

LinkedIn is one of several online business tools that have emerged just within the past few years that allow you to research your potential customers. LinkedIn gives you a full profile of your contact, with information supplied by the contacts themselves. Because your contacts edit their own profiles, LinkedIn offers some of the most accurate, up-to-date information about who is in which position at your target company. (*Note:* Some LinkedIn users employ privacy settings to block information from appearing on their profiles.)

You can research each contact on LinkedIn to make sure you will be talking to the right person at a target company. You want to make sure your contacts are people who have a need for your products or services, and who have the power to buy from you. Even if a contact on your list is not the right person to call, the chances are that they have a close connection with the right person through their LinkedIn profile.

For example, say you decide that regional sales directors are the best people to talk to about your products or services at a target company. A certain name, John Swanson, is listed on your initial contact list as the regional director of sales for the company's Northeast region. But when you check John Swanson's LinkedIn profile, you find out he has moved on to another division of the company.

However, John Swanson is probably still connected on LinkedIn to other regional sales directors at his company. You can find their names (including, probably, the name of the new regional sales director for the Northeast) by looking through John Swanson's list of LinkedIn connections or by looking in the "People Who Viewed This Profile Also Viewed . . ." section of links on the side of the profile page. You can view the LinkedIn profiles of other regional sales directors at the company, get a sense of their background, and add them to your contact list.

Using LinkedIn, you can also learn about any relationship that you might have with a potential contact. For example, you might notice that you have a shared LinkedIn connection with a certain regional sales director—let's say, Sarah Kinzer—at the contact company. Maybe Gary Cattell, a sales manager at another company—someone you've met at a conference and with whom you have a LinkedIn connection—is also connected to Sarah Kinzer via LinkedIn.

You might ask Gary Cattell to introduce you to Sarah Kinzer through a LinkedIn introduction. This can help you to get a foot in the door with Sarah Kinzer, so that she might be more willing to listen to your pitch about your products or services when you call her. You will often get better responses from contacts when they've received a warm introduction to you from a colleague than if you make your own cold introduction.

OTHER ONLINE RESEARCH TOOLS

In addition to LinkedIn, other data-enhanced services are available that will allow you to get more information about a potential client than just their standard demographics. Gist (www.gist.com) is an online service (owned by Blackberry) that provides social customer relationship management (CRM) and contact management. If you subscribe to Gist, you can search for and get regular updates about the social media activities of your business contacts and potential customers.

For example, you can type in the job title of a target customer and their company in the search engine on Gist (e.g., "Chief Marketing Officer—Dell"). You'll get a profile of that person that might include their blog address, Twitter feed, and any relevant articles they've written, or in which they've been quoted. Using rich data like this can help you to make a connection with persons when you cold-call them.

On a Gist search report, you might see a news article that says your contact recently accepted an award for helping to make their company more energy efficient. If your company specializes in "green" technology, you can customize your cold call introduction to tell your contact about how your products or services work to help companies increase their energy efficiency. You can make a connection with your contact on the initial call by talking about a subject that you know the person is passionate about.

USING E-MAIL AND OTHER RESEARCH METHODS

Another online research tool that you can use to check the accuracy of your list is Xobni (www.xobni.com), which is now owned by Blackberry. The name *Xobni* (pronounced *zob-nee*) is "Inbox" spelled backward. Xobni offers e-mail applications that can be attached to Microsoft Outlook or Gmail, or to the address book of your Blackberry, iPhone, or Android. These applications let you search or navigate e-mail archives to find the e-mail addresses of people on your contact list.

If you have the e-mail addresses of contact names on your list, you can use e-mail to check the accuracy of the list as well. For example, you might send out an e-mail marketing blast to your contacts on the list and discount any names that bounce back. You can also prioritize anyone who opened the e-mail and clicked through as likely interested buyers. Companies such as Eloqua and Marketo offer marketing automation tools to help you automate this process.

Other ways of improving the accuracy of your contact list are very simple. For example, you can go to the website of any company on your list to confirm basic contact information. While you're at the website, you can search for any context information about a contact name on your list.

CREDITING YOUR LIST

Even with your research to verify the contacts, chances are that a number of dud names will still be on your list. The person you call will have left the company, been fired, moved to another position, etc. A general rule of thumb is, even on a good list that matches your target criteria, one out of every three names will be a dud. If you buy a list with 1,000 names, for example, between 300 and 350 of those names will turn out to be duds. List owners use time-based methods to acquire contact information for people at various companies, so the list you buy may have contact records that are up to a year old.

Fortunately, it's a standard practice for most list owners to offer a make-good to credit their clients for dud names. As you verify the data on your list or make the calls, keep careful track of bad or inaccurate contact names, and ask the list owner for a refund on those names. (See Chapter 11 for more information about the make-good process.)

You'll be surprised how variable pricing is for contact lists used for cold calling. Since purchased lists are often less accurate, they are usually less expensive. With contact lists, the value and the risk of the list are usually pre-assessed and factored into the price.

Step 3: Create Your Cold-Calling Script

In cold calling, the creative asset of your campaign is the script for the call. Like a direct mail piece or e-mail offer, the cold-calling script includes a pitch, a CTA, and possibly an offer.

I *strongly* recommend that the marketing department should be in charge of creating the cold-calling script, and should have total control over it, whether a sales or marketing person will be making the cold call. By controlling the script, the marketing department can ensure that the pitch, offers, and other features in the script are in line with the marketing elements being used in other lead-generation tactics, and ultimately in line with the brand.

You don't want to let salespeople develop their own cold-calling script because they have a tendency to go off-message when they don't understand your company's marketing goals. When off-message salespersons call customers, they stray away from the company's pre-defined marketing messages and concentrate on the wrong features of the product or service when describing it to customers.

For example, you may have built your marketing campaign around the fact that your product provides a great cost savings to the customer. You've built your ads and other marketing collateral to highlight this cost savings advantage. But when off-message salespersons call a customer, they concentrate instead on the *physical* features of the product (the color, design, etc.), and on the fact that you can order it in bulk. Their message is not consistent with the company's marketing message for the product, and, as a result, they lose many sales opportunities. There is nothing worse for a marketing manager than a rogue salesperson who is off-message.

With a cold-calling script, the information must be very quick and succinct, and it must concentrate on the value of the product or service. You have about 30 seconds to convince the person you are calling to stay on the phone with you and hear you out. Therefore, in the first 15 seconds, you should:

1. Introduce yourself

2. Briefly describe your company, and say why its brand or purpose is relative to the person you are calling (assuming the potential customer is not already familiar with you)

3. Tell them why your product or service is relevant to them

4. Give your offer and its value proposition

5. Give the potential customer your call-to-action to accept the offer

You should center the script around your value proposition and call-to-action. Most potential customers have the attitude of "What's in it for me?" (which marketers often describe as "WIIFM" or "Whiff-'em!"). If you can't convince the customer why they should care, you won't convert them to leads. Your script will be very effective only if you can quickly show them how using your products or services will benefit them.

In terms of branding, the more well-known your company is, the more willing the person you call will be to listen to you. If you don't have a well-known brand, however, you can still make cold calling work for you. Your chances for success will increase if you have a compelling script with an attractive offer, and if you target the right audience for the cold call.

For example, say you are a new company that sells software tools for online recruiting. Your name is not well-known, but you have great products and are offering a 30-day free trial of your recruiting tools to prospective customers. When you begin cold calling, you want to have a targeted list of company recruiters, executive recruiters—the types of people who have a need for your tools.

When you call your prospective customers, explain how the tools work, but focus on your CTA: "You can use our system for 30 days free of charge." Chances are the recruiters you call will at least listen to you, and possibly take you up on the offer.

Try to lead with a case example from a similar client that has a brand that your audience cares about. For example, if you are calling an executive recruiter at Acme Computers, and one of your clients is Legend Software (an Acme competitor), you might say, "By using our online research tool, Legend Software was able to fill six executive positions in just under two months."

Step 4: Test and Execute Your Campaign

To be effective, cold calling must be well-rehearsed. Your cold callers must be able to speak clearly and enthusiastically, in addition to delivering your value proposition and offer quickly and accurately. Your cold callers also need to know how to handle the follow-up to the offer—that is, how to qualify the potential customer and set the follow-up action in motion *while they have them on the phone.*

REHEARSING YOUR SCRIPT

Once your cold callers have the script, they need to rehearse it. When calling potential customers, they have that 15 seconds to catch the caller's attention and convince them to stay on the phone. So it's extremely important that your cold callers know how to deliver the value proposition and offer in a clear, enthusiastic way. They should be cheerful and confident about the product or service when they make the calls, but not overly salesy and pushy.

Note: *Think back to the days of telemarketing. How often did you hang up on telemarketers because they kept pushing a product that you didn't want and wouldn't take "No" for an answer? Or, worse, how often did you hang up on telemarketers who mumbled through their call script and didn't have any real enthusiasm for what they were selling? These same problems—too much salesmanship and not speaking clearly—can spell disaster for a cold-calling campaign.*

Your cold callers should rehearse the script until they have a feel for the language and can speak the words clearly and precisely. Once they have confidence in their delivery, you should try a role-playing exercise to help them refine it. Have your cold callers call each other. Each caller can listen as the other practices the delivery of the script over the phone.

You can also have your cold callers call other people in your company and record the script on their voice-mail. Listening to each other, and to the voice-mail recordings, will give your cold callers insights as to how to improve their delivery of the message, and the people who have been called can provide feedback on the message.

Eventually, you hope, the cold callers will get so comfortable with the script that they will "make it their own." They will be able to speak the words naturally and spontaneously, without sounding as if they are reading from a script. They can improvise while still staying on-message and make their interactions with the potential customer more conversational. If the cold caller can give customers calls that are more of a one-on-one conversation (and less of a product pitch), customers are more likely to view the calls as a positive experience and to be interested in the product or service.

TESTING AND REFINING YOUR MESSAGE

How do you test and refine your message in cold calling? Start off your campaign by calling smaller or not so important potential clients. For example, from a contact list of 1,000 names, you might select 100 less important clients as a test sample. You don't want to call your "dream" clients first and try to sell them on your product or service before you know whether your cold-calling message works. If the message doesn't work, you may end up losing an opportunity to land a valuable client.

For example, say you're selling a new software tool for online recruiting. You know this tool could be very useful to Fortune 500 companies (General Motors, Aetna Insurance, Kimberly-Clark, etc.). But you shouldn't call those companies to try to pitch your product until you are sure your cold-calling message, value proposition, offer, and all the other elements are good enough to attract major clients.

In this case, start out by calling small to midsized companies, which might bring you less business but which might still have a need for your software tool. If your message gets a good response from these companies, you can move on to larger or more important clients. If your message gets a poor response in the initial calls, you can change your offer or refine your message before taking it to the more important clients on your list.

DEALING WITH VOICE-MAIL

Voice-mail has become a fact of life in the business world. When you call people at work, at least 80% of the time, you get their voice-mail. Unfortunately, a large number of calls left on voice-mail—especially cold calls that pitch new products or services—go unreturned. As a society, we have allowed voice-mail to take the place of one-on-one business communication. (And people wonder why our economy is growing at such a slow and languid pace!)

If you do cold calling, you need to decide how your callers will handle voice-mail. At the highest level, there are two possibilities to consider. First, you can tell your callers to ignore voice-mail completely. If they get someone's voice-mail, they should not leave a message, but should keep calling back at various times of day until they get the intended person on the phone. This may be more time-consuming, but you have a better chance of selling your product or service if you can actually speak to the person you are calling, rather than leaving a message.

The second option is to develop a message that your cold callers can leave on someone's voice-mail. This message should give a brief summary of the benefits of your product or service, along with maybe a short case example from one of your well-known clients (e.g., "Acme Software was able to cut their recruiting time in half by using our online recruiting tools"). You should also include a short, one-sentence offer. (For example, "Call us back, and we'll let you try our software free of charge for 30 days.") The point is to entice persons to call you back by giving them just enough information so that your offer will be of interest to them.

QUALIFYING THE LEAD

When the cold caller has practiced the script enough to become comfortable with it, their next step is to start calling potential clients. But once the cold caller connects with a prospective customer on the phone and confirms the customer's interest, their job changes. As the cold caller continues to sell the customer on your company's products or services, they must also qualify the customer as a potential client.

First, the cold caller needs to confirm that the client has a genuine interest in your offer, and a need for your types of products or services. They also need to confirm that the person they've called is the right person to talk to, and that this person has the authority and buying power to purchase your company's products or services for their company. And most important, the cold caller should confirm that the client has the budget to spend money on your type of product or service!

You should include the need to qualify the prospective customer as a lead in the cold-calling script. You shouldn't necessarily script the qualifying process because it needs to be done subtly. Instead, you should include a series of questions in the script that allow your cold callers to confirm certain points of information with prospective customers during the call. For example:

- *"I understand that you're the director of recruiting for Acme Company. Is that correct?"* This question confirms that the prospective customer is in the right position at the company to have a need for your products or services.

- *"Do you have a regular need for [type or function of product, e.g., online recruiting software tools]?"* This probe confirms that the prospect uses or has a need for your type of product. This question determines whether you need to sell the listener on the concept in general or just sell your own product.

- *"Are you looking to buy new [online recruiting software]?"* This question not only verifies interest, but also verifies two important points about the person: The person has (1) the authority to purchase your product and (2) the budget.

- *"Would you like to try our product for 30 days, free of charge?"* The caller makes your offer and/or call-to-action to see whether they are accepted.

Turning Them into a Lead

If the prospective customer qualifies as a lead, the cold caller's next step should be to convert them into actual leads. The caller can do this in several ways. The way you choose to do it depends on the type of product or service you are selling.

- *Drive them to an online experience such as a landing page:* As you talk with the prospective customer, give them the URL to a landing page for signing up for your special offer. (See Chapter 6 for details on how to create a good landing page.)

- *Send them a follow-up e-mail:* You can send the potential client a follow-up e-mail that summarizes your conversation and includes a link to a landing page where they take the next step (e.g., sign up for the offer, download a white paper, etc.).

- *Transfer them to a salesperson who can drive the lead into a sale.*

On this last option, there are several ways to turn the potential customer over to a salesperson:

- *Log the lead into a CRM tool:* Using CRM software, the cold caller can create a lead for the sales team. Usually, a lead in a CRM tool is a record with the potential customer's contact information. Salespersons using the same CRM software receive the lead record, and can then call the potential customers back at their convenience to convert them into opportunities.

- *Set an appointment:* On the initial call, the cold caller can ask customers to schedule an appointment for a salesperson to call or visit them at an appropriate day and time. The salesperson can then do a product demo, re-verify the customers as leads, give them the free trial, etc.

- *Transfer the call directly to a salesperson:* A cold caller who confirms the potential customer's interest can transfer the call directly to an available salesperson. This is a warm transfer, and it's the best, most effective way to turn the customer into a lead. The salesperson can continue the conversation while the customer's interest is still piqued. Depending on the offer, the salesperson may be able verify the customer as a lead or even turn the customer's interest into an actual sale or transaction.

Note: The entire cold-calling process should take less than a few minutes. A cold caller should be able to make 30–100 cold calls in a day.

THE UNQUALIFIED LEAD

What do you do if the persons you call are not qualified as leads? Maybe they are the right persons at their companies. They meet your target criteria. They have a need for your type of product or service and the authority to buy it. But they just don't have the budget to buy it right now. Or maybe the company is using a competitive product or service, and they won't make a decision about whether to use a new product or service for another year.

These potential customers still qualify as marketing leads, in the sense that they may have a need for your products or services in the future. But you shouldn't pass them over to the sales team right away. (The sales team should focus only on leads who are ready to buy.)

Instead, put potential customers who are not ready to buy into a "drip bucket." Continue to do nurture marketing with them. By sending them e-newsletters, e-mails with special offers, case studies, occasional sales letters, and other materials, you keep your company and your brand in their mind for the day when they might be ready to try your products or services.

In another scenario, you might discover the lead is the wrong person at the company altogether. The person has neither the job title/position that you have listed for them on your contact list nor the authority to purchase your products or services. Or the person doesn't even have a need for your types of products or services in their department at the company.

In this case, you should still use the phone call as an opportunity to find the right person at that company. Ask the person you've called if they know which person or department at their company might have a need for your type of product or service. Or, if the receptionist says the person you are calling has left the company, ask for the replacement's name.

BUILDING YOUR COLD-CALLING TEAM

You might ask: "What if I don't have a cold-calling team to use for lead qualification? My marketing guys are shrinking violets, and they don't like to be on the phone. How do I use cold calling to my advantage?"

You can solve this problem in several ways. One way is to create your own cold-calling organization under the direction of the marketing department. A typical internal cold-calling organization is made up of entry-level employees who don't require a degree or direct job experience. The callers do need to be eager, friendly on the phone, and not afraid of rejection. These types of organizations are fairly inexpensive to create. All you need is a computer, a phone, a desk, and a chair for each individual caller.

Also, many external, third-party companies will do cold calling for you. Some are located in the United States; others are overseas, in places like India and Malaysia. These companies will collaborate with you to set up a call center structure, where they will make calls on your behalf using your script, lead-qualification questions, and other materials. The callers will then pass on any qualified leads to your sales team.

Usually, when third-party callers receive leads, they will either enter the leads directly into your CRM tool or, more commonly, record the leads in a daily/weekly spreadsheet, which they then pass on to your company. If your third-party callers are recording leads on spreadsheets, your marketing team will often have to manually enter the leads from the spreadsheets into your CRM tool.

A third option is to work with your sales organization to have them make cold calls according to a script provided by marketing. However, this gives marketing less control over the cold-calling experience.

Step 5: Measure Your Results

With cold calling, measuring success is a lot less straightforward than with other lead-generation tactics. When you calculate your CPA, you not only need to include the cost of the contact list you buy, but also the cost of the employee doing the cold calling. Although many of the costs are tangible, it can become a slippery slope. Let's say you pay each cold caller $3,000 per month (or $36,000 per year), and each caller generates an average of 1,000 leads per month. You can argue that each caller contributes $3 to the CPA. But wait! Are you adding in things like computer and telephone costs, office space allocations, taxes, benefits, the average two complimentary soft drinks each employee takes per day from your food and drink pantry, and other, not-so-visible costs? Sometimes, it's tough to know where to draw the line.

In calculating your CPA for cold calling, it may help you to use the concept of a cost-per-click (CPC), as you would use with online lead-generation tactics like SEM. Even though cold calling is an offline process, and you don't have a metric like a "click" when you call a prospective customer, you can apply online measurement tactics. For example, think of each cold call you make as being an impression, similar to the impression someone gets when they see a PPC ad for your product on a search engine. The persons you call may not buy your product, but at least they become aware of it.

Think of each lead you get from cold calling as being a "click." Every time your cold callers pass on a warm transfer to a salesperson, or every time the prospective customer puts down the phone and visits a landing page, you have a lead. So if a cold caller is doing 300 calls per day, and approximately 30 of these calls become a warm transfer, you have a 10% conversion rate. If that list cost you $600, then your CPL is $20.

Measuring the number of calls, or impressions, your cold callers make per day, as well as the number of leads, or "clicks," they receive, should be easy. Most CRM tools have components that allow cold callers to log the number of calls they make, and to keep track of the number of leads that each caller is able to generate.

There are a lot of ways to measure the productivity of your team, but, at the end of the day, what really matters is how many leads they are generating. Often, their success or failure is not based on how many calls they are making but *how they are making the calls.* For example, a cold-calling team might average 100 calls per member per day but produce very few leads. But if they change tactics and do a little research on the people and companies on the list before making each call, they can often make fewer calls but yield a greater number of leads.

> > > **What You Should Know** < < <

Here's what you need to know to plan a cold-calling campaign:

- For lead-generation purposes, cold calling is a tried-and-true tactic. It is extremely appropriate for businesses whose purchasing audience is very small. Cold calling works best when the marketing department controls it.

- For cold calling, you need to purchase a targeted list of clients from a trustworthy source. The initial list should include contact and demographic information for your potential customers, such as their phone numbers and job titles. Even after purchasing the list, you will need to improve it, either by having your marketing team research and verify the names and contact information on the list, or by hiring a third party to do it for you. Use tools like LinkedIn and Gist to research your prospects and gain as much context about them as possible before calling them.

- Cold callers should have a script to follow when making their calls. The script is the creative asset of the cold-calling tactic, and marketing should be in charge of writing it. The script should introduce your company or brand, give your value proposition, and make your call-to-action/offer to the potential customer in about 30 seconds.

- The script should also include follow-up questions that will allow the cold caller to qualify the potential customer as a lead during the call. If the customer qualifies, the cold caller should then convert them into a lead by directing them to a landing page, sending them a follow-up e-mail, setting an appointment, or making a warm transfer of the call to a salesperson.

- When potential customers don't qualify as leads but still have an interest in your company's products, they should be placed in a "drip bucket," so that marketing materials and special offers can be sent to them in the future. If the person called is the wrong person altogether, the caller should take the opportunity to find out who the right person is at the company—that is, who might have a need for your products.

- Measuring your success can be tricky in cold calling because you have to factor in the expense of the employees who are doing the calling. In measuring your CPA, you should measure the number of calls made against the number of qualified leads you receive from those calls.

15

Trade Shows

A **TRADE SHOW**, on a basic level, is an opportunity to meet face-to-face with people who might be interested in your products or services, and to display your goods in person. A trade show might be held at a convention center, an exhibition hall, a stadium or sports arena, inside a hotel ballroom, or in a public park or fairground.

I love trade shows. They're a lot of fun, and a very effective form of lead-generation marketing. A trade show is network marketing at its finest. It's a way for like-minded people to get together for a few days to talk about topics that are specific to their particular industry or personal interests.

For attendees, a trade show provides a "one-stop-shop" opportunity to buy or learn about products or services, and to talk directly with the people who make or sell them. In just a few days, the customer can get a good overview and understanding of their options. They can walk the floor at the trade show, talk in person with company reps, and compare products and services from different companies to see which are the best for their needs. They can speak to other attendees, who may serve as customer references for these products and services. They can see live product demonstrations, check out the newest and coolest products, and pick up valuable tips and information at seminars and panel discussions.

For the company or marketer, the trade show offers a great opportunity for in-person marketing and interaction with potential customers. In other lead-generation tactics such as direct mail, the company reaches out to customers, who may or may not be in the market for the product. At a trade show, the opposite happens: Customers come to see your company (and other similar companies). Often, the customers have a *vested interest* in learning all they can about your types of products or services. Depending on their needs, they may travel thousands of miles and pay thousands of dollars in travel expenses to attend a certain trade show. In addition, customers must pay an admission registration fee for the show, and the fees for some high-ranking industry shows can range from $2,000 to $10,000.

This is good news for your company because trade show attendees are more likely to have a need for your products or services, or at least a willingness to listen to what you have to say. Attending a trade show as a vendor provides an opportunity to put your products or services in front of thousands, if not tens of thousands, of potential customers who are *looking to buy*.

Trade shows are the oldest lead-generation marketing tactic. They've been around in one form or another for centuries! In medieval times, farmers, merchants, and craftspeople would go to annual town fairs and festivals to sell their goods and wares in makeshift booths or out of the backs of carts. Following the industrial fairs of the 19th century, where inventors and industrialists came to display the latest advances in science and technology, the trade show started to evolve into its current form around the beginning of the 20th century.

Even as we advance through the digital age, trade shows will continue to be widely used. Occasionally, such as in the aftermath of the 9/11 attacks and in the years following the recent financial meltdown, attendance at major trade shows briefly drops off. But the companies and the customers always come back.

There have been some attempts to develop virtual trade shows, where companies display their goods online while holding live chats with potential customers. But these have largely failed, because a virtual show lacks the personalized experience and one-on-one human connection that potential customers get by attending trade shows in person. Companies know the value of demonstrating their products or services in live demonstrations, and potential customers are always eager to come back to the show to see what new products or services their favorite companies have to offer *this* year.

To Show or Not to Show?

The good news is, there's a trade show for just about every kind of industry these days: software, wireless communications, dental equipment, farm machinery, industrial marine products, etc. Also, many types of services can be marketed at trade shows. For example, insurance companies that specialize in homeowners' insurance often attend local trade shows for home and garden products.

But trade shows are also the most expensive form of lead-generation marketing. Attending a show as a vendor often requires a considerable investment. You have to rent space for your booth, build your creative assets (the booth, marketing collateral, etc.), cover travel costs (airline fees, hotel rooms, rental car, etc.) for getting your company representatives to the show, and incur other types of expenses.

Some companies spend hundreds of thousands of dollars to attend a single annual trade show. Some larger corporations may even spend *millions* of dollars to make a big splash at a certain national or international show. Other companies may spend millions per year, but they spread out the expenses over dozens of trade shows.

Companies that know how to *justify the cost* of trade shows will use them to their best advantage. In other words, these companies know that making a decent display at a trade show will bring them enough new sales and/or

- Close to the booths of high-profile brands that attract crowds of people

- In the flow of traffic between the entrances and/or the high-profile brand booths

The worst place to have your booth is at the far edges of the convention hall, where many people are not likely to go. A booth space next to the restrooms may or may not work to your advantage, depending on the circumstances. (There's a theory that more people will notice you as they come out of the restrooms.)

Also, you need to be aware of the companies in the area of your booth space. Trade shows have different strategies for how they organize the layout of booth locations at each show. Some trade show organizers will group companies with similar products or services in the same area. For example, at a software or high-tech show, they may create a "Web Design Alley," so that all traffic interested in Web design can visit that area and get a quick evaluation of each company's products or services.

Other trade show organizers want to spread out the competition, to give vendors the full attention of the traffic flowing through. Where you are located in relation to other companies depends on the product you are selling and the dynamic of the trade show. Most trade shows will let you know which companies are around certain booth spaces if you request the information. When you select your booth location (see next section), they will often show you a billboard or a computerized display showing the open booth locations, the taken locations, and locations of the various companies at the next show.

You want to know where your competitors are. There are two competing arguments when it comes to how close you want to be to them:

1. You want to make sure you're *not* near a competitor because, if they are too close to you, they may take customers away from you, especially if they have a well-known brand and products that everyone flocks to see at the show. Also, if you have a similar brand or product, you may find your brand being confused with theirs.

2. On the other hand, you may *want* to have a booth near your competitors so your potential customers can compare products or services. If you can demonstrate that you have a superior product, you may be able to pull customers from your competitors' booths.

THE BOOTH LOCATION LOTTERY

Selecting a good booth location is one of the most competitive aspects of trade shows, because every company wants the best location possible. Each trade show has its own priority system for how vendors choose their locations for the next show. Several factors affect priority in choosing your booth location:

Timing Some shows assign booth locations on a first-come/first-serve basis, and give priority to the show's current vendors. As soon as this year's show is over, usually on the last day of the show the trade show organizers will approach vendors at the show, offering to let them keep the same space for next year's show. After the current vendors make their decision, the organizers open up additional spaces to newcomers.

This sometimes means that, literally, the minute this year's trade show is over, vendors are booking their booth locations for next year. The trade show organizers may invite vendors to come into a conference room and pick next year's location right then and there. In this case, the earlier you can get to the last show to book your space for next year, the better, even if it's one minute after the last show concludes.

Seniority At some shows, the organizers give vendors priority for space based on their loyalty to the show. The more years you've exhibited, the better the space you get for next year's show. If you attend the show as a vendor over several years, you may get better chances for booth opportunities as you continue to exhibit.

Booth Size Many shows assign priority for selecting booth location according to booth size. Companies with the largest booths get first priority because, of course, they're paying the most money.

Each trade show has its own style of assigning priority and determining which companies get first pick of their booth locations. For example, the National Retail Federation (NRF) Show, one of the largest trade shows in the country, gives each vendor a lottery number. Based on a combination of the preceding factors, your retail company may be assigned as the first, the 500th, or the 1,200th company to have the opportunity to select your booth location for next year's show. Newcomers to the NRF Show get any location space that's left over after this lottery.

For some major shows, it's really hard for newcomers to get good locations, unless, of course, they come in with sponsorship money and a good-sized booth. If you have money to spend, the trade shows will do more to accommodate you, even if you're not at the top of their priority list for booth location. ("It's a business," as they say, and trade shows are in it to make money.)

Creating Your Booth

Even before reserving your booth space, you need to start thinking about what kind of booth you need. Of course, you should have an initial idea of booth size (e.g., 10 × 10 or 30 × 30 feet) so that you can reserve an appropriate space at the show.

You have several options in terms of the booth itself:

- You can rent a ready-made, turnkey booth from the trade show itself and customize it to your brand and company.

- You can buy a pre-made booth, which you customize to your brand and company. Once you own the booth, you can carry it to multiple trade shows, as needed. (Usually, these booths will have ready-made blank-slate panels to which you can attach or silkscreen your logo.)

- You can have a custom-made booth or display built for you by a trade show display company.

A lot of fantastic companies out there, such as the Godfrey Group and Smash Hit Displays, specialize in trade show displays. They will create custom displays or turnkey booths for you at very competitive prices.

It's important to understand what trade shows give you, and what they don't. At some shows, you can get peppered with nickel-and-dime expenses for providing extras to your booth. For example, you may rent a booth space, but the trade show will charge you extra to provide electrical power, carpeting, and Internet access. Often, this is not the trade show's fault. Usually, the convention center or exhibition hall dictates the cost for these items, based on local power and Internet rates and on labor union guidelines.

Also, be aware that you may have to pay union rates to have things set up or moved that you can't handle yourself. Unions tend to mark up the price of work quite a bit with their various union rules, and sometimes these markups can get pretty ridiculous. For example, according to union rules, you may be required to have *two union workers* (and pay both of them) to set up a simple audiovisual display, when one worker could set up the display in about five minutes!

Some trade shows offer booth package deals that may include a booth table, two stools, a backboard, some carpeting, a wastebasket, and basic electricity and Internet access. Look at the trade show's vendor information packet to see what kinds of booth package deals may be available. And be sure to examine your rental space or booth package contract to find out *exactly* what you get when you rent your booth space and/or turnkey booth.

Your Displays, Tchotchkes, and Other Marketing Materials

Once you have your booth in place, you need a way to demonstrate your product or service. How you do this depends on what you offer. If it's a software product, you should have computer monitors at your booth and do software demos. If you can demonstrate the product in a short (e.g., 3-minute) corporate video or computer animation, have TV monitors running the video. If your product is more tactile—something you can demonstrate on the spot—have a makeshift stage or theater where the audience can stand or sit and watch a manual demonstration.

If your product is small or something you can produce inexpensively in mass quantities, you might hand out product samples. A friend told me he once attended a maritime trade show. The vendors at this show included boat manufacturers and sellers of boat engines, propellers, marine navigational equipment, and other products for the marine industries. One booth belonged to a company that specialized in catching and processing fish bait for fishers and fishing companies. At this booth, the company reps were giving away free samples of fish bait—squid and small minnowlike fish. The fishermen who attended the show were walking up to the booth to examine the fish samples. (Yes, some of the fishermen were actually tasting the fish bait samples, presumably to see whether the fish would like them.)

Even if you don't have a product sample to give away, you should have some kind of takeaway, such as a brochure or sell sheet with extra information about your product or service. Be sure to have an abundance of copies so that you don't run out. And be sure any brochure or sell sheet you use has the necessary contact information for your company, such as your address, phone number, or website URL.

And then there're your tchotchkes. The tchotchkes are little knickknacks or giveaways that people can take away with them. Printed somewhere on them should be your brand and contact information (e.g., your website URL).

The purpose of the tchotchke is to bring people to your booth so that you can give them your product or service pitch. Never underestimate the value of a good tchotchke. I've seen some really creative takeaways that helped to drive traffic to booths that might not otherwise have had as many visitors. Some of my favorite tchotchkes are:

- *A branded pencil or ballpoint pen.*

- *A branded zip drive.*

- *Branded candy:* Many trade show booths have a bowl of candy to entice visitors to stop by. But really smart companies give out chocolate bars with their brand and contact info printed on the wrapping.

- *Toys:* Some companies hand out a branded stuffed animal. At one show I attended, a company had a toy monkey that screeched when you pushed its belly. Other companies might hand out a small, branded toy made of plastic or foam rubber. For example, an aviation company might hand out a branded toy airplane. A shipbuilding company might hand out a small model of a cargo ship. Toys are very popular with people who bring their kids to the show.

- *Hats or other apparel:* Many companies give out baseball caps or even T-shirts with their brand and contact info. I once saw a company giving out branded scarves at a trade show. It was a hit because it was wintertime, and everyone had forgotten their winter clothes.

Finally, you need to consider whom you want to represent your company at the trade show. Selecting the right people to represent your products and services is critical. Who you choose to be your "faces" at the trade show sometimes depends on your products or services, and on who can effectively sell or market them to potential customers. Many companies use sales or marketing people as trade show representatives, but you have other options. For example:

- If you have a CEO who is well-known in the industry—or just an enthusiastic promoter of your products or services—they can represent you.

- Some companies send the product designers to demonstrate a product at a trade show.

- Companies may hire a celebrity spokesperson, or a person well-known in their industry, to host a product demonstration.

- Other companies send satisfied customers to give testimonials on why they use and like the company's products.

- Some companies hire professional models to model clothes or give product demonstrations. I've seen companies hire these "booth babes" for every occasion, even when it isn't absolutely necessary. For example, I've seen them at video game conventions, demonstrating the latest video games. Often, the models don't even understand how to play the games they are demonstrating. But they attract the male fans to the booth to try out the games. The reality is, using a pretty face is a good way to attract people to your booth to hear your pitch or try out the product.

Capturing Leads

Capturing leads is the most important aspect of attending a trade show. You need to have a method in place at the show to do this. Just as you want your landing page for an e-mail or online ad to collect a potential customer's contact information, you also need a way to collect information from potential customers at a trade show.

You can do this in several ways. You might have a signup sheet at your booth for a freebee or special prize (e.g., "Sign up now for our daily drawing. Every day at the trade show, we give away 10 free copies of our latest software."). If it's a B2B trade show, you might also keep a bowl or basket at the booth where people who are interested in your products or services can leave their business cards.

Some trade shows are making it easier for companies to collect contact information from attendees. The attendees wear special badges with embedded microchips or bar codes. Each vendor at the show gets a scanner, and the company reps need only to scan badges to capture the attendee's essential information.

Your goal should be to capture as many leads as possible at the trade show. After the show, you should make sure that your marketing or sales staff follows up on those leads promptly. *It amazes me how many companies don't do this.* They spend thousands of dollars to attend a trade show. They collect business cards or other contact information from hundreds of potential customers who visit their booth. And then, after the show, they don't follow up on those costly leads!

This is the same as flushing money down the toilet. The people you meet at trade shows usually have a good reason to be there; they are very likely to have a need or interest in your types of products or services. If you don't follow up with them after the show to gauge their interest, you are throwing away valuable leads that could easily turn into potential long-term customers! Therefore, you should treat the leads from a trade show with the same importance and urgency as leads from any other lead-generation tactic. Follow up on those leads as soon as possible!

Sponsorships

Sponsorships are the second way to participate in a trade show. As a sponsor, your company pays a certain amount of money to the show. In return, you get to display your brand or logo in various places at the show.

Sponsorships give you two advantages: First, they give you opportunities to build your brand with the attendees. Second, they allow you to use your brand to drive potential customers to your booth. Once the attendees at the trade show know you are there, they may be more inclined to visit your booth to see what you have to offer.

Sponsorships operate on a pay-to-play model: The more money you pay, the more opportunities you get to display your brand at the show. Trade shows usually provide different levels of sponsorship, such as Platinum, Gold, Silver, and Bronze levels. A Platinum-level sponsorship might be in the $100,000 range, whereas a Bronze-level sponsorship might be in the $10,000 range.

For a Platinum-level sponsorship, your brand receives the most exposure. For example, your company might be able to put your brand on all marketing materials for the show, including the attendees' badge. You might get a full-page color ad in the event guide, promoting events and takeaways at your company booth. You might get your brand or logo displayed on the special bag of freebees that the show gives out to attendees along with the registration packet, and be asked to provide a gift (e.g., a free zip drive with your brand on it) in the event bag. You may be able to sponsor or put your name on certain events like receptions, keynote speeches, or panel discussions. Usually, you want to pick an event that ties in well with your brand, so your target customers will be in the audience at the event, and will associate your brand with it.

A Bronze-level sponsorship will be less expensive but will get you less coverage for your brand. For example, you might get a quarter-page ad in the event guide, be provided with on-site signage, and get your brand featured on the show's website.

Sponsorships are usually sold on a first-come/first-serve basis. The shows typically have a limited number of spaces in the event guide, on the website, and in other places where they can put company brands. So it's a good idea to find out the show's deadlines for registering as a sponsor.

Usually, you can find information about sponsorships in the show's vendor information guide. Also, once you sign up as a sponsor, the trade show will usually give you all sorts of feedback on where you can place your brand.

One more thing about sponsorships: Even though the shows sell sponsorship packages at different levels and prices, you have more control over the contents of these packages. After all, you're the one paying the money. You can often negotiate with the trade show to build your own package of branding opportunities, so you can maximize your brand's impact at that trade show.

Speaking Engagements

Being a keynote speaker or a panelist at a panel discussion is the most valuable way you can participate at a trade show. It positions you (or a spokesperson or representative for your company) as a thought leader, front and center, in view of everybody who matters at that particular show.

Being a keynote speaker gives you more credibility than anything else you will do at a trade show, because attendees don't perceive public speaking as marketing. They perceive it as you, an expert, offering valuable advice to them, free of charge. But if you're a good keynote speaker—if you can get your message across about your product, or impress everyone with your expertise in the industry—you can really drive people to your booth at the trade show.

The best thing about speaking engagements at trade shows is that they are usually free. Unlike a booth or sponsorship, you don't have to pay for the privilege of speaking at the trade show. The hardest part about public speaking is convincing the trade show managers that you're the best person for the job. Trade shows are very selective in picking speakers for their events. They want someone who will give good value in the information they provide, not just a sales pitch for the company's latest product release.

What do you need to become a keynote speaker? It helps if you or someone in your organization has outside credibility such as having written a book, or having a well-known blog, about a popular subject in your field. It helps if you have a well-respected brand in the industry, or if you are well-known from prior speaking engagements. (Obviously, Bill Gates and Tom Peters don't have any problems getting a keynote speakership.)

If you're relatively unknown, the key is to create a compelling and relevant topic that you're willing to speak on, one that really meets the needs of the conference. For example, if you're attending a conference of lawyers, you might create a presentation that focuses on FCC guidelines and changes, and on their impact to Internet regulations. If you're an expert on a subject, and you have enough credibility to give a decent talk on that subject before a live audience, the trade shows will be more interested in what you have to offer as a potential speaker.

The goal of the trade show organizers is to get as many attendees to the show as possible. They do this by offering content that matters to the attendees. You can help them by offering to speak about a topic of interest to the industry, thereby attracting more attendees in your field to the show. In this respect, being a keynote speaker will provide benefits for both you and the trade show.

> > > *What You Should Know* < < <

Here's what you should know about attending trade shows:

- A trade show provides opportunities for marketers and potential customers to interact on a personal level. As a marketer, you can talk one-on-one with potential customers who have come to the show because they have a reason to buy your types of products or services.

- If you've never attended a trade show before, start the first year with the smallest booth available (e.g., 10 × 10 feet). Make sure that trade shows will be a cost-effective form of lead generation for you before you think about having a larger booth at future shows.

- To determine whether a trade show is right for your business, look at the demographic profile that is usually made available on the show's website. If the people who have attended the show in the past match your target customer profile, the show is probably a good fit for you.

- You want a booth location in the flow of traffic at the show, where your target customers can come to you. To find out about the priority system for how vendors pick their locations for the next show, contact the show or download their vendor information packet.

- You can construct your own booth or rent one from the trade show or rental agency. Usually, the trade show will offer a package deal for a rental booth that includes extras such as electricity and Internet access.

- Your marketing materials, giveaway tchotchkes, and your company representatives all play an important part in driving traffic to your booth.

- Have a method for collecting contact information from potential leads at the trade show, and *follow up on those leads as soon as possible after the show.*

- Sponsorships allow you to pay a certain amount of money to have your brand displayed prominently at the show. Sponsorships help you to build your brand and drives traffic to your booth at the show.

- Being a keynote speaker or panelist is the most valuable way you can participate in a trade show. If you can make a presentation with relevant information on a topical subject that attendees are interested in, it will position you as the expert in that topic and, again, bring traffic to your booth.

16

Integrated Lead-Generation Marketing

AN INTEGRATED lead-generation marketing campaign is a campaign that uses two or more lead-generation tactics at one time. I recommend that you use as many of the seven lead-generation tactics as you can. If all seven tactics will work for your type of business, try to use them all. If only four or five tactics are appropriate, use those four or five (assuming you have the budget and resources to do so).

You can, of course, use lead-generation tactics individually, and create separate marketing campaigns for each tactic you use. But your lead-generation efforts will be so much more effective if you take an integrated approach, using several tactics in conjunction with each other. You can simplify planning for your campaign by targeting several tactics to the same target demographic and generating the creatives for each tactic around common themes. Also, the results of each tactic will be easier to measure.

With an integrated approach, you will get better, overall increased performance by using more than one tactic at a time. The overall benefits to your business will be greater than if you use lead-generation tactics separately, on a tactic-by-tactic basis.

The Benefits of Integration

Using your lead-generation tactics in an integrated campaign allows you to plan and coordinate your lead-generation efforts around common themes and goals. To begin with, you can do all your up-front planning for the campaign in a single stroke. Once you determine your target audience and their demographics, you can coordinate a series of tactics toward gaining leads from that audience.

If you do an integrated campaign of multiple tactics, you can create a common message, call-to-action, etc., and build your creatives for each tactic around those themes. You can create one creative brief that each of your internal marketers can work from in developing marketing collateral for each tactic. Or you can share this creative brief with agencies, consultants, interns, and other participants, who can then do the work for you.

Also, if you use a series of tactics, you don't necessarily have to spend equal budget, time, and energy on each of them. You can spend the bulk of your time and money on a primary tactic that you know will work well for you, while devoting a little less time and money to secondary tactics. You can even test one or two test tactics against a baseline primary tactic (see Chapter 5) to see how well the test tactics work.

Synchronizing Your Goals

Even if you do multiple tactics at various budget and effort levels, the results for each tactic should be measured around the same goals. If you have a $50 target CPA, for example, that goal should be *universal across all your tactics;* the success of each tactic should be measured according to that $50 target CPA.

You should compare your actual CPAs (the ones you actually get) among tactics in order to find out which tactic gives you the best ROMI. The closer the actual CPA is to your target CPA, the more cost-effective the tactic is for your company, and the better your ROMI will be for that tactic.

> **Note:** *Let me caution you: Do not to try to measure your actual CPA among tactics too early in the campaign. For example, if you're just starting up and you compare the costs of using display advertising against the costs of attending trade shows, you may find that your initial CPA is very out of balance in favor of display advertising.*
>
> *But further down the road, when you get to the point where your customers are actually buying the products, your CPA may even out between trade shows and display advertising. You may have a $100 CPA on trade shows but an 80% conversion rate. And you may have a $20 CPA on display advertising but only a 2% conversion rate. In other words, don't discount a tactic too early because you think that the initial costs are too high. (See the case example in Chapter 5 for a more complete analysis of the comparison of trade shows and display advertising.)*

In an integrated campaign, it's imperative to create a measurement tool that lets you compare the results of each tactic on an apples-to-apples basis. It should be a spreadsheet, a CRM tool, or a lead-scoring tool that will help you to quantify the effectiveness of a tactic. Without some kind of tool that enables you to compare your results of one tactic with those of the others, you may end up wasting a lot of money on less efficient and cost-effective tactics. Only by comparing the results among tactics can you tell how well a certain tactic works for your business.

A Case Example

Here is a case example of how integrating marketing strategies can work for you. Let's say you're an insurance company that is currently using five different lead-generation tactics: direct mail, e-mail marketing, SEM, display advertising, and occasional cold calling. You want to coordinate these tactics so they can work together.

You develop a special campaign for advertising a new insurance plan called Platinum Choice. This plan is designed for luxury car owners (e.g., Cadillac owners), and it includes a number of perks to help them save money on car insurance. As part of this campaign, you plan to advertise a special offer: "Act now, and get a 25% savings on your premium for one year." All of your lead-generation tactics for this campaign are built around this product and offer.

You put together and execute a direct mail campaign, sending out a direct mail piece to 100,000 luxury car owners. The piece explains the Platinum Choice program, gives details about how the program saves money, and includes the special offer.

At the same time, you coordinate with the post office to find out the expected delivery date for the direct mail piece. On that day (or the day before), you send out an e-mail notifying the target customers to be on the lookout for the direct mail piece in their mailboxes. The e-mail tells your target customers that, in addition to the special offer, the direct mail piece will have full details about how they can save money on insurance by switching to your Platinum Choice plan.

A few days later, your sales representatives make follow-up calls to the target customers who received the direct mail piece. "Hey, I know you just received our special offer. I wanted to know if you had any questions about the Platinum Choice plan?"

At the same time, you are also using SEM and display advertising. When potential customers search for "Insurance for Cadillacs" on Google, they see an SEM ad about your new Platinum Choice plan. Potential customers click on the ad, read the details about how the plan saves money, but don't sign up for it then. They decide they will check other options for car insurance.

But thanks to display advertising, you are able to track potential customers' click trail, using a cookie they downloaded while reading about the Platinum Choice plan on your website. You can now use redirecting technologies to present that potential customer with display ads about the Platinum Choice plan. Your Platinum Choice ads will appear to them on other websites.

The more your potential customers learn about your Platinum Choice offer and the more they see it advertised, the more it will be in their consideration set when they are looking for luxury car insurance, or if they are thinking of switching to a better car insurance plan. The more you advertise your Platinum Choice plan through different lead-generation tactics, the higher your response rate to those tactics will be.

Integrating Lead-Generation Marketing with Brand Marketing

Used in the right way, all your lead-generation tactics should support your brand initiatives. Your lead-generation tactics should have the same look and feel and use the same logos and imagery, so that every time someone sees one of your lead-generation tactics at work, it should reinforce your brand and build brand recognition.

Many major companies do this well. Banks like Bank of America and credit card companies like Visa and Discover use their logos extensively in their lead-generation efforts. Every time people see a direct mail piece, a marketing e-mail, or an online ad from one of these companies, it reinforces the company logo in their mind, building awareness of the brand.

You can also strengthen your brand if you tie the look and feel of your lead-generation tactics to your current branding campaign. If you can find ways to use brand imagery to personalize your lead-generation tactics, it will help you to create familiarity with your brand and company among potential customers. The more personalized your lead-generation tactics are, the more they will engage customers, and the higher your response will be for those tactics.

Geico Insurance has found numerous ways to integrate their mascot, the Geico Gecko, into their lead-generation tactics. The talking Gecko became an advertising star through TV commercials. But Geico also uses the Gecko mascot in marketing e-mails, on the envelopes and letters in direct mail offers, and in online display and social media ads. Usually, the Gecko mascot is giving a call-to-action in the marketing creative. In some cases, Geico can even use the Gecko brand image to personalize the creative for the target recipient. For example, a direct mail piece may have a picture of the Gecko printed at the top of the letter, with a speech balloon that says, "Hey, Dave. Act now to save on car insurance."

By using the Gecko in their lead-generation creatives, Geico is able to extend the brand a step beyond simply using the logo. They are using the *personality* of the brand. This allows them to better engage potential clients, and it probably results in a higher response to the lead-generation tactic being used.

The Halo Effect

What I love about integrated marketing campaigns is the halo effect (which I mentioned in Chapter 1). A *halo effect* occurs when the positive effect of one marketing tactic provides a performance boost for other marketing tactics.

Time and again, marketers have proven that when it comes to marketing tactics, 1 + 1 = 3, not 2. The more you target your customers through different marketing mediums, the more you create an *impression* of your brand and company in the target customers' minds. And the more inclined they are to seriously consider your products or services as a solution to their needs.

For example, say target customers read an article about one of your company's executives (e.g., your vice president of sales) in a newspaper or trade magazine. A few days later, they see a display ad for your company on a website. A couple of weeks go by, and they get a call from one of your salespeople. They remember seeing your company name in the article they read, and in the display ad they saw online. So they listen to the salesperson and sign up as a lead.

In this example, your use of several integrated tactics created a halo effect that added value to your lead-generation marketing campaign. At first glance, you might think your display ads didn't work because the cold call captured the lead. But the display ads and the article about your executive caught the target customers' *attention,* and helped to create an initial *impression* of your brand and company in their minds. When your salesperson called, this initial impression was enough to spark *interest* in their minds. (Remember the AIDA curve from Chapter 2.)

This is how an integrated campaign gives momentum to your brand and company, and how it can help to make your lead-generation efforts more successful. If customers had not seen your display ads, they might have dismissed an out-of-the-blue sales call from you with a "Thanks, but I'm not interested." But because they had heard of your company and seen your brand, the customer was more inclined to listen to the salesperson's offer. The first or second touch you make with the customer—in this case, a display ad—may reap benefits in future touches, such as the cold call.

When I combine multiple lead-generation tactics, I often see a quantitative, measurable lift in overall performance. For instance, an SEM campaign may be humming along at a 2% CTR. Then I do an e-mail marketing push, sending out 50,000 marketing e-mails. In addition to the traffic generated from the e-mail campaign, I'll also see at least a 50% increase in my SEM performance. People who received the e-mail may not have clicked on it. But some of those people will search for the company on Google and Bing to find out more about it. A percentage of those people will click on the search engine ad.

You can also build momentum for your brand using nurturing campaigns. In Chapter 5, I mentioned the concept of the "drip bucket." Using this strategy, you keep sending e-mails to qualified leads over time, keeping them informed about special offers and company events. Again, the more they see of your brand, the more they will take you seriously. Using a variety of lead-generation tactics in an integrated marketing campaign helps to accomplish this same goal, and integrated lead-generation marketing works as well, if not better, than nurture marketing.

Testing an Integrated Marketing Campaign

How do you test an integrated marketing campaign? How do you measure how well your lead-generation and brand marketing tactics work in tandem with one other? And how do you measure the ROMI that you get from combining several tactics?

The best way to measure the results of an integrated marketing campaign is to add the dimension of time. Use the same testing principles discussed in previous chapters to measure each tactic on its own. For example, if you use e-mail marketing or online lead-generation ads (SEM ads, social media ads, etc.), you should measure your CTR, the cost-per-action, etc.

But now you want to measure what kind of return the *integration* of these tactics has provided for your marketing campaign. In other words, how did using the tactics together provide a different return from using each tactic individually? In the car insurance example of the previous section, I first received a 2% CTR with the SEM campaign. That's a pretty good initial result. When I added an e-mail marketing campaign, it increased the CTR for the SEM ads to 3%. That's better by 50%.

Now how does that affect my ROMI for the SEM tactics? Or for the e-mail marketing tactic? Let's say that my original target CPA was $50 per action. When I examine the actual CPA for e-mail marketing, I find it was $60, which is above my target CPA. However, the actual CPA for the SEM ads has dropped to $25, which is half my original target CPA.

In this scenario, my e-mail marketing campaign results in a loss, but the benefits of improving my SEM campaign more than make up for it. Thanks to the e-mail push, I saw a 50% lift in the performance of the SEM ads. Even though the secondary tactic may not have hit my target CPA and may not be as profitable, the e-mail marketing campaign was worth it because it created a halo effect that helped to make my SEM campaign more profitable. Thanks to the boost provided by e-mail marketing, the success of the SEM campaign produced a better overall ROI for my marketing efforts.

In Conclusion

I hope that, after reading this book, you've acquired a new outlook on lead-generation marketing. The purpose of the book is to help you to devise a lead-generation strategy that makes sense for your company so you can build your campaigns intelligently and cost-effectively.

Any business can use these tactics effectively. If you use the tools I've provided in this book, you can easily scale up your lead-generation efforts to provide more quality leads to your company. And if you continuously test and measure your results to determine how well the tactics are working and how cost-effective they are, you'll be able to do it without breaking the bank.

When I started out in lead-generation marketing, I didn't have these tools. I had to create them myself. But once I did, the marketing departments I directed were able to achieve a positive ROMI for our lead-generation results within a very short time. We were able to acquire more leads without losing a lot of money or expending a lot of effort. Also, by continuously testing and measuring our results, I was able to communicate our success to my superiors. This allowed me to justify a larger marketing budget and to increase my organization's marketing initiatives.

Hopefully, you can do the same in your company's marketing organization, using the tools given you in this book. I wish you success and good luck.

> > > *What You Should Know* < < <

To review, here is what you should know about integrated lead-generation marketing campaigns:

- An integrated marketing campaign is one that uses two or more lead-generation tactics in conjunction with each other. You should use as many of the seven lead-generation tactics as will work for your type of business and as many as you have the budget and resources to use.

- When you use lead-generation tactics in an integrated campaign, it becomes easier to plan and execute the campaign. You can build the creatives for all the tactics you plan to use around a common marketing theme, offer, call-to-action, etc.

- You don't need to spend equal time and resources on each tactic in an integrated campaign. You can have a primary tactic that receives the largest amount of time and budget, and also use secondary tactics that receive less time and budget.

- An integrated campaign also makes it easier to measure the results of each tactic, and to compare those results on a tactic-by-tactic basis. However, it is important that you measure the results for each tactic around the same goals (e.g., a $50 target CPA) in an apples-to-apples comparison.

- Your lead-generation tactics can support your brand initiatives as well. Your lead-generation creatives should all use the same logos and imagery to help reinforce your brand and build awareness. Look for ways to tie the look and feel of your lead-generation tactics to your current branding campaign.

- When you use several tactics at once, it can produce a "halo effect." If your target customer sees your brand and hears about your company through several different mediums (direct mail, display ads, etc.), they will take your products or services more seriously as a possible solution to their needs. They will then be more inclined to listen to your offer when you make it to them.

- To test the results of an integrated marketing campaign, you should use the same testing tools discussed in previous chapters to measure the results of each individual tactic. But you also need to measure how using the tactics together provided a different return from using each tactic individually.

- If you use the tools provided in this book, you will be able to deploy a successful lead-generation strategy in your marketing organization. By continuously testing and measuring your results, you will be able to increase your lead-generation efforts and provide more quality leads for your company in an efficient, cost-effective way.

Notes

CHAPTER 1: What Is Lead-Generation Marketing?

1. "How Companies Are Marketing Online: A McKinsey Global Survey," *The McKinsey Quarterly*, Vol. 2007, July 2007.

CHAPTER 4: Using Lead-Generation Tactics

1. Geoffrey A. Moore, *Inside the Tornado: Marketing Strategies from Silicon Valley's Cutting Edge* (New York: HarperCollins Publishers, 1995), 14.

CHAPTER 12: E-Mail Marketing

1. Jim Dickie and Barry Trailer, *2011 Lead Management Optimization Key Trends Analysis* (CSO Insights, 2011), 3.

2. Morgan Stewart, *2009 Channel Preference Study* (ExactTarget, 2009), 7.

3. *The Power of Direct Marketing: ROI, Sales, Expenditures, and Employment in the U.S.*, 2011–2012 Edition (Direct Marketing Association, 2011), 7.

CHAPTER 13: Direct Mail Marketing

1. John Mazzone and John Pickett, *The Household Diary Study: Mail Use & Attitudes in FY2010* (United States Postal Service, April 2011), 39–40.

2. Ibid., 44.

3. 2012: Email in Action Study (Collaboration between Direct Marketing Association and Econsultancy.com Ltd., February 9, 2012), 23–24.

Index